Westward Expansion Biographies

Westward Expansion Biographies

Tom Pendergast
and Sara Pendergast

Christine Slovey, Editor

U·X·L®

AN IMPRINT OF THE GALE GROUP

DETROIT · SAN FRANCISCO · LONDON
BOSTON · WOODBRIDGE, CT

Westward Expansion: Biographies

Tom Pendergast and Sara Pendergast

Staff

Christine Slovey, *U•X•L Senior Editor*
Carol DeKane Nagel, *U•X•L Managing Editor*
Tom Romig, *U•X•L Publisher*

Rita Wimberley, *Senior Buyer*
Dorothy Maki, *Manufacturing Manager*
Evi Seoud, *Assistant Production Manager*
Mary Beth Trimper, *Production Director*

Shalice Shah-Caldwell, *Permissions Specialist*

Michelle DiMercurio, *Cover Art Director*
Pamela A.E. Galbreath, *Page Art Director*
Kenn Zorn, *Product Design Manager*

Kelly A. Quin, *Image Editor*
Pamela A. Reed, *Imaging Coordinator*
Robert Duncan and Dan Newell, *Imaging Specialists*
Randy Bassett, *Image Database Supervisor*
Barbara J. Yarrow, *Graphic Services Supervisor*

Marco Di Vita, Graphix Group, *Typesetting*

Cover photographs reproduced by permission of the Granger Collection (Sarah Winnemucca) and from the Collections of the Library of Congress (George Armstrong Custer, Geronimo, and Buffalo Bill Wagon).

Library of Congress Card Number: 00-109475

ISBN: 0-7876-4863-9

Printed in the United States of America

10 9 8 7 6 5 4 3 2

Contents

Biographies

Sarah Winnemucca. *(The Granger Collection, New York. Reproduced by permission.)*

William "Buffalo Bill" Cody. *(Archive Photos, Inc. Reproduced by permission.)*

Reader's Guide

The westward expansion of the United States, which took place between 1763 and 1890, is at once one of the most romantic sagas of human accomplishment and one of the bleakest tragedies of human cruelty. In just over one century, American settlers, soldiers, and diplomats helped the United States expand from a mere thirteen British colonies clinging to the eastern seaboard to a sprawling nation stretching 3,000 miles from the Atlantic to the Pacific Oceans.

Westward Expansion: Biographies presents the life stories of twenty-eight individuals who played key roles in the westward expansion of the United States. Individuals were selected to give readers a wide perspective on this era of American history. Included are diplomats, entrepreneurs, explorers, frontiersman, Native American leaders, politicians, pioneers, and outlaws. *Westward Expansion: Biographies* includes well-known figures such as Daniel Boone, James Fenimore Cooper, and Annie Oakley, as well as lesser-known individuals such as Benjamin "Pap" Singleton, a leader of the "Kansas Exodus," and Mariano Vallejo, a Mexican rancher and politician who campaigned for the U.S. annexation of California.

Format

The entries in *Westward Expansion: Biographies* contain sidebars that highlight people and events of special interest; each entry offers a list of additional sources students can go to for more information, including sources used in writing the chapter. More than sixty-five black-and-white photographs and maps help illustrate the material covered in the text. The volume begins with a timeline of important events in the history of westward expansion and a "Words to Know" section that introduces students to difficult or unfamiliar terms (terms are also defined within the text). The volume concludes with a subject index so students can easily find the people, places, and events discussed throughout *Westward Expansion: Biographies*.

Dedication

To our children, Conrad and Louisa, who have journeyed with us on our own westward trek.

Special Thanks

Special thanks are due to Lynne E. Heckman, teacher of American history at Valley View Middle School in Snohomish, Washington, for helping us understand the needs and interests of middle school students and teachers, and to the many historians and writers whose work on the West we filtered through our minds as we prepared this collection.

Comments and Suggestions

We welcome your comments on *Westward Expansion: Biographies* and suggestions for other topics in history to consider. Please write: Editors, *Westward Expansion: Biographies*, U•X•L, 27500 Drake Rd., Farmington Hills, Michigan 48331-3535; call toll-free: 1-800-877-4253; fax to (248) 414-5043; or send e-mail via http://www.galegroup.com.

Timeline of Events in Westward Expansion

1622 Indian chief Powhatan's younger brother, Opecha-nough, starts the first Indian war by attacking colonists in Jamestown, Virginia, to protest white use of Indian land.

1754 The French defeat George Washington and American colonists fighting for the British at the Battle of Fort Necessity on July 3–4, beginning the French and Indian War.

1763 The first Treaty of Paris is signed, ending the French and Indian War. Under the treaty, France relinquishes its claim to Canada and the Ohio Valley to England

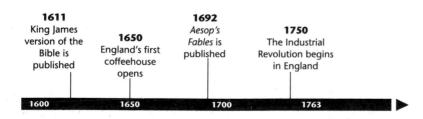

1611
King James version of the Bible is published

1650
England's first coffeehouse opens

1692
Aesop's Fables is published

1750
The Industrial Revolution begins in England

1600   1650   1700   1763

and hands over its holdings west of the Mississippi River to Spain.

1763   Hoping to end Indian attacks in the Ohio Valley, the British issue the Proclamation of 1763, which recalls all settlers from west of the Appalachian crest and forbids further emigration into the area.

1769   Catholic missionary Father Junipero Serra and the Spanish army establish the first of twenty-one missions along the coast of California. Serra directs soldiers to round up the Native North Americans and bring them, by force if necessary, to the missions.

1775   After years of hunting in and exploring the rich forests of Kentucky, **Daniel Boone** cuts the first road over the Cumberland Gap to found Boonesborough in Kentucky in 1775.

1776   The Revolutionary War begins. Among the many factors contributing to the war are clashes between colonists and the British over access to land west of the Appalachians.

1783   The Revolutionary War ends. The second Treaty of Paris grants the newly formed United States of America its independence. The United States gains all of the territory from the Great Lakes south to the Gulf of Mexico and from the Appalachian Mountains west to the Mississippi River.

1783   To raise funds, the newly formed U.S. government claims all of the Indian lands east of the Mississippi River (consisting of present-day Indiana, Kentucky, Ohio, and Tennessee) to sell to settlers. The Chippewa, Delaware, Kickapoo, Miami, Ottawa, Potawatomi, Shawnee, and Wyandot nations and some Iroquois

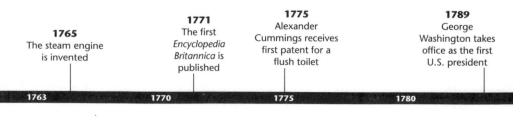

1765
The steam engine is invented

1771
The first *Encyclopedia Britannica* is published

1775
Alexander Cummings receives first patent for a flush toilet

1789
George Washington takes office as the first U.S. president

1763   1770   1775   1780

warriors join together to oppose the invasion of U.S. settlers into their territory.

1803   The United States purchases from France more than 800,000 acres of land west of the Mississippi River for $15 million. The Louisiana Purchase doubles the size of the United States. This territory today makes up the states of Arkansas, Iowa, Kansas, Louisiana, Missouri, Montana, Nebraska, North Dakota, Oklahoma, and South Dakota and parts of Colorado, Minnesota, and Wyoming.

1804   **Meriwether Lewis, William Clark,** and their entourage set out from St. Louis, Missouri, on May 14 to determine whether the Gulf of Mexico and the Pacific Ocean are linked by a river system. Finding no such water connection, they pioneer an overland route across the Rocky Mountains.

1806   The Lewis and Clark expedition returns to St. Louis on September 23 after nearly twenty-eight months of exploration. The expedition had been given up for lost, and its return is celebrated throughout the country.

1810   Governor of Indiana territory William Henry Harrison and Shawnee warrior **Tecumseh** meet in Vincennes, Indiana, to try to negotiate a peace agreement. Their efforts are unsuccessful.

1812   The War of 1812 begins. In a war that is often called the Second War for Independence, Americans seek to finally eliminate the British presence in the Old Northwest and to end British attacks on American ships carrying goods to France.

1813   Shawnee warrior Tecumseh is killed at the Battle of the Thames in Ontario.

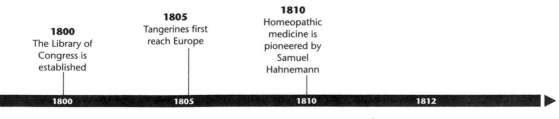

1800
The Library of Congress is established

1805
Tangerines first reach Europe

1810
Homeopathic medicine is pioneered by Samuel Hahnemann

1800   1805   1810   1812

Andrew Jackson. *(Reproduced from the Collections of the Library of Congress.)*

James Bridger. *(Reproduced from the Collections of the Library of Congress.)*

1814   The Treaty of Ghent ends the War of 1812. The British agree that all the territory south of the Great Lakes to the Gulf of Mexico belongs to the United States. The British also agree not to give any help to their Indian allies in this territory.

1820   The U.S. Congress approves the Missouri Compromise, which outlaws slavery within the Louisiana Purchase territory north of 36" 30' latitude. Missouri enters the Union as a slave state, while Maine enters as a free state.

1821   Mexico gains its independence from Spain and opens its borders with the United States.

1821   **Stephen Austin** moves to Texas.

1823   *The Pioneers*, the first of **James Fenimore Cooper**'s Leatherstocking Tales, is published.

1823   William Ashley begins the annual mountain man Rendezvous for American fur trappers in the Rocky Mountains. Trappers gather at the annual Rendezvous to sell their pelts and gather a year's worth of supplies.

1826   *The Last of the Mohicans*, the most widely read of James Fenimore Cooper's Leatherstocking Tales, is published.

1828   **Andrew Jackson** becomes the seventh president of the United States.

1830   The Church of Jesus Christ of Latter-Day Saints is founded April 6 at Fayette, New York, by local farmhand Joseph Smith, Jr., who has *The Book of Mormon* published in Palmyra, New York. The first gathering of the church occurs in April 1830.

1830   The U.S. Congress votes in favor of the Indian Removal Act on May 28. The act calls for the removal—

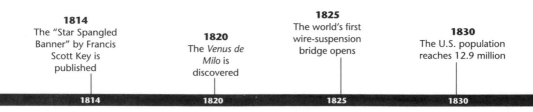

1814
The "Star Spangled Banner" by Francis Scott Key is published

1820
The *Venus de Milo* is discovered

1825
The world's first wire-suspension bridge opens

1830
The U.S. population reaches 12.9 million

1814   1820   1825   1830

voluntary or forced—of all Indians to lands west of the Mississippi.

1830   **James Bridger, Thomas "Broken Hand" Fitzpatrick**, and Milton Sublette establish the Rocky Mountain Fur Company.

1832   The Black Hawk War begins in May. It ends in August 1832 with **Black Hawk**'s surrender.

1834   Congress establishes Indian Territory, which covers parts of the present-day states of Oklahoma, Nebraska, and Kansas, far smaller than the "all lands west of the Mississippi" that whites had once promised.

1835   **Mariano Guadalupe Vallejo** is named military governor of the "Free State of Alta California."

1836   The mission system in California collapses. Devastating epidemics and slave labor are responsible for killing the majority of Native California people who come into contact with the Spanish colonists. Native Americans leave the missions to find that their former land has been changed forever. Animals and crops introduced to the area by the Spanish make it virtually impossible for California Indians to live off the land in the way they had before the Spanish came.

1836   On April 21, Mexican president Antonio López de Santa Anna and a large army lay siege to a band of Texans holed up at the Alamo Mission. After a ten-day battle, every American man is killed. "Remember the Alamo" becomes the battle cry of Texans who fight back against Santa Anna and win independence for the Republic of Texas on May 14, 1836.

1836   The Republic of Texas claims all land between the Rio Grande and Nueces Rivers. Sam Houston is sworn in as president on October 22.

Black Hawk. *(The Granger Collection, New York. Reproduced by permission.)*

The Alamo. *(Courtesy of the U.S. Department of Interior and National Parks.)*

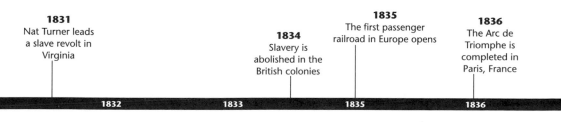

1831
Nat Turner leads a slave revolt in Virginia

1834
Slavery is abolished in the British colonies

1835
The first passenger railroad in Europe opens

1836
The Arc de Triomphe is completed in Paris, France

1832   1833   1835   1836

1836   **Narcissa Prentiss Whitman** and Eliza Spalding, two Protestant missionaries, become the first white women to cross the Rocky Mountains when they travel westward with their husbands.

1838   The U.S. Army forms the Corps of Topographical Engineers to look at western lands with an eye toward settlement. The corps makes maps and surveys of the frontier until the 1860s.

1838–39 The removal of the Cherokee Indians from Georgia to Indian Territory (present-day Oklahoma) begins in October. General Winfield Scott and seven thousand federal troops are sent to the Cherokee's homeland to insist that the Cherokee leave. Scott's troops imprison any Cherokee who resist and burn their homes and crops. The Cherokee remember the trek as the "Trail Where They Cried," while U.S. historians call it the "Trail of Tears." More than four thousand Cherokee die on the forced march before they reach their destination in March 1839.

1839   **John Augustus Sutter** establishes the community of New Helvetia in present-day California.

1840   The U.S. fur-trapping system deteriorates due to beaver depletion and shifts in fashion toward silk hats.

1842   **John Charles Frémont** leads his first expedition to the West to explore the country between the Missouri River and the Rocky Mountains from May to October.

1843   The Oregon Trail is opened from Idaho to the Grande Ronde Valley in Oregon. The Great Migration, the name given to the first major exodus of emigrants westward, draws one thousand settlers onto the Oregon Trail.

1838
Slaves mutiny on the
Spanish ship *Amistad*

1837
Blacks are given the right
to vote in Canada

1840
A worldwide cholera epidemic that
will last twenty two years begins

1843
A Christmas Carol by Charles
Dickens is published

1830   1840   1842   1843

1844 Mormon leaders Joseph and Hiram Smith are killed after the governor of Illinois orders their arrest. **Brigham Young** succeeds Smith as the leader of the Church.

1844–45 The U.S. Congress passes laws to build military posts to protect settlers moving from the East to California and Oregon. These forts cause conflict with Indian tribes along the route.

1845 Mormon leader Brigham Young leads his followers from Nauvoo, Illinois, more than 1,000 miles to the Salt Lake Valley in present-day Utah.

1845 John C. Frémont's *Report of the Exploring Expedition to the Rocky Mountains* is published.

1845 In March, President John Tyler signs a resolution to bring Texas into the Union. Because the border of Texas is still contested, Tyler's action angers the Mexican government and it breaks off diplomatic relations with the United States.

1845 As war with Mexico looms, John L. O'Sullivan, editor of *The United States Magazine and Democratic Review,* defines Americans' faith in the expansion of their nation as their "manifest destiny." The idea of manifest destiny implies that Americans have the God-given right to acquire and populate the territories stretching west to the Pacific.

1846 The Mexican-American War officially begins on May 11. The United States and Mexico go to war to settle their disagreement over the southern border of Texas. Texas and the United States claim the Rio Grande as the southern border. Mexico argues that the Nueces River is the actual border.

1844
Samuel Morse sends the
first telegraph message

1845
The Great Irish
Famine begins

1846
The Smithsonian
Institution is founded
in Washington, D.C.

1844   1845   1846

1846 California's Bear Flag Revolt begins on June 14 when settlers claim their independence from Mexico and raise a flag at Sonoma bearing a black bear and a star.

1846 The Oregon Treaty is signed with Britain on June 15 giving territory south of the forty-ninth parallel to the United States. Though the British had occupied the area since 1818, the American population of Oregon Country has grown to 5,000 by 1845 while the British claim only 750 inhabitants.

1847 In November, members of the Whitman mission in Washington territory are massacred by Cayuse Indians, who believe the missionaries have started a devastating measles epidemic.

1848 James Marshall discovers gold at Sutter's Mill in California on January 24, thus beginning the California gold rush.

1848 The Treaty of Guadalupe Hidalgo is signed on February 2 ending the Mexican-American War. The treaty grants the United States all or part of the present-day states of Arizona, California, Colorado, New Mexico, Utah, and Wyoming. It is a territorial addition second only to the Louisiana Purchase and virtually doubles the size of the country.

1850 The U.S. Congress passes a series of laws to address the growing divisions over the slavery issue and disputes over the land acquired in the Mexican-American War. The famous Compromise of 1850 addresses the problem of slavery in the new territories of New Mexico and California. It outlaws the slave trade in Washington, D.C., but allows it everywhere else throughout the South. In addition, California is admitted to the Union as a free state, and a new and

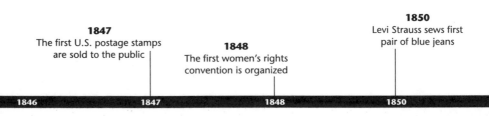

1847
The first U.S. postage stamps are sold to the public

1848
The first women's rights convention is organized

1850
Levi Strauss sews first pair of blue jeans

1846　　　　1847　　　　1848　　　　1850

tougher fugitive slave law replaces the poorly enforced Fugitive Slave Act of 1793.

1851   **James P. Beckwourth** guides the first wagon train through Beckwourth Pass in the Sierra Nevada Mountains.

1859   Chiricahua Apache warrior **Geronimo** begins his personal crusade to avenge the death of his family at the hands of Mexican troops and settlers.

1861–72 The Apache Wars begin in southern Arizona in 1861 when Apache chief Cochise escapes from an army post in Arizona with hostages. In 1871 Cochise opposes efforts to relocate his people to a reservation in New Mexico. In 1872 he finally agrees not to attack the U.S. Army in exchange for reservation land in eastern Arizona.

1862   The Homestead Act of 1862 is passed by the U.S. Congress. Nearly 470,000 homesteaders apply for homesteads in the next eighteen years.

1864   The "Long Walk" of the Navajo begins. Forces led by **Christopher "Kit" Carson** trap a huge number of Navajo in Canyon de Chelly in present-day Arizona, a steep-sided canyon in which the Navajo had traditionally taken refuge. The Navajo are marched southeast to Bosque Redondo, with many dying along the way.

1866   The first of the great cattle drives begins in Texas. Cowboys round up cattle and drive them northward to rail lines that reach into Kansas. In the years to come some eight million longhorn cattle travel the trails north to Kansas from ranches across Texas and throughout the Great Plains.

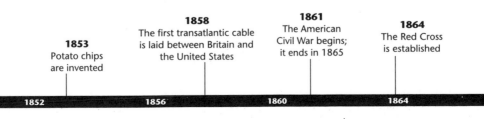

1853
Potato chips
are invented

1858
The first transatlantic cable
is laid between Britain and
the United States

1861
The American
Civil War begins;
it ends in 1865

1864
The Red Cross
is established

1852   1856   1860   1864

Jesse James.

1866   **Jesse James** and his brother Frank rob their first bank, the Clay County Savings and Loan in Liberty, Missouri.

1868   U.S. military authorities force Navajo chiefs to sign a treaty in which the Navajo agree to live on reservations and cease opposition to whites. The treaty establishes a 3.5 million-acre reservation within the Navajo nation's old domains (a small portion of the original Navajo territory).

1869   The completion of the first transcontinental United States railroad is celebrated with the Golden Spike ceremony on May 10. The railroads joining the Atlantic and Pacific coasts are linked at Promontory Point, Utah, north of the Great Salt Lake.

1870   The U.S. Supreme Court, in the case of *McKay v. Campbell,* decides that Indians are not U.S. citizens since their allegiance is to their tribe, not to the United States. Because of this ruling Indians are denied protections guaranteed by the U.S. Constitution.

1871   The U.S. Congress stops the practice of making treaties with Indians. Congress allows "agreements," which do not recognize tribes as independent nations. At the end of the treaty era, American Indian tribes still control one-tenth of the forty-eight states, or about one-fourth of the land between the Mississippi River and the Rocky Mountains. By the early 1900s much of this land is owned by the U.S. government.

1873   **Benjamin "Pap" Singleton** leads a group of more than three hundred African Americans to settle in Kansas.

1874   An expedition led by **George Armstrong Custer** discovers gold in the Black Hills of South Dakota, sacred

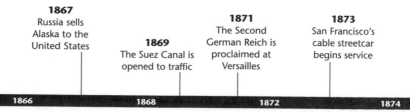

1867
Russia sells Alaska to the United States

1869
The Suez Canal is opened to traffic

1871
The Second German Reich is proclaimed at Versailles

1873
San Francisco's cable streetcar begins service

1866   1868   1872   1874

land for the Lakota Sioux, Cheyenne, and other tribes. In violation of the Fort Laramie Treaty, gold miners flood the Black Hills. Soon Indian and U.S. Army forces are fighting over this land.

1875   U.S. president Ulysses Grant vetoes a bill that could protect the buffalo from extinction.

1876   At the Battle of Little Bighorn on June 25 forces led by George Armstrong Custer are defeated by combined Native American forces. The Indians' victory is their last major triumph against the whites.

1877   After the Battle of Little Bighorn, all of the Nez Percé Indians are ordered to report to reservations. Chief Joseph of the Nez Percé leads a band of his people on a long, torturous journey to elude army forces, but they are eventually captured just 40 miles from the Canadian border.

1877   Oglala Sioux warrior and tribal leader **Crazy Horse** is killed by U.S. soldiers at Fort Robinson, Nebraska.

1878   **James J. Hill**, in partnership with several investors, takes over the Saint Paul and Pacific Railroad, renaming it the Saint Paul, Minneapolis, and Manitoba Railway.

1879   Native American rights advocate **Sarah Winnemucca** gives her first lecture on the plight of the Native Americans in the United States.

1881   **Wyatt Earp**, his brothers Virgil and Morgan, and Doc Holliday get into a gunfight with the Clanton brothers and McLaury brothers at the O.K. Corral in Tombstone, Arizona.

1882   Jesse James is shot in the back by Charles and Robert Ford, members of his own gang who hope to collect the ten-thousand-dollar reward offered for James's capture.

George Armstrong Custer.
(Reproduced from the Collections of the Library of Congress.)

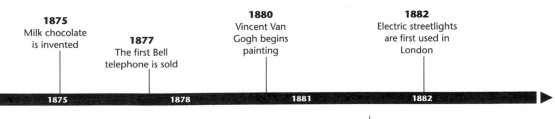

1875 Milk chocolate is invented

1877 The first Bell telephone is sold

1880 Vincent Van Gogh begins painting

1882 Electric streetlights are first used in London

1875   1878   1881   1882

Annie Oakley performing in the Wild West Show. *(The Corbis Corporation. Reproduced by permission.)*

1883 **William "Buffalo Bill"** Cody's Wild West Show opens to a crowd of eight thousand spectators in Omaha, Nebraska.

1884 **Annie Oakley** joins Buffalo Bill's Wild West Show.

1885 The cowboy era ends. Increased settlement of Kansas leads to the closing of the cattle towns, and expanding railroad lines mean that ranchers no longer have to drive cattle to railheads.

1886 On September 4, Chiricahua Apache warrior Geronimo surrenders for the last time to U.S. general Nelson A. Miles.

1889 Western rancher and cattle rustler **Belle Starr** is killed by an unknown assailant.

1890 The Battle of Wounded Knee takes place on December 29, ending the last major Indian resistance to white settlement in America. Nearly 500 well-armed soldiers of the U.S. 7th Cavalry massacre an estimated 300 (out of 350) Sioux men, women, and children in a South Dakota encampment. The Army takes only 35 casualties.

1890 The Superintendent of the Census for 1890 declares that there is no longer a frontier in America. The census report's conclusion about the closing of the frontier later encourages President Theodore Roosevelt to begin setting aside public lands as national parks.

1897 **Mifflin Wistar Gibbs** is named U.S. consul to the African country of Madagascar.

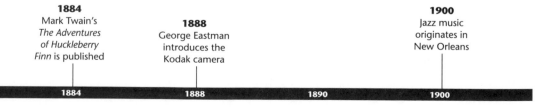

1884 Mark Twain's *The Adventures of Huckleberry Finn* is published

1888 George Eastman introduces the Kodak camera

1900 Jazz music originates in New Orleans

1884   1888   1890   1900

Words to Know

A

Annexation: The addition of territory to a country. Annexation became an issue in westward expansion when Southerners called for the United States to annex the Republic of Texas.

C

Californios: Descendants of the original Spanish settlers in California.

Cattle drive: Moving a herd of cattle from the open range to a railroad line. Cattle drives were led by bands of cowboys who tended the cattle.

Cholera: An acute intestinal infection. Cholera causes violent vomiting, fever, chills, and diarrhea. This infection killed hundreds of emigrants making their way west.

Colonies: Regions under the political control of a distant country.

Continental Divide: The line connecting the highest points of land in the Rocky Mountains. Waters on the west side of the divide flow into the Pacific Ocean, while waters on the east side flow into the Gulf of Mexico.

E

Emigrants: People who leave one region to move to another. Those who moved from the East to settle in the West during westward expansion were known as emigrants.

F

French and Indian War: A war between the British and combined French and Indian forces from 1755 to 1763 over control of the fur-trading regions of the American interior.

Frontier: A term used by whites to refer to lands that lay beyond white settlements, including lands that were already occupied by Indians and Mexicans. In the United States the frontier existed until 1890 when Americans had settled the entire area between the Atlantic and Pacific Oceans.

G

Great Migration: The mass movement of emigrants westward on the Oregon Trail that began in 1843 and eventually carried some 350,000 settlers to the West.

Great Plains: The vast area of rolling grasslands between the Mississippi River and the Rocky Mountains.

H

Homestead Act of 1862: An act passed by Congress that gave settlers up to 160 acres of free land if they settled on it and made improvements over a five-year span. This act was responsible for bringing thousands of settlers into the West.

I

Indian Removal Act of 1830: An act passed by Congress calling for the removal—voluntary or forced—of all Indians to lands west of the Mississippi.

L

Louisiana Territory: More than 800,000 acres of land west of the Mississippi that was acquired from France for $15 million by President Thomas Jefferson in the Louisiana Purchase of 1803.

M

Manifest Destiny: The belief that by acquiring and populating the territories stretching from the Atlantic Ocean west to the Pacific Ocean, Americans were fulfilling a destiny ordained by God. This idea has been criticized as an excuse for the bold land grabs and the slaughter of Indians that characterized westward expansion, but those who believed in it thought they were demonstrating the virtues of a nation founded on political liberty, individual economic opportunity, and Christian civilization.

Mexican-American War: This war between the United States and Mexico, fought between 1846 and 1848, began as a battle over the southern border of Texas but soon expanded as the United States sought to acquire the territory that now includes Arizona, California, Colorado, Nevada, New Mexico, Utah, and Wyoming.

Missionaries: Proponents of a religion who travel into unexplored territories to try to convert the indigenous peoples to the missionaries' religion. Spanish missionaries had an important influence in California; Protestant missionaries in Oregon and Washington; and Catholic missionaries throughout the French-influenced areas of the East.

N

Northwest Passage: A mythical water route that linked the Atlantic Ocean to the Pacific Ocean; this passage was long sought by explorers of North America.

Northwest Territory: The unsettled area of land surrounding the Great Lakes and falling between the Ohio River and the Mississippi River that was given to the United States in the Treaty of Paris (1783). It included the present-day states of Ohio, Indiana, Illinois, Michigan, Wisconsin, and part of Minnesota.

O

Old Northwest: The area of land surrounding the Great Lakes and between the Ohio River and the Mississippi River; it included the present-day states of Ohio, Indiana, Illinois, Michigan, Wisconsin, and part of Minnesota.

Oregon Country: The name given to a vast expanse of land west of the Rocky Mountains and north of the Spanish territory containing the present-day states of Washington, Oregon, Idaho, and western Montana. This territory was jointly occupied by the British and the United States until 1846, when England ceded the territory to the United States.

Oregon Trail: A 2,000-mile trail that led from St. Joseph, Missouri, to the mouth of the Columbia River in Oregon. Thousands of settlers traveled on the trail from the 1830s to the 1890s. A major branch of the trail, the California Trail, led settlers to the gold fields of California.

R

Rendezvous: A gathering or meeting. The annual mountain man Rendezvous was a gathering of trappers and traders in the Rocky Mountain region. At the Rendezvous, fur trappers sold the furs and bought the goods that would allow them to survive through the next year. The mountain men entertained themselves during the Rendezvous with drinking, singing, dancing, and sporting contests.

S

South Pass: A low mountain pass over the Continental Divide located in present-day Wyoming; this pass was a major milestone on the Oregon Trail.

T

Territory: The name given to a region before it became a state. The Northwest Ordinance paved the way for the orderly admission of territories into the Union.

Trans-Appalachian West: The area of land that stretched west from the crest of the Appalachian Mountains to the Mississippi River.

Treaty of Guadalupe Hidalgo: This treaty with Mexico, signed on February 2, 1848, ended the Mexican-American War and granted to the United States territory including all or part of the present-day states of Arizona, California, Colorado, Nevada, New Mexico, Utah, and Wyoming.

W

War of 1812: A war fought between England and the United States from 1812 to 1814 that was aimed at settling control of the trans-Appalachian west and shipping disputes between the two countries. Many Indian tribes sided with the English. The American victory established complete American control of the area.

Westward Expansion Biographies

Stephen F. Austin

Born November 3, 1793
Wythe County, Virginia
Died December 27, 1836
Columbia, Texas

Diplomat and colonizer of Texas

S tephen F. Austin earned the title "Father of Texas." For almost two decades, Austin worked, to the exclusion of almost everything else, to create an American colony in Texas.
But unlike other western heroes, Austin was not a hardy soul
using his muscle strength to carve out civilization. Instead he
was a slight man who suffered severe depression and contin-
ual bouts of sickness and who won his fame as a savvy diplomat. Austin shrewdly nurtured friendships with people of
various political leanings who could push through the policies he wanted. The result of Austin's efforts culminated in a
revolution that won Texas its independence from Mexico.

"I make no more
calculations except to
spend my life here,
[whether] rich or poor,
here (that is in this
colony) I expect to
remain permanently."

Groomed to be a businessman

Austin grew up on the American frontier. But unlike
many of his peers, he grew up in the lap of luxury. Stephen
Fuller Austin was born on November 3, 1793, in Wythe
County, Virginia, where his father operated a lead mine 250
miles from Richmond. By the time Stephen reached his third
birthday, his father Moses entertained the idea of moving

Stephen Austin.
*(Reproduced from the Collections
of the Library of Congress.)*

into Spanish territory, which would eventually become the state of Missouri, upon word of large lead deposits there.

Moses Austin was a very successful businessman and planned to make his son one too. After successfully negotiating with Mexican authorities, he described his actions to his son in a thirty-eight-page letter that would be the blueprint from which Stephen Austin would later conduct his business dealings. According to biographer Gregg Cantrell, author of *Stephen F. Austin: Empresario of Texas,* the elder Austin advised "maintaining proper appearances, going through official channels, courting influential officials … [and] appealing to the national interests of a foreign government."

An education fit for a gentleman

Moses moved his family to the Spanish territory on June 8, 1798. The family lived in a two-and-a-half-story mansion called "Durham Hall," which was comparable to the grandest southern plantations. Around 1804, Austin traveled East to get a proper education and learn to be a gentleman. Austin entered Bacon Academy and began studying to be a "man of business" as his father wished, according to Cantrell. For years, Austin kept a letter from his father that said, "I hope and pray you will improve Every moment of time to the utmost advantage and I shall have the satissfaction [sic] of seeing that my expectations are not Disappointed," according to Cantrell. Within three years, Austin passed his examinations and continued his education at Transylvania University in Lexington, Kentucky, in 1808 or 1809. But within about a year, Moses called for Stephen to quit school and join him at his mine.

Dedication to family

Instead of getting an education to make his own way in the world, Austin got an education to further his family in the world. He never flagged in his commitment to the Austin name. He would dedicate his entire life to preserving his family's name, never even taking the time to marry and start his own family. When Austin returned to his family in 1810 at the age of seventeen, he quickly proved an adept manager and took on more and more responsibility at the mines over the next few years. By 1817, Moses granted Stephen full control over the mines for a five-year period while Moses nurtured other financial opportunities. The mines suffered greatly over the next few years, and the Austin family fell deeply in debt.

As the family business flagged, Stephen Austin developed his political talents and joined the Missouri legislature. But by 1819, with an economic crisis called the Panic of 1819 making money scarce, Austin decided to close the mines in Missouri and buy nine thousand dollars' worth of Arkansas land on credit to develop a town. His scheme was designed to free his family from debt, but it failed; other speculators had purchased the best land. On March 11, 1820, Moses Austin was jailed for his debts, and his mines were sold at auction. In Arkansas, Stephen Austin won an appointment as a circuit court judge, but the salary could barely begin to repay his family's debts. Mortified that he could not help his family, Stephen began looking for more lucrative opportunities.

Moving to Texas

In February 1820, Moses had traveled to Texas, which was at the time Spanish territory, to investigate emigration possibilities. In the meantime, Stephen moved to Louisiana, where a wealthy friend, Joseph Hawkins, gave him room and board and provided him with a legal education. Austin regarded Hawkins as an adopted brother and would soon get his help to start colonizing Texas.

In Texas Moses quickly obtained a grant to permit him to settle three hundred families on the Colorado River. Moses returned home to persuade Stephen to join him in the venture. Soon after notifying his son of his plans, Moses succumbed to an illness he had been battling and died on June 10, 1821. Stephen and his younger brother Brown left for Texas and publicized the venture in newspapers throughout the United States. Arriving in the Texas countryside, Austin declared it to be "the most beautiful I ever saw," noted Cantrell. Once Austin learned of his father's death, he decided to fulfill his father's dying wish to create an American colony in Texas.

Sam Houston

Sam Houston (1793–1863) had earned quite a reputation before he moved to Texas. Serving under Andrew Jackson (1767–1845; see entry) in the War of 1812 (1812–14; a conflict between the British and the Americans over the control of the western reaches of the United States and over shipping rights in the Atlantic Ocean), Houston distinguished himself in battle and became a general of the Tennessee militia. He then became a congressman and governor, a post he resigned after a public humiliation over his failed marriage. He exiled himself to live among the Cherokee before going to Texas in 1832 to practice law and dabble in politics. A charismatic man, Houston quickly gained the confidence of Texans and stirred their enthusiasm for independence.

Houston would serve two terms as president of the Republic of Texas. After the annexation of Texas to the United States, he served as a senator for thirteen years. Then in 1859 he was elected governor of Texas. He was ejected from office in 1863 when he refused to swear allegiance to the Confederacy.

Becoming "empresario"

As Austin entered Texas, he noticed rejoicing Mexicans who were celebrating Mexico's independence from Spain. Austin quickly offered his allegiance to the new government and went about securing sole authority to offer settlers permission to emigrate into the area. The Mexican government granted him the title of "empresario," giving him authority over the settlers as his colony's highest ranking official. As "empresario" Austin would be granted large tracts of prime land and, for some of his contracts over the years, would be able to charge a fee for the settlers' land. He and his brother Brown would soon establish a system for providing the steady influx of immigrants with land.

Immigration to Texas proved very popular in the United States. Starting in 1820 settlers had to pay cash up front for land in the United States. But in Texas, land was cheaper and settlers could buy on credit. Most immigrants to Texas needed credit; most settlers left the United States because of bad credit. Austin himself owed nearly ten thousand dollars to creditors in the United States.

Winning influential friends

Austin moved quickly to make sure the policies he needed to successfully encourage people to move into his colony were approved by the appropriate government officials. He applied for Mexican citizenship and would arrange to meet with influential men in his territory, including the various Mexican presidents over the years. He gained the friendship of many people who helped him continue with his colonization plans as Mexico established its independent government. In April 1824 Texas became part of a state of Mexico. By this time Austin had decided to spend his life in Texas. He wrote to his sister saying, "I make no more calculations except to spend my life here, wheither [whether] rich or poor, here (that is in this colony) I expect to remain permanently," according to Cantrell.

During this time of political upheaval, Austin freely and frequently wrote to his friends and advised them on policies of import to him. The policy most important to Austin was the ability to allow settlers to bring slaves into Texas. Although Austin felt slavery was "that curse of curses" he considered it to be a business necessity and held slaves himself. When Mexican officials threatened settlers' ability to keep slaves, Austin spoke out, demanding that "Texas *must be* a slave country." He wrote that "color forms a line of demarcation between [blacks] and whites. The law must assign their station, fix their rights and their disabilities and obligations—something between slavery and freedom, but neither the one nor the other. Either this, or slavery in full *must* take place."

By 1828, Texas had more white inhabitants than Tejanos, or Spanish Mexicans. And in the next two years the population of Texas would more than double. Mexican officials noted that Texas was largely populated by foreigners and began to hedge on their approval of continued immigration. The Mexican government passed the Law of April 6, 1830, which prohibited further immigration of Anglo-Americans into Texas. Austin did not take the news well. The cash flow from the fees he was able to levy on the settlers' land provided Austin with enough wealth to start repaying his debts. And Austin was committed to the colonization of Texas to such an extent that it took on, as he described it, the "character of a religion," according to Cantrell. Austin found a loophole in the new law and won the right to continued immigration into the colony.

Pushing for independence

Events in the early 1830s pushed Mexico into a state of chaos, as President López de Santa Anna (1794–1876) forcefully changed the role of government. Austin found the

The Alamo.
(Courtesy of the U.S. Department of Interior and National Parks.)

president a "sort of Mad Cap difficult to class" and continued courting allies of opposing political views. But in December 1831, Austin became persuaded that Texas should "go for *Independence,* and put our trust in our selves, our [rifles], and –our god," according to Cantrell.

By 1832, Austin had repaid his debts and began making plans to retire. But Cantrell notes that "private matters could never come first" for Austin; he quotes an acquaintance of Austin who claimed that Austin was a "kind of slave" and that Texas was his master. Public outcries came for Texas to push for independent statehood, and Austin heard the call. Austin served as president of the first convention to discuss the possibility of independence. More conventions followed, and soon the settlers had drafted a proposal for the Mexican government. These conventions were illegal in Mexico, and Austin was arrested and jailed for a year for his part in the affair.

While Austin was in jail, immigrants flooded into Texas. Cantrell estimates that the population of Texas reached nearly thirty thousand. Upon Austin's return to the colony, Austin's nephew reported that Austin was greeted "as one risen from the dead," according to Cantrell. Shortly after arriving home, Austin assessed the situation and declared that "war is our only resource" on September 19, 1835. The Texans went to war with Mexico to win their independence. Austin served for a short time commanding troops, but his weak body was prone to illness and he soon proved to be more of a diplomat than a soldier. Sam Houston (1793–1863) took over command of the army, and Austin became a commissioner to the United States. He traveled to the United States to win money for the Texas cause.

Meanwhile after American forces suffered terrible defeats at Alamo and Goliad, Houston captured Santa Anna at a battle at San Jacinto on April 23. Austin returned to Texas and quickly prepared to run for president of the new republic. He appeared to be the most qualified of the candidates, but the victorious general Houston entered the race late and won by a landslide. Houston did appoint Austin secretary of state, but Austin's health soon failed him and he died on December 27, 1836. His last words were: "The independence of Texas is recognized! Don't you see it in the papers?" according to Cantrell. Houston publicized the news of Austin's passing as "the Father of Texas is no more!" and insisted that government officials wear black armbands for thirty days "as a mark of the nation's gratitude for his untiring zeal, and invaluable service," according to Cantrell.

For More Information

Cantrell, Gregg. *Stephen F. Austin: Empresario of Texas*. New Haven, CT: Yale University Press, 1999.

James P. Beckwourth

**Born c. 1800
Fredericksburg, Virginia
Died September 25, 1866
Near Denver, Colorado**

**Fur trapper, Indian chief,
and mountain man**

Jim Beckwourth led an extraordinary life. Born to a slave mother, he grew up to become a skilled fur trapper, a mountain man, an expedition leader, an army scout, and an Indian chief. Near the end of his life he recorded the details of his life in an autobiography that made him famous and fueled Americans' ideas about the excitement and danger of life in the West.

James P. Beckwourth claimed to have been born on April 26th, 1798—but like many elements of his life, this date is disputed. Diligent biographers suggest that a better date would be 1800. The identity of Beckwourth's father is certain: he was Sir Jennings Beckwith, a member of a prominent white Virginia family and a veteran of the recent Revolutionary War (Jim later changed his name from Beckwith to Beckwourth). Less is known of his mother. She was certainly an African American, and probably one of Beckwith's slaves known as "Miss Kill." In any case, Beckwith took his entire brood—slaves, children, and livestock—and moved to a large farm on the American frontier, near St. Charles in Missouri Territory, where the Missouri and Mississippi Rivers meet. In

"The restless youthful mind, that wearies with the monotony of peaceful every-day existence, and aspires after a career of wild adventure and thrilling romance, will find, by my experience, that such a life is by no means one of comfort."

James P. Beckwourth.
(© Hulton Getty/ Liaison Agency. Reproduced by permission.)

9

St. Charles, young Jim grew up not as a slave but as the free son of a fairly prosperous farmer.

A youth on the frontier

Jim Beckwourth grew up on the frontier. He and his family cleared the land, and along with several other families, they built blockhouses—small forts—in which they would take shelter in the case of Indian attack. The boy learned a variety of skills, including how to hunt and fish and track animals in the woods. He also learned that the frontier was sometimes a harsh and violent place.

When Beckwourth was about ten his father entrusted him with carrying a sack of grain from their settlement into the local mill. He recounted the experience in his autobiography, *The Life and Adventures of James P. Beckwourth, Mountaineer, Scout, and Pioneer, and Chief of the Crow Nation of Indians:*

> On my way I rode joyously up to the little fence which separated the house from the road, thinking to pass a word with my little playmates. What was my horror at discovering all the children, eight in number, from one to fourteen years of age, lying in various positions in the door-yard with their throats cut, their scalps torn off, and the warm life-blood still oozing from their gaping wounds! In the door-way lay their father, and near him their mother, in the same condition; they had all shared the same fate.

Jim hurried back home to tell his father, and his father and some other men set off to hunt down the band of Indians who had attacked their neighbors. They returned several days later with eighteen scalps. Jim learned how quickly one's fate could change on the frontier—but he didn't grow up to hate Native Americans. With the help of his father, he came to realize that both the Indians and the settlers were capable of both kindness and cruelty. It was a lesson that would serve him well.

Between the ages of ten and fourteen Jim attended a school in St. Louis, Missouri, where he learned to read and write and studied math and history. St. Louis bustled with the trade that coursed down the Mississippi River, the major transportation route for the interior of the growing United States. Beckwourth dreamed of one day exploring the West he heard so much about. When he was fourteen he was apprenticed to (sent to learn a trade with) a local blacksmith. Jim learned a valuable trade and became a strong man in the process. But by the time he was eighteen Jim was convinced that he was cut out to be neither a blacksmith nor a farmer like his father. He longed for adventure.

Expeditions and Indians

Beckwourth soon joined an expedition led by Colonel Richard M. Johnson that was setting out to negotiate a treaty with the Sac Indians for access to lead mines on their land. Camped along a bluff of the Mississippi River, the band of men spent over a week with the Sac and Fox tribes. Beckwourth joined the Indians' hunting parties and grew to appreciate Indian culture and religion. He spent nearly eighteen months in the area and earned his first real money working in the mines.

James P. Beckwourth loved the difficulties and challenges of the life of a trapper and mountain man. *(The Granger Collection. Reproduced by permission.)*

Beckwourth soon found more opportunities for exploration, and in 1824 he joined a trapping and trading expedition to the Far West sponsored by William Henry Ashley's Rocky Mountain Fur Company. The party was making slow progress on its journey and soon recognized that they would need more horses. Beckwourth joined an experienced adventurer named Moses Harris in a two-hundred-mile march to buy horses from the Pawnee Indians. Beckwourth not only passed the test of keeping up with Harris; he saved both their lives by finding the trail of the departing Pawnees—or so he told the story in his autobiography. Others challenged this account and other tales Beckwourth told, leading some historians to distrust the reliability of the autobiography as a historical document. True or not, Beckwourth's book remains one of the few firsthand accounts of the life of a trapper and an American man living with Indians.

Beckwourth loved the difficulties and challenges of the life of a trapper and mountain man, so he continued to trap and work for William Sublette, who had purchased Ashley's fur trading business. Under Sublette, Beckwourth enjoyed his share of battles with Indians, killing a number of Blackfeet Indians over the years. Around 1827, when the white men wanted to establish a trading post among the Blackfeet, Beckwourth volunteered for the duty and was welcomed by the Indians, who respected him. "I soon rose to be a great man among them," recalled Beckwourth, "and the chief offered me his daughter for a wife. Considering this as an alliance that would guarantee my life as well as enlarge my trade, I accepted his offer, and, without any superfluous ceremony, became son-in-law to *As-as-to,* the head chief of the Black Feet."

A few years later Beckwourth left the Blackfeet tribe and went to live among the Crow tribe, who claimed him as a long-lost tribe member who had been captured by enemies. Soon his fighting skills against the Crow's enemies earned him the title "Chief Medicine Calf." In later years, Beckwourth led the Crow in a great battle against their Blackfeet enemies in which he claimed that all the Blackfeet were killed and the Crow lost thirty or forty warriors. For a time Beckwourth's life with the Crow was ideal: he had gained the kind of respect that he could never earn as a black man in a racist country, and his Indian "brothers" led him to rich hunting and trapping grounds inaccessible to most American trappers. Beckwourth sold his furs to the American Fur Company of St. Louis until 1837, when he was dropped from the company's books and decided to look elsewhere for a livelihood.

Beckwourth left the Crow tribe and worked for a time as a scout and mule driver for the U.S. Army in its military campaign against the Seminole tribe of Florida. Beckwourth fought against the Seminole in the Battle of Okeechobee on December 25, 1837, but the soldier's life didn't suit him and he soon returned to Missouri and the fur trade. Hired by Andrew Sublette, the younger brother of William, he traded for a time on the Santa Fe Trail and married a local Mexican woman. In October 1842, the couple opened a trading post on the Arkansas River that later became the town of Pueblo, Colorado.

Beckwourth again grew restless, and he left Pueblo for California in 1843. Through the 1840s Beckwourth bounced

around the Southwest, joining Los Angeles residents in their battle against Mexican officials in 1845. (California was still Mexican territory at the time; this battle was a precursor to the Mexican-American War, which lasted from 1846 to 1848.) Beckwourth traded along the Santa Fe Trail and worked as a guide for the U.S. Army in 1848—always on the lookout for adventure. In 1849 he traveled to northern California to participate in the booming California gold rush.

But Beckwourth did not dig for gold. Ever resourceful, he made a living gambling, trading horses, and profiting from the needs of prospectors. His adventures eventually took him into the Sierra Nevada Mountains, to a mountain pass that now bears his name. Beckwourth Pass lies just west of the California-Nevada border about thirty miles north of Reno. Beckwourth hoped to make the pass a major entrance from the east into the gold mining region in California, and he and his companions set about building a road through the pass. Beck-

Seminole Indians attacking a fort during the Seminole War of 1837. Beckwourth fought with the U.S. Army against the Seminole in the Battle of Okeechobee on December 25, 1837.
(© Hulton Getty/ Liaison Agency. Reproduced by permission.)

wourth guided the first wagon train through the pass in late July or early August 1851.

By 1852 he had built a road and established a trading post just west of Beckwourth Pass, hoping to profit from the stream of immigrants coming to California. In October 1854, T. D. Bonner, a justice of the peace in nearby Butte County, California, met up with Beckwourth and agreed to write up Beckwourth's stories and publish them as his "autobiography." *The Life and Adventures of James P. Beckwourth*, published in 1856, became a best-seller and made Beckwourth an instant celebrity.

Beckwourth's days as an adventurer were over by the late 1850s. After leaving California in 1858, he moved to Denver, Colorado, managed a general store, and was briefly married (though it is unclear what happened to his previous wife). After his new wife's death Beckwourth lived with a Crow woman. In the 1860s he briefly joined the U.S. Army in several battles against Cheyenne Indians. On September 25, 1866, while on an extended visit at the Crow Indian reservation in Colorado, Beckwourth died of mysterious causes.

Beckwourth knew that he had lived a remarkable life, one not available to many men. In closing his autobiography he declared:

> The restless youthful mind, that wearies with the monotony of peaceful every-day existence, and aspires after a career of wild adventure and thrilling romance, will find, by my experience, that such a life is by no means one of comfort, and that the excitement which it affords is very dearly purchased by the opportunities lost of gaining far more profitable wisdom. Where one man would be spared, as I have been, to pass through the perils of fasting, the encounters with the savage, and the fury of the wild beasts, and still preserve his life ... it is not too much to say that five hundred would perish, with not a single loved one near to catch his last whispered accent, would die in the wilderness, either in solitude, or with the fiendish savage shrieking in revolting triumph in his ear.

Though historians doubt the truthfulness of some of the stories in Beckwourth's autobiography, there can be no doubt that Beckwourth led a nearly legendary life. His many exploits—his brushes with death in the wild; his battles against and alongside Indians; his travels with some of the trailblazers of the West—make him a central figure in the opening of the West. Beckwourth's life was all the more remarkable because he was an African American man who enjoyed the riches of freedom at a time when so many of his race were enslaved.

For More Information

Blassingame, Wyatt. *Jim Beckwourth: Black Trapper and Indian Chief.* New York: Chelsea House, 1991.

Bonner, T. D. *The Life and Adventures of James P. Beckwourth, Mountaineer, Scout, and Pioneer, and Chief of the Crow Nation of Indians.* 1856.

Reprint. University of Nebraska Press, 1972.

Locke, Raymond F. *James Beckwourth: Mountain Man.* Los Angeles: Holloway House, 1995.

Marvis, B. *James Beckwourth: Legends of the West.* New York: Chelsea House, 1996.

Sabin, Louis. *Jim Beckwourth: Adventures of a Mountain Man.* New York: Troll, 1993.

Wilson, Elinor. *Jim Beckwourth: Black Mountain Man and War Chief of the Crows.* Lincoln: University of Oklahoma Press, 1972.

Black Hawk

Born c. 1767
Saukenuk, Virginia Colony
(present-day Rock Island, Illinois)
Died October 3, 1838
Iowaville, Iowa

Native American resistance
leader and warrior

Black Hawk was a powerful leader of the Sauk (also called Sac) and Fox American Indians located in northwestern Illinois and southern Wisconsin in the early nineteenth century. Black Hawk was one of the few Sauk who urged his people to fight the settlement of whites in the region. Despite his fierce resistance, Black Hawk was forced to surrender after the Massacre at Bad Axe River in 1832. His autobiography is one of the best records of the Native American experience.

"I fought hard, but your guns were well aimed. The bullets flew.... My warriors fell around me; it began to look dismal. I saw my evil day at hand."

Becoming a warrior

Black Hawk was born around 1767 in Saukenuk, a village of approximately one thousand people located near the convergence of the Rock River and the Mississippi River in present-day Illinois. He was given the name *Ma-ka-tai-me-she-kia-kiak* (Black Sparrow Hawk); his father, Pyesa, a member of the Thunder clan, was the keeper of the Sauk band's medicine bundle (a bundle containing items associated with the religious life of the tribe).

Black Hawk.
(The Granger Collection.
Reproduced by permission.)

In his autobiography Black Hawk recalled that "Few, if any, events of note, transpired within my recollection, until about my fifteenth year." However, that changed when Black Hawk joined his father in a war party against the Osage Indians. Black Hawk described his first kill: "Fired with valor and ambition, I rushed furiously upon another [Osage], smote him to the earth with my tomahawk—run my lance through his body—took off his scalp, and returned in triumph to my father! He said nothing, but looked pleased. This was the first man I killed!" In the years that followed Black Hawk killed several other enemies, and led war parties of his own in battle against enemy groups.

When Black Hawk was nineteen years old, his father died in a battle against the Cherokee. As was the custom among his people, Black Hawk blackened his face with charcoal, put aside all his belongings, and went into a period of mourning (grieving for the dead). According to biographer Maggi Cunningham, "Black Hawk spent five years alone in the forest and on the plains seeking strength and guidance from the Great Spirit.... During that hard and lonely time, Black Hawk learned about the ancient laws of nature, healing powders and herbs, and signs from Mother Earth and Father Sky." When he returned to his people he was the keeper of the medicine bundle and during his twenties and thirties became a famed warrior and leader of his people.

The white enemy

For many years, the Sauk people traded with the French and Spanish traders who traveled throughout their region. But their attitude toward white people began to change after 1803 when the United States purchased a vast tract of land from the French for fifteen million dollars. This land purchase, called the Louisiana Purchase, brought numerous American settlers into the territory that stretched from the Mississippi River to the Rocky Mountains. In 1804 Black Hawk encountered his first problems with U.S. government representatives. A group of leaders from the southern Sauk and Fox tribes had traveled to St. Louis to negotiate the release of a member of their tribe held captive by the whites; yet somehow the leaders ended up signing a treaty, the Treaty of St. Louis, that gave all tribal lands east of the Mississippi—some fifty million acres—to the United States in exchange for one thousand dollars a year. Black Hawk and other tribal leaders were outraged, for such a treaty could not be made without the approval of all tribal leaders. To the Americans, however, the deal was done, and the Indians no longer held claim to the land. Thus began the conflict with the United States that would shape the rest of Black Hawk's life.

In the years following the Treaty of St. Louis, the Sauk lands—parts of Illinois, Iowa, Wisconsin, and southern Minnesota—were still considered the frontier of the United States and were home to few white settlements. Therefore, Black Hawk and others in his tribe still hoped that they could keep their land. With the start of the War of 1812 (1812–14; a conflict between the British and the Americans over the control of the western reaches of the continent and over shipping rights in the Atlantic Ocean) Black Hawk and his people sided with the British forces in their attempt to keep Americans out of the Midwest. Black Hawk and his warriors, known as the British Band, helped the British take several forts in Ohio before the British surrendered to the Americans. Though Black Hawk and his warriors had helped the British control the entire Upper Mississippi Valley, the British signed a treaty that gave the Americans full control over all the land south of the Great Lakes.

In 1816 the U.S. Army built Fort Armstrong at Rock Island, Illinois, in the heart of Black Hawk's traditional homeland. The protection of the army paved the way for white settlement, especially in the eastern half of the territory. Two years later, the Illinois Territory became the twenty-first state. Though Black Hawk and his followers continued to oppose white settlement, another group of Indians listened to the advice of a Sauk leader named Keokuk. Keokuk had long believed that his interests lay with the Americans, and he had become rich by trading with them. It was Keokuk who sold American whiskey to the Sauk, which led to widespread alcoholism among the Sauk. (Black Hawk was strongly opposed to alcohol use.) By 1829 Keokuk and two other chiefs had sold the remainder of the Sauk lands east of the Mississippi to the United States in exchange for land in Iowa and cash payments. The treacherous Keokuk also warned the Americans that Black Hawk would resist with force white occupation of the land.

The Black Hawk War

In the spring of 1829 Black Hawk led his people from their winter hunt back to their village of Saukenuk, only to discover their homes and land occupied by white squatters. Though the whites and Indians lived in close proximity for some time, eventually the white squatters called on Illinois governor John Reynolds to remove the Indians. On June 26, 1831, army troops prepared to remove Black Hawk's people from Saukenuk. Hearing of the army's advance, Black Hawk peacefully removed his people across the river into Iowa to avoid conflict. While staying in Iowa, Black Hawk came under the influence of two men—Neapope and White Cloud—who urged him to fight back against the Americans. Black Hawk became determined to reclaim his people's homeland.

On April 5, 1832, Black Hawk and a band of one thousand people crossed the Mississippi River back into Illinois and headed north, looking for a place to settle as well as for support from other tribes in the area. The Winnebago and Potawatomi Indians, however, wanted to avoid war with the U.S. military and refused to support Black Hawk. Soon, the U.S. Army and state militias (volunteer armies that served for a short time, usually thirty days) were ordered to round up the Indians. A month later, hungry and discouraged, Black Hawk was ready to admit defeat and surrender. On May 14, 1832, as his group approached the U.S. troops under a white flag, nervous soldiers fired on them. Black Hawk's warriors attacked and handily won the battle, which became known as Stillman's Run (after the panicked flight of Major Isaiah Stillman's men). Happy in their victory—but fearful of further attacks—Black Hawk and White Cloud headed north. For the next two months, the U.S.

forces kept Black Hawk's band on the run. With little aid from other tribes, lacking food, and losing troops to desertion, Black Hawk continued to press north into Wisconsin.

Black Hawk surrendering.
(The Corbis Corporation. Reproduced by permission.)

On July 21, 1832, the U.S. forces, aided by Winnebago informers, attacked Black Hawk in the Battle of Wisconsin Heights, northwest of Madison. Many Sauk were killed, but others escaped by raft across the Wisconsin River, pushing westward toward the Bad Axe River that flows into the Mississippi. On August 1, 1832, the U.S. steamship *Warrior,* armed with cannon and supported by soldiers on the riverbank, attacked Black Hawk's group at the mouth of the Bad Axe River, even though the group approached under a white flag. Approximately twenty-eight Native Americans were killed. The following day Black Hawk pushed for a northward march to the land of the Anishinabe and the Chippewa. Most of his band refused to follow him, so Black Hawk left with White Cloud and around fifty followers. On August 3, 1832, the army forces attacked with cannon, artillery, and sharpshooters, slaughtering three hundred Native Americans who had stayed behind. Dakota tribesmen killed those Sauk, Fox, and Winnebago who reached the western bank of the Mississippi. This slaughter became known as the Massacre at Bad Axe River.

Prisoner of war

Exhausted and demoralized, Black Hawk, White Cloud, and the remaining native resistance fighters surrendered at Fort Crawford (present-day Prairie du Chien), Wisconsin, on August 27, 1832. In his surrender speech, Black Hawk stated, "I fought hard, but your guns were well aimed. The bullets flew.... My warriors fell around me; it began to look dismal. I saw my evil day at hand. The sun rose dim on us in the morning, and at night it sank in a dark cloud, and looked like a ball of fire. That was the last sun that shone on Black Hawk. His heart is dead, and no longer beats in his bosom. He is now a prisoner to the white men."

Imprisoned for a time in St. Louis, Black Hawk and a few of his men were sent to Washington, D.C., in April of 1833 to meet with President Andrew Jackson (1767–1845; see entry). Black Hawk expected that he would be treated with respect, but Jackson berated Black Hawk for his attacks and sent him and his men to another prison at Fort Monroe, Virginia. In 1833 Black Hawk was allowed to return to his people, but not before he was taken on a tour of eastern cities that was meant to show him how powerful America had become.

Shortly after his return to Iowa in 1833, Black Hawk dictated a moving account of his life story to interpreter Antoine LeClaire. Published as *Life of Ma-ka-tai-me-she-kia-kiak, or Black Hawk,* the book offered Black Hawk's version of the wrongs that had been done to him and his people. Black Hawk died on October 3, 1838, at the age of seventy-one. Not long after his death, Black Hawk's remains were stolen from his burial ground by a man who wanted to display them in museums and traveling shows. The governor of the Iowa Territory protested and eventually secured the remains at the Iowa Historical Society. When the society's building burned to the ground Black Hawk was finally free of the white man's grasp.

After Black Hawk's death, the United States, with Keokuk's cooperation, took the remaining six million acres of Sauk and Fox lands. By 1842 the tribes were forced to give away all their land in Iowa as well and move to a smaller reservation in Kansas. Finally in 1867, the Sauk and Fox were moved to their final destination in Indian Territory in Oklahoma.

For More Information

Books

Black Hawk. *Black Hawk, an Autobiography*. Edited by Donald Jackson. Champaign-Urbana: University of Illinois, 1990.

Cunningham, Maggi. *Black Hawk*. Minneapolis, MN: Dillon Press, 1979.

Hargrove, Jim. *The Story of the Black Hawk War*. Chicago: Children's Press, 1986.

Nichols, Roger. *Black Hawk and the Warrior's Path*. Wheeling, IL: Harlan Davidson, 1992.

Oppenheim, Joanne F. *Black Hawk: Frontier Warrior*. New York: Troll, 1979.

Vonvillain, Nancy. *Black Hawk: Sac Rebel*. New York: Chelsea House, 1993.

Web Sites

"Black Hawk (Ma-ka-tai-me-she-kia-kiak)" [Online] http://www.rsa.lib.il.us/~ilalive/files/wi/htm1/wi000002.html (accessed May 2, 2000).

"'Black Hawk' entry from Hodge's *Handbook*" [Online] http://www.prairienet.org/prairienations/blackhwk.htm (accessed May 2, 2000).

Daniel Boone

Born November 2, 1734
Exeter Township, Berks County, near
present-day Reading, Pennsylvania
Died September 26, 1820
Near St. Charles, Missouri

Frontiersman

Daniel Boone is considered the most famous American frontiersman in history. He guided settlers to establish the first American settlement west of the Appalachian Mountains in present-day Kentucky. At the time of Boone's early adventures, Native Americans vigorously defended their homeland west of the Appalachian Mountains against the encroaching waves of white settlers. Boone's efforts to carve out settlements in what he called "the dark and bloody ground" of Kentucky came to symbolize American efforts to tame the West, according to J. Gray Sweeney in *The Columbus of the Woods.*

Artist George Caleb Bingham captured Boone's legend in one of the most enduring images of the great man, *Daniel Boone Escorting Settlers Through the Cumberland Gap.* In the portrait, Boone is illustrated leading a group of settlers over a stormy mountain pass into a lush valley. Indeed, many early stories promoted the idea that, despite hostile Indians and wild animals, the frontier was safe as long as Boone was there. Though his real adventures were impressive, his sensational image in paintings, magazines, and novels obscured the facts of his life. His image was used to popularize the notion of

"Even in his own time the tale of Boone's role as the leader of colonists migrating through the Cumberland Gap into the Kentucky territories had begun to assume larger-than-life status. Boone came to be considered the consummate symbol of the American pioneer."

J. Gray Sweeney, in The Columbus of the Woods: Daniel Boone and the Typology of Manifest Destiny

Daniel Boone.
(The Corbis Corporation. Reproduced by permission.)

25

westward expansion, and he was the first American hero promoted to the entire nation.

Early life

Born the sixth of eleven children to Squire and Sarah Boone near Reading, Pennsylvania, in 1734, Boone led an active childhood, trapping, fishing, and camping in the forest. Given a rifle at age twelve, he became a superb shot and an excellent hunter. He had little formal education, but he did learn how to read and write. As a young man, Boone moved with his family to Virginia and North Carolina, working on his father's farm and blacksmith shop. In 1755 he served as a teamster (a wagon driver) and blacksmith for General Edward Braddock during the French and Indian War (1754–63). After the war, Boone married Rebecca Bryan on August 14, 1756. The couple would eventually have ten children together. Rebecca also gave birth to one illegitimate daughter, whom Daniel loved and cared for as his own.

So many stories of Boone's adventures have been written that it is difficult to separate fact from fiction. Nevertheless, the following story highlights what is generally accepted as his real adventures. From his daring deeds, it is easy to understand how Boone became the most renowned American frontiersman.

Exploring Kentucky

During the French and Indian War, Boone became acquainted with John Findley, a friend who intrigued Boone with his stories of the wilds of Kentucky. In the winter of 1768–1769, Findley convinced Boone to join him on a hunting trip to Kentucky. Boone hoped to gather enough furs to repay his debts to Judge Richard Henderson (1735–1785). Some sources indicate that Henderson financed Boone's first trip to Kentucky. By 1770, Boone and his companions had accumulated enough hides to pay the debt.

Boone's first attempt to settle in Kentucky occurred in 1773. Describing the rich, fertile valleys, he persuaded five families to join him. He then led his small group along nar-

row buffalo and Indian trails in search of a place to settle. En route, Native Americans attacked the trespassers as they slept. Most of the settlers were murdered, including Boone's seventeen-year-old son.

Soon after that unsuccessful attempt, Boone began work as a land agent for Henderson's Transylvania Land Company. His main duty was securing land from the Shawnee

Daniel Boone rescuing his daughter from North American Indian abductors. *(The Corbis Corporation. Reproduced by permission.)*

tribe for white settlement. Eventually, Henderson succeeded in buying what is now Kentucky for about fifty thousand dollars. In 1775 Boone and a party of thirty men employed by Henderson began cutting a road across the Cumberland Gap and building a settlement they called Boonesborough. As work progressed, nearby Native Americans grew angry at the invasion and raided the workers, killing some. Although the attack would have driven others off in fright, it strengthened Boone's group's resolve. According to Sweeney in *The Columbus of the Woods*, Boone wrote the following to Henderson:

> My brother and I went down and found two men killed and sculpted [scalped].... My advice to you, Sir, is to come or send [reinforcements] as soon as possible.... For the people are very uneasy, but are willing to stay and venture their lives with you; and now is the time to flusterate [frustrate] their [the Indians'] intentions and keep the country whilst we are in it. If we give way to them now, it will ever be the case.

Indian captivity

Boone and his companions were determined to fight for their town and the surrounding territory. They defended Boonesborough against several devastating Indian raids between 1776 and 1778. During one raid, Boone's daughter was among the captured. Within two days, Boone and a small group had ambushed the abductors, killed two men, and saved the girl. The rescue became the stuff of legend. James Fenimore Cooper (1789–1851; see entry) based his 1826 novel, *The Last of the Mohicans,* on a glorified version of the story.

In 1778 Boone was captured by Shawnee Indians. Some sources indicate he was captured by Indians four times, managing to escape unharmed each time. During this particular time in captivity, Boone's excellent marksmanship and natural curiosity about Indian culture endeared him to the tribe. In John Filson's "autobiography" of Boone's life, Boone describes his time with the tribe:

> I was adopted, according to their custom, into a family, where I became a son, and had a great share of affection of my new parents, brothers, sisters, and friends. I was exceedingly familiar and friendly with them, always appearing as cheerful and satisfied as possible, and they put great confidence in me.

Return to civilization

Approximately one year after his capture, Boone learned of a planned attack on Boonesborough and escaped to warn the residents and lead them in a successful resistance to the Indians. Upon his return, he discovered that his wife had assumed that he was dead and had returned to her family in North Carolina. Although he eventually reunited with his family and brought them back to Boonesborough, he felt uneasy with the townspeople; he was suspected of being a "white-Indian," a man who lost his civilized ways and should be feared, according to Sweeney. Over the next few years, Boone settled in several spots in Kentucky. He operated a tavern and tried to profit from land speculations; both ended in financial failure. Though he did not fight with American soldiers during the Revolutionary War (1776–83), his efforts on the frontier helped to secure America's eventual claim to that land. His popularity as a strong leader helped him to be elected to the Virginia legislature in 1771 and 1791, but political life didn't suit him.

Boone's skill on the frontier contrasted greatly with his inability to manage his lands or money. After the Revolutionary War (1776–83) the Virginia legislature negated Henderson's agreement with the Native Americans, and Henderson and Boone lost legal claim to thousands of acres of land in 1784. When Kentucky became a state in 1792, Boone tried to reclaim his lost land, but the government denied his claim.

Boone's last move

Without money or land, Boone decided to leave Kentucky for the new frontier. In 1799 he settled in present-day Missouri in the Louisiana Territory (a vast expanse of land that stretched from the Mississippi River west to the Rocky Mountains and from the Canadian border in the north to the Gulf of Mexico). Hoping to profit from Boone's fame, the Spanish government, which controlled the Louisiana Territory at that time, offered Boone a grant of land for encouraging others to settle the area. When the United States bought the land in the Louisiana Purchase of 1803, the United States initially denied Boone's right to the land. Congress reversed its decision in 1814, a year after Rebecca Boone's death. Supposedly, Boone sold the lands to repay previous debts. Without his wife, he continued to live on the frontier, taking his last hunting trip at the age of eighty-two in 1816. Boone died almost penniless on September 26, 1820, at the home of his son Nathan in Missouri.

Hero status

Boone's popularity grew throughout his lifetime. After the 1784 publication of John Filson's book *The Discovery, Settlement and Present State of Kentucke,* which devoted an entire chapter to "The Adventures of Col. Daniel Boone," more and more accounts of Boone's life were repeated and embellished in magazines and novels. Filson even acted as ghostwriter on Boone's "autobiography." Moreover, artists soon began depicting Boone's adventures as well. Some of the most famous illustrate his role as a pathfinder, showing him directing settlers toward lush, wild landscapes. Monuments of Boone were erected in the Frankfort cemetery in Kentucky and in Tuque Creek, Missouri, to commemorate his important contributions.

For More Information

Bakeless, John. *Master of Wilderness: Daniel Boone.* 1939. Reprint. Harrisburg, PA: Stackpole Co., 1965.

Faragher, John Mack. *Daniel Boone: The Life and Legend of an American Pioneer.* New York: Holt, 1992.

Filson, John. *The Discovery, Settlement and Present State of Kentucke ...[and] The Adventures of Col. Daniel Boon.* Wilmington, DE: John Adams, 1784.

Lofaro, Michael A. *The Life and Adventures of Daniel Boone.* Lexington: University Press of Kentucky, 1986.

Slotkin, Richard. *Regeneration Through Violence: The Mythology of the American Frontier, 1600–1860.* Middletown, CT: Wesleyan University Press, 1973.

Sweeney, J. Gray. *The Columbus of the Woods: Daniel Boone and the Typology of Manifest Destiny.* St. Louis, MO: Washington University Gallery of Art, 1992.

James Bridger

Born March 17, 1804
Richmond, Virginia
Died July 17, 1881
Missouri

Mountain man, trapper, guide

One of the American West's most infamous mountain men and scouts, Jim Bridger also operated a key trading post on the trail to California and served as a guide for mapping expeditions and military crusades against the Indians. He is credited with discovering the Great Salt Lake in present-day Utah, as well as the pass that was later used by the Overland Mail and the Pony Express.

Difficult early life

Bridger was born on March 17, 1804, in Richmond, Virginia, where he spent his youth working at the family business, a tavern (restaurant and bar). When he was eight years old, his family journeyed westward to Missouri Territory in a covered wagon, finally settling on a farm in Six-Mile-Prairie, which was not far from the booming city of St. Louis. Jim quickly learned the skills of a frontier boy—hunting, fishing, learning the lay of the land, and keeping a sharp eye out for Indians. However, his life was turned upside down when his mother, his brother, and then his fa-

"Only a man with extraordinary and relentless powers of observation, only a man with an utterly reliable memory could possibly gain and retain exact knowledge of the mighty welter of mountains, the endless tangle of streams and valleys which formed Bridger's vast hunting grounds."

Stanley Vestal in Jim Bridger: Mountain Man

James Bridger.
(Reproduced from the Collections of the Library of Congress.)

31

ther died, leaving fourteen-year-old Jim and his younger sister alone.

To earn a living, Bridger got a job operating a flatboat that ferried people across the Mississippi River. He was then hired as an apprentice to a blacksmith in St. Louis. It was there that he overheard the stories of the trappers and traders who flowed in and out of the bustling city. He soon hungered for adventures of his own. When trapper William Henry Ashley posted a notice seeking "enterprising young men" to join his expedition to the West in 1822, Bridger was quick to sign on.

To the mountains!

Ashley's expedition would become legendary, for it launched the careers of several renowned mountain men, including Jim Beckwourth (1800–1866; see entry), Tom Fitzpatrick (1799–1854; see entry), William Sublette, and Jim Bridger (1804–1881). Many men who had no experience living in the wilderness soon found themselves dressing in buckskins (leather clothes), trapping beaver, and shooting guns. It was a difficult life on the trail, but for a young man who liked hard work and adventure it was a great life.

By 1824 Bridger believed that he knew enough about living off the land to become a "free trapper." Beaver were plentiful in the Rocky Mountains, and a man could make a good living if he knew how to read the land and find good rivers. According to biographer Stanley Vestal, "Only a man with extraordinary and relentless powers of observation, only a man with an utterly reliable memory could possibly gain and retain exact knowledge of the mighty welter of mountains, the endless tangle of streams and valleys which formed Bridger's vast hunting grounds." Bridger was that man, and he became known even among other mountain men for his exceptional knowledge of the present-day states of Wyoming, Montana, Idaho, Utah, and Colorado.

In 1824, while camping with other trappers along the Bear River, in present-day Idaho, Bridger volunteered to find out where the river ended. He built himself a "bullboat," a round basketlike boat covered in buffalo hide, and set off down the turbulent stream. Miles later the stream emptied

James Bridger was known for his exceptional knowledge of the West. *(Reproduced from the Collections of the Library of Congress.)*

out into a huge lake. When Bridger dipped his hands in for a drink, he was surprised to find that it was salty. When he returned to meet his friends they all swore that he had reached the Pacific Ocean. In truth, he had discovered the Great Salt Lake and the Salt Lake Valley in present-day Utah. Bridger always felt a special connection to the Great Salt Lake area, and his detailed memory of its layout would come in handy to the Mormons who traveled there some years later.

In 1830 Bridger, Fitzpatrick, Milton Sublette, and several other mountain men founded a fur trading company of their own, known as the Rocky Mountain Fur Company. Competition from the Hudson's Bay Company and the American Fur Company was fierce, and the situation worsened when the market for furs began to decline. By 1834 the company—which had lost nearly one hundred thousand dollars in property and had seen seventy of its trappers killed in accidents or fights with Indians—was dissolved. Bridger trapped on his own for a few more years, but by 1840 the fur trade had collapsed due to overtrading and changes in the fashion industry. There was no more money to be made; Bridger had to find another way of life.

Fort Bridger

In 1842 Bridger settled at Fort Laramie in present-day Wyoming, the main trading post on the Oregon Trail. The travelers passing through were eager to soak up the advice of an experienced mountain man like Bridger. He decided to take advantage of that need, and with partner Louis Vasquez he built a fort on Black's Fork of the Green River, in the southwest corner of present-day Wyoming. The fort, called Fort Bridger, was situated near the point where the Oregon Trail forked, sending some travelers to Oregon and others south toward California. It was, writes Vestal, "not only 'an oasis in the desert' for all travelers, the haven of all the swarming emigrants who needed repairs, supplies, and fresh livestock, but also the trading post for all the tribes around, the rendezvous for wandering Mountain Men, and a great information bureau for all and sundry."

In 1847 Brigham Young (1801–1877; see entry) led a large group of Mormons westward on the Oregon Trail. The Mormons were a religious group fleeing persecution in the eastern United States. They believed that in the Salt Lake Valley they might be free of religious intolerance. They consulted Bridger, who praised the Salt Lake Valley as a place for settlement; according to Vestal, Bridger told Young, "It's my paradise, but you kin settle in it along with me." He provided the Mormons with maps and tips for avoiding trouble with Native Americans living in the region. However, Brigham

Whose Valley Was It?

From the moment they first met in 1847, Jim Bridger and Mormon leader Brigham Young were at odds. Bridger claimed the Salt Lake Valley as his own, but offered to share it with the Mormons. Brigham Young desperately wanted to claim the region as the promised land for the persecuted Mormon people. Though Bridger helped the Mormons find their way to the Salt Lake Valley, Young suspected him of inciting Indian attacks on Mormon settlements and of spying on the Mormons for the U.S. government, which was somewhat threatened by the separatist Mormon community. According to Bridger biographer Stanley Vestal, Young wrote in 1849, "I believe that Old Bridger is death on us."

In 1853 the Mormons sought to end Bridger's influence in "their" valley.

They sent a band of men to take over Bridger's lucrative ferry service across the Green River but were driven off by the well-armed mountain men. Then, charging that Bridger was inciting Indian raids, a Mormon sheriff led a posse of 150 men to capture Jim Bridger and take his fort. They took the fort, but not Bridger, who had left the scene. After looting the fort and killing some of Bridger's men, the Mormons left and Bridger returned—but his influence in the valley was never the same. The Mormons built Fort Supply to maintain their influence, and in 1855 they bought Fort Bridger for the sum of eight thousand dollars. In 1857, during the so-called Mormon War (see box on p. 36), the Mormons destroyed the fort in order to slow down U.S. forces marching on Salt Lake City. For his part, Bridger disputed Mormon ownership of the land around the fort until his death.

Young didn't invite Bridger to be their guide. Young wanted the area just for the Mormons.

Guide to the West

In the summer of 1849 Bridger accepted a huge challenge. Captain Howard Stansbury of the U.S. Army asked if Bridger could blaze a shorter trail from Fort Bridger to the South Platte River, thus shortening the route of the Oregon Trail. "Bridger stared," writes Vestal, "but had the grace not to laugh in the officer's face. *Find* it! Without leaving his seat, in five minutes' time, Jim told the Captain where that wagon road must run, scratching a map ... on the earthen floor."

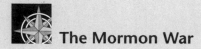
The Mormon War

The Mormon community lived in the Salt Lake Valley free from interference from the U.S. government until 1850, when Utah became a U.S. territory. Mormon leader Brigham Young was named governor of the territory. Over time, non-Mormon public leaders began objecting to the amount of power that the religious figure held over the territory. Government officials appointed to positions in Utah soon complained that Young's influence was too strong and that he was leading a theocracy (a government in which church and state are one). Moreover, non-Mormons were uncomfortable with some of the church's practices. The Mormon Church's official adoption of plural marriages (marriage to more than one partner at a time) in 1852 created a public outcry against Mormon immorality. Some charged that Mormons believed that they could live outside U.S. law. In 1857, convinced that the Mormons were considering rebellion, President James Buchanan (1791–1868) sent two thousand troops to Utah to install a new governor, Alfred Cumming. Fearful of renewed persecution and bloodshed, Young ordered the Mormons to evacuate Salt Lake City and hide in communities to the south. In June 1857, after the U.S. troops marched without resistance into Salt Lake City, a peace commission negotiated a deal that made Cumming governor but left the real power in Young's hands. The Mormon War was over, and life returned to normal.

Bridger soon led Stansbury over this trail, which later became the route used by the Overland Stage Coach, the Pony Express, the Union Pacific Railroad, and Interstate 80.

From 1849 to 1868 Bridger served as a guide in various capacities throughout the West. He led Captain William Raynolds of the U.S. Army Corps of Engineers on his journey to the Yellowstone area. (For years Bridger had told stories of the geysers and bubbling hot springs at Yellowstone, though most people wrote them off as the "tall tales" of a mountain man.) In 1861 he led Captain E. L. Berthoud and his survey party west from Denver through the mountains to Salt Lake City, and for the next several years he aided army units guarding the overland mail. With his encyclopedic knowledge of the western landscape, Bridger was the best guide in the West.

Bridger continued to serve as a guide after the end of the Civil War (1861–65; a war fought between the Northern and Southern United States over the issue of slavery). Meanwhile, the army was determined to protect gold seekers and settlers who were traveling on the Bozeman Trail, which extended across northeastern Wyoming and into Montana. However, they faced the determined resistance of the Sioux and Cheyenne. Bridger counseled the soldiers about how to deal with these Native American groups, but the eager young military men did not take the advice of the aging mountain man. They ignored Bridger with fatal consequences in 1866, when Captain William Fetterman led a party of eighty soldiers into an Indian ambush; all eighty soldiers were killed. When the army abandoned the Bozeman Trail in 1868, Bridger knew that his days as a guide were over.

Eventually, Bridger settled with his children in Missouri. He had been married three times to Native American women. His grandchildren loved to hear the stories told by their grandfather. By 1875 he was totally blind. He died on July 17, 1881, and was buried in Kansas City. Unable to read or write, Bridger left no written record of his life, but the Bridger Mountains, Fort Bridger, and Bridger's Pass all bear his name. Perhaps more importantly, he helped lead numbers of Americans into the West, thus paving the way for white settlement.

For More Information

Books

Alter, Cecil J. *Jim Bridger: A Historical Narrative.* Norman: University of Oklahoma Press, 1986.

Gowans, Fred R., and Eugene E. Campbell. *Fort Bridger: Island in the Wilderness.* Provo, UT: Brigham Young University Press, 1975.

Hafen, LeRoy R., and Harvey L. Carter, eds. *Mountain Men and Fur Traders of the Far West.* Lincoln: University of Nebraska Press, 1982.

Luce, Willard, and Celia Luce. *Jim Bridger: Man of the Mountains.* New York: Chelsea House, 1991.

Vestal, Stanley. *Jim Bridger: Mountain Man.* 1946. Reprint. Lincoln: University of Nebraska Press, 1970.

Web Sites

"Mountain Man Jim Bridger." [Online] http://xroads.virginia.edu/~HYPER/HNS/Mtmen/jimbrid.html (accessed on May 9, 2000).

Despain, S. Matthew, and Fred R. Gowans. "James Bridger." [Online] http://www.media.utah.edu/medsol/UCME/b/BRIDGER%2CJAMES.html (accessed on May 9, 2000).

Christopher "Kit" Carson

Born December 24, 1809
Madison County, Kentucky
Died May 23, 1868
Colorado

Frontiersman and guide

The ultimate frontiersman, Kit Carson spent his career on the edge of the American frontier, exploring, taming, and conquering it. Guts and determination turned Carson from an illiterate runaway into a brigadier general. Fortunate to be friends with one of the greatest promoters of the American West, John C. Frémont (1813–1890; see entry), Carson was a humble man whose amazing exploits would become known to the world—in embellished form—and make him a national hero.

Growing up on the frontier

Christopher "Kit" Carson was born on December 24, 1809, in Madison County, Kentucky, the third son of Lindsay and Rebecca Carson. The family soon moved to Howard County, Missouri, which was considered the frontier at the time. Carson remembered in his autobiography that "for two or three years after our arrival, we had to remain forted and it was necessary to have men stationed at the extremities of the fields for the protection of those that were laboring." As a

Kit Carson was "a symbol of the daring and intelligence by which the frontier was being extended."

Thelma S. Guild and Harvey L. Carter in Kit Carson: A Pattern for Heroes

Christopher "Kit" Carson.
(Reproduced from the Collections of the Library of Congress.)

boy, Carson thrived on the frontier, learning to shoot, hunt, and protect himself. A quick learner, Carson seemed to have a bright future.

In 1818, when Carson was just nine years old, his father was killed when a tree branch fell on him. Although Carson's father had recognized his son's intelligence and hoped Kit would get a good education, Carson had to leave school to look after his family when his father died. Carson's mother remarried in 1822, and Joseph Martin became a second father to Kit. Because Carson could not read or write, his stepfather sent him off to learn a trade at age fifteen. While working as an apprentice saddle maker in Old Franklin—the western-most outpost in Missouri—Carson heard prospectors, trappers, and scouts telling stories of trailblazing, hunting, and camping on the frontier and of fighting and trading with various Native American tribes in the untamed West. After two years of learning the saddler's trade, Carson decided that he could not spend his life as a saddler. Instead, he would join a party headed for the Rocky Mountains and see the world.

Makes his home in Taos

Finding an expedition to the Far West did not take long. Carson joined a scouting expedition headed for Santa Fe, New Mexico, in August 1826. Arriving in Santa Fe in November, Carson then traveled to Taos, New Mexico, to find more work. Carson enjoyed the diversity of the New Mexican inhabitants, quickly learning Spanish and some American Indian languages from the Spanish and Mexican settlers, and the Pueblo, Ute, and Apache Indians who were among Taos's 3,606 residents. The dusty, barren New Mexican landscape so appealed to Carson that he made it his home base for many years to come.

Falling in love with adventure

Carson worked for a few months as a cook and hunter for Colorado's first cattleman, David Kinkead, who had begun a ranch in Taos. He then joined American army colonel Philip Trammel's expedition to Chihuahua, Mexico, as an interpreter. After the expedition, he mined copper in Mexico for a while. But Carson's real love was of adventure, and he soon landed his first job as a guide, the career that would make him a popular American hero figure. In 1829 Carson accompanied Ewing Young's trapping party through the Rocky Mountains. Carson's easy ability with languages and his hunting and cooking skills quickly proved his value to the expedition. In addition, he soon became an able beaver trapper.

Although he stood only 5 feet 7 inches tall and weighed only about 160 pounds, Carson also established himself as an aggressive and effective Indian fighter. An example of his unrelenting drive occurred near San Rafael in northern California when some Navajo stole sixty head of cattle and horses from the expedition. Within a matter of days, Carson had tracked the Indians more than one hundred miles through territory unfamiliar to him in the Sierra Nevada Mountains. He recalled in his autobiography: "We surprised the Indians while they were feasting off some of our animals they had killed. We charged their camp ... and recovered all of our animals, with the exception of six that were eaten."

Etching of Kit Carson. Explorer John C. Frémont, who valued Kit Carson as a guide, called Carson "one of the finest pictures of a horseman."
(Archive Photos, Inc. Reproduced by permission.)

Establishing himself as a guide

Carson displayed such impressive abilities in the wilderness on his first expedition that his reputation as a skillful guide was established. He readily found more guide work over the next several years with fur trappers who were enjoying very profitable business in the 1830s. As a guide during this time, Carson's tracking abilities were continually tested. Indians would harass trappers, stealing their horses and mules or their animal skins. Although Carson showed a genuine appreciation for the customs and values of Native Americans, learning many Native American dialects, he would always protect those in his charge against Indian attacks or theft.

Carson's first wife was an Arapaho woman named Waanibe whom he married in 1835. The couple had two daughters. Waanibe died shortly after the second birth, sometime between 1839 and 1841. Carson then married a Cheyenne woman named Making-Out-Road, but she apparently did not enjoy being a stepmother, and she ended the marriage by placing Carson's belongings outside their home, which was the traditional Cheyenne method for divorcing a spouse. Carson's youngest daughter died unfortunately after falling into a pot of boiling soap in Taos in the early 1840s. Unable to care for his remaining daughter and pursue his work as an explorer, Carson made arrangements for his sister to raise his elder daughter, Adaline, in Missouri.

Carson meets Frémont

Carson found it increasingly difficult to find rivers with enough beaver for the trappers he guided throughout the West in the early 1840s. After settling his daughter with his sister in April 1842, Carson set off for St. Louis to look for new prospects as a guide. Uncomfortable in the city, Carson left St. Louis after only two days; he left on a riverboat headed up the Missouri River. On the same boat was John Charles Frémont, who Carson knew was looking for a guide. Approaching Frémont, Carson recalled saying "that I had been some time in the mountains and thought I could guide him to any point he wished to go," according to *Kit Carson: A Pattern for Heroes.* Frémont was in charge of an expedition to survey the Platte or Nebraska River to the headwaters of the Sweetwater River for the U.S. government, and he was intent on reaching the Rocky Mountains. After inquiring about Carson's abilities, Frémont hired him as a guide for one hundred dollars a month. As Frémont's guide, Carson validated his reputation as an invaluable member of any expedition, speaking with Indians in sign language, scaling snowy mountain peaks that others could not climb, and being what Frémont described as "one of the finest pictures of a horseman," according to *Kit Carson: A Pattern for Heroes.* Frémont immediately made plans for Carson to join his next expedition to California.

After the expedition, Carson returned to his home in Taos in 1843 and married Josefa Jaramilla, a beautiful fifteen-year-old girl from a prominent New Mexican family. Although Carson spent much of his married life in the wilderness, Josefa was a "magnet that always drew him back to Taos," according to Thelma S. Guild and Harvey L. Carter in *Kit Carson: A Pattern for Heroes*. Carson and Josefa saw each other only between his expeditions, but they had several children together.

Joins the Mexican-American War

Carson joined up with Frémont again and explored from the Great Basin across the Sierra Nevada Mountains to the Sacramento Valley of California between 1843 and 1844. During the journey, Carson protected the expedition from hostile Sioux who were warring against American trappers in the South Pass area of the Rocky Mountains. Carson prevented fights and facilitated trade with his knowledge of Spanish and Native American languages. His adventures on this expedition made Carson "a symbol of the daring and intelligence by which the frontier was being extended," according to Guild and Carter.

Carson returned and stayed near Taos until 1845. But by August 1845, Carson had once again joined Frémont, whose expedition was speeding toward California, which at the time was still Mexican territory. When Congress voted to annex Texas in 1845, many anticipated that war with Mexico would soon follow. Carson joined Frémont with the knowledge that the expedition might soon engage in a fight for American control of California.

Although first greeted warmly by Mexican officials in California, by 1846 Frémont's group was ordered to leave. The group headed toward Oregon but soon returned to California. Some sources indicate that they had received correspondence from Frémont's father-in-law, Senator Thomas Hart Benton, indicating that the United States wished to take California. Other historians insist that Frémont was acting without the consent of the U.S. government. Upon returning to California, Frémont and his group were instrumental in the success of the Bear Flag Revolt of 1846, in which Americans tried to take the territory from Mexico. Less than one month after these rebels raised the bear flag over California, the Mexican-American War began. This conflict started as a dispute over the southern border of Texas and became an opportunity for the United States to take much of Mexico's land in the Southwest. Carson worked as a guide, fought in some of the most significant battles, and by 1847 had become an official bearer of dispatches for the War Department, carrying some messages between California and Washington, D.C, until the Mexican-American War ended in 1848.

Staying near home

After the war, Carson returned to Josefa and their numerous children, including adopted Navajo children in addition to their own. To unite his entire family, Carson traveled to St. Louis to bring his daughter Adaline to Taos in 1851. For the longest stretch in his marriage, Carson stayed close to home, running a ranch on the Santa Fe Trail, forty miles south of Rayado, with some partners. Their enterprise proved quite profitable and increased trade in the region.

Works as an Indian agent

In 1853, Carson received news that he had been appointed Indian agent for the Mohuache Utes in New Mexico. As Indian agent, Carson was responsible for the lives of the Indians on the reservation and keeping the peace between the Indians and the surrounding white settlers. His compassion for the differences between Native American and white cultures proved valuable in maintaining relatively peaceful relations on the reservation. Though Carson believed "It would promote the advance of civilization among the Indians if ... I could live with them," note Guild and Carter, the reservation had no proper buildings for his residence. But Carson did not believe that Indians should assimilate into American society. Instead he maintained that Indian and white populations should live apart from each other. Quoted in *Kit Carson: A Pattern for Heroes,* he observed that the "one mode of saving them from annihilation" was to teach them to support themselves without the need for government aid. He added that "they will continue to sink deeper into degradation, so long as a generous government, or their habits of begging and stealing, afford them a means of subsistence."

Kit Carson in Fiction

Kit Carson gained fame first as John Frémont's scout during his expeditions into the Far West and then as Frémont's dispatch bearer during the Mexican-American War (1846–48; a war fought over the position of the southern border of Texas). In Frémont's reports of his expeditions into the Rocky Mountains, Oregon, and northern California, published in the 1840s, Carson appears as a brave but humble man of the wilderness. Frémont considered Carson a man who would always do more than was required of him. Carson became the subject of a number of biographies, novels, and other stories. Like such American heroes as Daniel Boone (1734–1820; see entry), Carson came to represent various interpretations of the West. In DeWitt C. Peter's *The Life and Adventures of Kit Carson* (1858), Carson is depicted as a virtuous man. Peter wrote that Carson "contracted no bad habits, but learned the usefulness and happiness of resisting temptation." Charles Burdett's 1862 biography of Carson supports this view of Carson as a moderate man who did not drink alcohol and did not gamble his money. Carson's reserved personal life contrasted greatly with his daring and bravery in the wilderness. In popular novels like Charles Averill's *Kit Carson, The Prince of the Gold Hunters* (1849), Carson's feats as a hunter and horseman are highlighted. Averill wrote that Carson had "a look of proud indifference to all, and the conscious confidence of ennobling self-reliance." But Averill exaggerated Carson's importance, even making the ludicrous claim that Carson was in fact the first to discover gold in California. Stories about Carson helped establish the model of a true Western hero that would be used again and again in popular books, films, and television programs depicting life in the American West.

Carson was also sympathetic to the plight of Indians on reservations. He urged the government to keep reservations far from white settlements because of the devastation that diseases carried by whites brought on Indian populations; to prohibit the sale of alcohol to Indians because of their particular difficulty with addiction to the substance; and to stop forcing unfriendly tribes to live on the same reservation. While becoming an advocate for Indian welfare, Carson developed a strong bond with the Indians. He gave them all the supplies the government sent for them (some Indian agents were known to keep the supplies or to sell them for a profit) and sometimes spent his own money to buy food and clothing for them. Without proper facilities on the reservation, Carson would meet and smoke with the Indians at his home in Taos. Carson served as Indian agent for eight years, until the beginning of the Civil War (1861–65; a war fought between the Northern and Southern United States over the issue of slavery).

Life as a soldier

With the outbreak of the Civil War, Carson resigned as Indian agent to serve as a soldier for the Union forces. In the Southwest, the greatest threat came from neighboring Indian tribes rather than hostile Texans supporting the Confederacy. Navajos and Apaches had begun raiding the territory so that the area was "virtually paralyzed with confusion and terror," according to Guild and Carter. Carson's vast experience with Indians made him an instrumental part of the army's campaign to subdue them. Carson could understand the various Native American languages; he knew how to negotiate with Indians by presenting gifts; he knew how to motivate Indians who helped the army; and he would relentlessly track Indians into desolate terrain.

Carson's skills were especially useful in the tragic Navajo campaign of 1863. Upset at being ordered to move from their homelands in present-day Arizona and New Mexico to the Bosque Redondo reservation in southern New Mexico, the Navajos determined to hold their ground near Fort Wingate in New Mexico. Carson was ordered by Colonel James Henry Carleton to round up the Indians who had refused to enter the reservation and to kill all Navajo men wherever they were found. Carson proved an excellent and relentless tracker of the Navajo. According to Robert Utley and Wilcomb Washburn in *Indian Wars,* "For six months, in summer and winter, [Carson's force] marched ceaselessly, burning hogans [Navajo houses], killing Navajo where they could but always keeping them on the run." The soldiers burned crops, slaughtered sheep and horses, and destroyed villages. Eventually Carson succeeded at trapping a huge number of Navajos in Canyon de Chelly, a steep-sided canyon in which the Navajo had traditionally taken refuge. The Indians were trapped with no food to eat. Carson's drastic method forced the surrender of nearly eight thousand Navajo early in 1864. The Navajo were marched to

Fort Defiance, and though many escaped during the journey and hid in the isolated canyons of northern Arizona, many more learned that they would be sent to a reservation far from their home. The Navajo resistance was broken.

Carson proved a masterful commander of his troops in several more campaigns. His efforts won him an appointment as brevet brigadier general. As thanks for the honor, Carson wrote to the secretary of war that "Though unsolicited by me, I accept with grateful pleasure, as a memento that during the late rebellion, the exertions of the New Mexico Volunteers [his troops], though restricted in its influence to its own territory, have not been overlooked by the United States," as quoted in *Kit Carson: A Pattern for Heroes.*

After the Civil War, Carson was made superintendent of Indian Affairs of the Colorado Territory, taking charge of the relations between the whites and the Utes there. When he arrived, tensions were high because both Indian and white inhabitants were short of supplies. Although his health was failing, Carson established peace in the area between 1866 and 1867, strengthening Fort Garland with arms and provisions and making friends with the Utes. Having secured peace for the area, Carson resigned from the army in 1867.

Even as he grew weaker, Carson made a trip to Washington, D.C., in 1868. During the trip he fell so ill that he quickly made arrangements to return home, fearful that he might not see his beloved wife before he died. On April 11, 1868, Carson was present as Josefa gave birth to their daughter, Josefita. But two weeks later, Josefa died.

After his wife's death, Carson's health and will to live rapidly faded. He spent his last days with a close friend, Dr. H. R. Tilton, making arrangements for his children's care after his death. On May 23, he called to Tilton from his bed, saying, "Doctor, Compadre, Adios," and died, according to Guild and Carter. Carson received a military funeral, and he and Josefa were buried side by side in Taos.

For More Information

Brewerton, George Douglas. *Overland with Kit Carson.* 1930. Reprint. Lincoln: University of Nebraska Press, 1993.

Carson, Kit. *Kit Carson's Autobiography*. Edited by Milo Milton Quaife. Lincoln: University of Nebraska Press, 1966.

Guild, Thelma S., and Harvey L. Carter. *Kit Carson: A Pattern for Heroes*. Lincoln: University of Nebraska Press, 1984.

Sanford, William R., and Carl R. Green. *Kit Carson, Frontier Scout*. Springfield, NJ: Enslow Publishers, 1996.

Utley, Robert M., and Wilcomb E. Washburn. *Indian Wars*. Boston: Houghton Mifflin, 1987.

William "Buffalo Bill" Cody

Born February 26, 1846
Scott County, Iowa
Died January 10, 1917
Denver, Colorado

Pony Express rider, army scout, showman

At the turn of the twentieth century, William F. Cody was known as "the greatest showman on the face of the earth," according to Nellie Snyder Yost in *Buffalo Bill: His Family, Fame, Failures, and Fortunes*. Growing up on the frontier, Cody loved the freedom and excitement of western life. But as more people settled the once "wild" West and as Indians were forced onto reservations, Cody saw that the way of life he had grown to love was disappearing. To preserve it, he turned his real life adventures into the first and greatest outdoor western show. Cody wanted to "bring the people of the East and of the New West to the Old West, and possibly here and there to supply new material for history," according to his autobiography. Buffalo Bill's Wild West Show presented eager spectators with reenactments of what Buffalo Bill considered true western life: battles between army soldiers and Indians, stagecoach ambushes, Pony Express deliveries, horse races, buffalo hunts, and trick shooting. Touring with his show for more than three decades, Buffalo Bill did more than any other person to both preserve and create the legend of the Wild West.

"Buffalo Bill was one of those men, steel-thewed and iron nerved, whose daring progress opened the great West to settlement and civilization.... He embodied those traits of courage, strength and self-reliant hardihood which are vital to the well-being of our nation."

Theodore Roosevelt, as quoted in Buffalo Bill: The Noblest Whiteskin

William "Buffalo Bill" Cody.
(Archive Photos, Inc. Reproduced by permission.)

Young man of the house

Born on a frontier farm in Scott County, Iowa, on February 26, 1846, William F. Cody did not enjoy a carefree childhood; he began working as a young boy. His family was one of the first to move to the Kansas Territory in 1847, where Cody saw men "dressed all in buckskin with coonskin caps or broad-brimmed slouch hats—real Westerners of whom I had dreamed," he remembered in his autobiography.

When Congress passed the Kansas-Nebraska Act in 1854, settlers began heated debates about whether Kansas should become a free or a slave state. Cody's father, Isaac, bravely announced his antislavery position among a group of proslavery supporters. As eight-year-old William watched, one of the proslavery supporters stabbed Isaac Cody in the back. Cody drove the wagon back home with his father's head in his lap. His father spent the next three years hiding from proslavery supporters who threatened his life. Cody took his father's place on the farm, tending the cattle, hunting, bringing water to the house, and riding to Fort Leavenworth for supplies. Cody's father died from pneumonia in 1857, and his mother rented out the farm and sold the livestock. The eleven-year-old William took a job driving an ox team to Leavenworth and delivering messages on the back of a mule.

Riding the range

While still a boy, Cody accompanied trail boss John Willis on a month-long cattle drive to Fort Kearny, Nebraska. On this trip Cody killed an Indian for the first time. Indians ambushed the cattle drive and three of the herders were killed. Cody wrote that he saw an Indian hiding by a nearby riverbank. "Instead of hurrying ahead and alarming the men in a quiet way, I instantly aimed my gun at the head and fired," he later wrote in *The Life of Hon. William F. Cody Known As Buffalo Bill*. Such an experience was part of Cody's job. Cody grew up at a time when white settlers were pushing American Indians out of their native lands. Though he did kill Indians, he later came to regret it, according to Karen Bornemann Spies in *Buffalo Bill Cody: Western Legend*.

Cody thrived on his experiences on the trail and continued to work on wagon trains. In 1858 he met Christopher

"Kit" Carson (1809–1868; see entry) and Jim Bridger (1804–1881; see entry) at Fort Laramie. Cody sat fascinated as the scouts talked in sign language with Indians. This meeting planted the seed of what would become Cody's next career, and he quickly began learning sign language by playing with Indian children from neighboring villages. Most of Cody's skills were learned in this way—by experience.

After a brief stretch of work in the Colorado gold mines, Cody took a job with the Pony Express. The express mail service, which lasted about eighteen months starting in 1860, needed brave men to ride horses at full speed between relay stations to carry mail across the country. One of the youngest riders, Cody logged one of the longest rides on his trip from Red Buttes to Rocky Ridge, in Wyoming Territory. Usually Cody would hand off the mail to another rider after the seventy-two-mile trip to Three Crossings, but one day Cody arrived to find the other rider dead. Undeterred, Cody hopped on a fresh horse and rode on to the next station. By

Although William Cody became a showman later in life, he had experienced the western frontier firsthand as a Pony Express rider, an army scout, a stagecoach driver, and a buffalo hunter. *(Reproduced from the Collections of the Library of Congress.)*

the time he returned to Red Buttes, twenty-one hours and forty minutes later, he had ridden twenty-one horses and logged 322 miles. On another ride he was pursued by fifteen Indians and escaped capture.

Becoming a scout

The Civil War (1861–65; a war fought between the Northern and Southern United States over the issue of slavery) broke out when Cody was fifteen years old. He initially joined a band of raiders who stole the horses of proslavery supporters, but his mother insisted that he quit the band. Cody found legitimate work with military wagon trains. And by 1864, he had signed up for the Seventh Kansas Volunteer Cavalry of the United States Army. During his year and a half in the army, Cody fine-tuned his skills as a scout.

After the war, Cody held several jobs, including that of stagecoach driver for Ben Holladay's Overland Mail Company and a short stint as a hotel owner. On March 6, 1866, Cody married Louisa Frederici. The couple would eventually have four children. But Cody was not one to appreciate the stay-at-home life; some scholars assert that Cody did not spend longer than six months at home during the entire marriage, according to Paul O'Neil in *The End and the Myth*. Shortly after his marriage, Cody left his wife in Leavenworth, Kansas, and went to Fort Ellsworth, Kansas, to begin life as a scout for the army.

Renamed Buffalo Bill

Cody's first assignment was to guide General George Armstrong Custer (1839–1876; see entry). Custer thought so highly of Cody's scouting skills that he extended an open invitation for Cody to serve as a guide for him. But Cody left scouting to start an ill-fated town along the Kansas Pacific Railroad. He lost all his money on this venture. Cody's fortune soon changed when he became a buffalo hunter for the railroad. In 1867 Cody had a contract to kill twelve buffalo each day to feed the railroad workers. The wage of five hundred dollars per month was significantly more than the thirteen dollars per month a private in the army was paid. After killing eleven buffalo with twelve shots, Cody earned the nickname "Buffalo Bill," a name he proudly answered to for the rest of his life. The railroad workers sang this song about the great hunter:

Buffalo Bill, Buffalo Bill
Never missed and never will.
Always aims and shoots to kill
And the company pays his buffalo bill.

By the time he finished his eight-month stint as a hunter, Cody claimed to have killed 4,280 buffalo, note Joseph G. Rosa and Robin May in *Buffalo Bill and His Wild West*. This number is probably an exaggeration. Karen Bornemann Spies states that three thousand is a more accurate number.

Living legend

Cody returned to scouting in 1868 by signing up with the Tenth Cavalry at Fort Hays, Kansas. He signed up for the most dangerous assignments in Indian Territory. His bravery won him a position as chief of scouts for the Fifth Cavalry. With this cavalry, Cody joined seven expeditions and fought in nine battles in the ongoing war with the Indians. He earned a reputation as the best army scout. Cody's fame spread quickly. He was the first scout to be honored with a one-hundred-dollar bonus. In 1872, Cody earned a Medal of Honor, the highest medal awarded in the armed services, for his work as a scout for Company B of the Third Cavalry.

In 1869, Ned Buntline wrote the first dime novel about Buffalo Bill, titled *Buffalo Bill, the King of Border Men*. Over the years, hundreds of dime novels would be written about Cody. His fame also won the attention of wealthy men from the East and Europe, who wanted to experience the thrill of the West. Starting in 1871, Cody led these rich men on planned hunting expeditions. The most memorable trip included Grand Duke Alexis, son of Czar Alexander II of Russia. Cody treated his royal guests to a five-day hunting trip, including a buffalo hunt and a wild ride in a stagecoach. The grand duke rewarded Cody with a fur robe, a stickpin, and buffalo-shaped, diamond cuff links.

Performers in Buffalo Bill's Wild West Show reenact an Indian attack on a stagecoach.
(The Corbis Corporation. Reproduced by permission.)

Life on stage

Cody took a leave of absence from scouting in 1872. On a trip to see Ned Buntline's theatrical production of his book *Buffalo Bill, the King of Border Men*, Cody soon found himself on stage. Buntline offered to pay Cody five hundred dollars each week for playing himself on stage. Cody persuaded a few of his friends to join him on stage on December 16,

1872, for a production of *The Scouts of the Prairie*. Although Cody couldn't act—a *New York Herald* review of the program noted that "Everything is so wonderfully bad it is almost good"—the play proved very popular. Cody soon formed his own company and moved his family to Rochester, New York, where he began touring in 1873. His program of *The Scouts of the Prairie* grew in popularity over the next three years and included trick shooting and western roping.

On April 20, 1876, Cody learned that his only son had died of scarlet fever. Depressed by the news, Cody closed the show and left for the frontier, rejoining the Fifth Cavalry as a scout. As his detachment prepared to move out, they learned of General Custer's slaughter by the Sioux at Little Bighorn. On July 17, 1876, Cody led men to fight the Cheyenne. During the battle Cody killed Chief Yellow Hair (sometimes referred to as Yellow Hand).

After this brief return to scouting, Cody returned to the stage. But now he included a reenactment of his battle with Yellow Hair in his show. Soon Cody organized his company to perform outdoors with live animals. While touring California in 1877, Cody persuaded some Sioux Indians to join the show. By 1882, Cody had begun to perfect what would become the formula for his lasting success. He wanted to present reenactments of western history. Cody organized the "Old Glory Blow Out" in North Platte for Independence Day. The show became one of the first rodeos, including horse and bronco riding, shooting contests, and a dramatic reenactment of a stagecoach robbery.

On May 19, 1883, Buffalo Bill's Wild West Show opened to a crowd of about eight thousand in Omaha, Nebraska. The cowboys, live animals, reenactments of famous battles, shooting exhibitions, and stagecoach and Pony Express deliveries proved a winning combination. By 1885, the show had about one million spectators and made a profit of one hundred thousand dollars. According to Walsh and Salsbury in *The Making of Buffalo Bill,* Mark Twain (1835–1910) wrote that the show "brought vividly back the breezy, wild life of the great plains and the Rocky Mountains ... Down to its smallest details, the show is genuine cowboys, vaqueros, Indians, stage coach, costumes, and all." The Wild West Show had garnered such fame in the United States that Queen Victoria

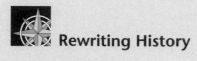

Rewriting History

Buffalo Bill represented his Wild West Show as an authentic slice of western life. But like the many books about Buffalo Bill, the Wild West Show exaggerated and embellished real events to rewrite history. Though Cody had been present at many events depicted in his show, the reenactments often embellished the truth. In the reenactment of Custer's Last Stand, for instance, Cody rode into the ring after the battle and the words "Too Late" flashed on a screen. In truth, Cody never attempted to save Custer at Little Bighorn.

While embellishing certain details, the Wild West Show also created stereotypes that would endure for generations. Buffalo Bill's depictions of cowboys and Indians are the most well known stereotypes he influenced. The Native Americans in the show, for example, were real Indians. Buffalo Bill had originally hired Sioux who wore their traditional feather headdresses and war paint and rode horses. Not all Native American tribes dressed this way before battle or rode horses. Nevertheless, the ornamentation was so popular that all Indians, whatever their tribe, dressed the same way in the Wild West Show. While Buffalo Bill introduced prominent Indians in the show with respect, the show portrayed Indians as a menace to whites on the plains. Some historians suggest that the show perpetuated a stereotype of Indians as vicious warriors. The cowboys of the Wild West Show did not show the wear and tear of lonely days herding cattle on the open plains. Instead, Buffalo Bill's cowboys and cowgirls exhibited impressive roping and shooting skills and performed fancy riding tricks.

of England requested that the show be featured at her Golden Jubilee in 1887 to celebrate fifty years of her rule. Cody loaded 200 passengers, 180 horses, 18 buffalo, 10 mules, 10 elk, 5 Texas steers, 4 donkeys, and 2 deer onto a ship called the *State of Nebraska* in New York and began a seventeen-day trip to England. The show traveled and performed for the next six months in England, returned to the United States for a year, and then toured Europe until 1892. The Wild West Show played to a crowd of nearly eighteen thousand outside the World's Fair grounds in Chicago in 1893.

The end of the glory days

By 1894, the slow economy made it difficult for people to afford tickets to the Wild West Show. Buffalo Bill was tired of traveling and his partner, Nate Salsbury, became ill. Salsbury died in 1902, but Cody couldn't retire because he had mismanaged his money and had lost a great deal in bad investments. To try to get out of debt, Cody took his show to Europe again and toured until 1906. By 1908, the show had regained its financial success. Cody gained the financial support of Major Gordon Lillie, known as Pawnee Bill. Pawnee Bill owned another show, which he combined with the Wild West Show. Cody was still unable to retire because he continually lost money in bad investments. Cody lost his show in 1913 when it was auctioned off to pay his debts. He then toured with a circus between 1914 and 1916. In his sixties, Cody no longer performed for audiences. Often helped onto his horse, he would merely ride into the ring and sit tall in the saddle while the spotlight lingered on him. His final appearance was on November 4, 1916. He died in the company of his wife and one remaining child, Irma, in Denver on January 10, 1917.

For More Information

Burke, John. *Buffalo Bill: The Noblest Whiteskin*. New York: Putnam, 1973.

Cody, William Frederick. *An Autobiography of Buffalo Bill (Colonel W. F. Cody)*. New York: Holt, Rinehart and Co., 1920.

Cody, William Frederick. *The Life of Hon. William F. Cody Known As Buffalo Bill*. Lincoln: University of Nebraska Press, 1978.

Havighurst, Walter. *Annie Oakley of the Wild West*. Lincoln: University of Nebraska Press, 1992.

O'Neil, Paul. *The End and the Myth*. Alexandria, VA: Time-Life Books, 1977.

Rosa, Joseph G., and Robin May. *Buffalo Bill and His Wild West*. Lawrence: University Press of Kansas, 1989.

Spies, Karen Bornemann. *Buffalo Bill Cody: Western Legend*. Springfield, NJ: Enslow Publishers, 1998.

Walsh, Richard J., and Milton S. Salsbury. *The Making of Buffalo Bill*. Indianapolis, IN: Bobbs-Merrill, 1928.

Yost, Nellie Snyder. *Buffalo Bill: His Family, Fame, Failures, and Fortunes*. Chicago: The Swallow Press, 1979.

James Fenimore Cooper

Born September 15, 1789
Burlington, New Jersey
Died September 14, 1851
Cooperstown, New York

Writer

James Fenimore Cooper was a pioneer of American literature and the first writer to popularize the American West. Frustrated that most novels available in America were about English society, Cooper penned several books that have since become American classics. In his Leatherstocking Tales, which include such favorites as *The Last of the Mohicans* and *The Deerslayer,* Cooper showed that American themes—the conquest of the West, the conflict between whites and Native Americans, and manifest destiny—could produce great literature. Cooper also created Natty Bumppo, the protagonist of these tales, a rugged, romantic, nature-loving hero who has been copied in novels, films, and television Westerns ever since.

James Fenimore Cooper introduced the themes of the frontier, white/Indian conflict, and America's westward expansion as proper subjects for literary works. Perhaps even more importantly, he began to shape the romantic idea of the American West.

James Fenimore Cooper.
(Drawing by Cacilie Brandt. National Portrait Gallery/Smithsonian Institution. Reproduced by permission.)

From privilege to poverty

Born on September 15, 1789, James Cooper was the twelfth of thirteen children born to William Cooper and Elizabeth Fenimore Cooper. Cooper's parents were of old Quaker stock, and they were part of the tight-knit world of wealthy New York families. With a partner, William Cooper purchased a huge tract of land near Otsego Lake, New York, northwest of the Catskill Mountains, and relocated there with his family. Cooper and his partner planned to sell the land to immigrants arriving in America, and they named the settlement Cooperstown.

In Cooperstown, young Cooper learned about the frontier firsthand. He grew up wild, playing and exploring in the surrounding woods with his brothers. But Cooper never encountered American Indians, except in books. At age eleven, Cooper was sent to boarding school in Albany, and from there, at age thirteen, he entered Yale College. He was such a wild boy that he was expelled two years later for blowing another boy's door in with gunpowder. Back in Cooperstown, Cooper spent his time reading novels, until his father determined that James would have a naval career. Cooper was sent to serve on a sailing ship, the *Stirling,* for a year-long voyage to England and Spain. The sea lore and nautical tall tales he heard on this voyage would later enter several of his novels.

Cooper's father died in 1809, leaving his son a very wealthy young man. Cooper married Susan De Lancey on New Year's Day of 1811 and decided to live the life of a gentleman farmer. For the next decade, Cooper and his steadily growing family lived mostly in Westchester County, New York, on Angevine Farm, which he built on his wife's family property. Involved in the social life of the region, Cooper also founded agricultural and Bible societies and was quartermaster and paymaster for New York's Fourth Division of Infantry, happily parading in his blue uniform and sword. But Cooper's wealth did not last. Land values decreased after the War of 1812 (1812–14; a conflict between the British and the Americans over the control of the western reaches of the United States and over shipping rights in the Atlantic Ocean), and Cooper's brothers lived beyond their means and invested their money foolishly. By 1818, Cooper had to sell the family's mansion in Cooperstown to pay off debts. By 1819, all of his brothers were dead, and their debts—and in some cases their children—had been left to Cooper's care.

"I could write a better book than that myself"

One day in 1819 or early 1820, Cooper was reading a new English novel that he felt was of poor quality. He became

frustrated; he threw down the book and proclaimed aloud, "I could write a better book than that myself." Cooper took up his own challenge, and the result was his first book, *Precaution,* a novel about the efforts of an English family to marry off its daughters. Though the novel sold few copies, it gave Cooper the confidence to begin his next novel, which he modeled on the adventurous romances of the famous British novelist Sir Walter Scott. This book, *The Spy,* appeared in 1821 and changed the course not only of Cooper's life but of American literature.

A proudly nationalistic book, *The Spy* tells the story of Harvey Birch, a peddler (traveling salesman) who operated behind the lines of General George Washington's army during the Revolutionary War (1776–83). The story mixed battle scenes, romance, mystery, and historical events in the first novel that was ever written about American themes for an American reading public. The book was an overnight success and instantly established Cooper as an important novelist.

Royalties from the book began to pour in, saving Cooper from bankruptcy. Cooper had found a way to make a living.

The Leatherstocking Tales

The Spy made a celebrity of Cooper and rescued him from financial disaster. For the next decade or so Cooper was a popular success. The first of what became known as his Leatherstocking Tales, *The Pioneers,* was published in 1823. The book explores the conflict between Judge Marmaduke Temple—representing progress and civilization—and Natty Bumppo, or Leatherstocking, an old scout and hunter who cannot abide the "wicked and wasty ways" of civilization. Leatherstocking's reaction to the growth of a town in what was once the frontier encourages readers to question the benefits of the westward march of civilization that was taking place across America. In the end, Leatherstocking heads off to join the Indians and wild animals.

After publishing two other novels that didn't fare as well as *The Pioneers,* Cooper returned to the Leatherstocking Tales in a series of books published over the coming years. *The Last of the Mohicans,* Cooper's most widely read book, was published in 1826. Natty Bumppo was a man in his thirties in that book. Then came *The Prairie* in 1827, featuring an eighty-year-old Natty. When Cooper returned to his hero in *The Pathfinder* (1840) and *The Deerslayer* (1841), he explored Leatherstocking's youth. Together these books dealt with a range of American and Western themes, earning Cooper a distinctive place in American literary history.

In *The Last of the Mohicans,* Cooper depicts Natty—here called Hawkeye—as a scout for the British during the French and Indian War in 1757. The title of the novel refers to two other main characters—Hawkeye's Indian friend Chingachgook and the Indian's son Uncas—who are "good" Indians (those who are friendly and helpful toward whites and don't resist whites' taking their territory). Chingachgook and Uncas are the last of their tribe and representatives of the "noble savage" (a stereotype of Native Americans that was common at the time; see sidebar on p. 64). Contrasted to them are the evil Magua and his Mingo or Iroquois brethren who represent the dark side of savagery. Magua twice captures

THE LAST OF THE MOHICANS.

Illustration from James Fenimore Cooper's *The Last of the Mohicans*.
(Archive Photos, Inc. Reproduced by permission.)

the white Munro sisters, Alice and Cora, and has designs on making Cora his wife. But Hawkeye, helped by his trusted friends Chingachgook and Uncas, saves the ladies from this fate. In the midst of several chase scenes is the violent massacre of the British at Fort William Henry by the native allies of the French. In the end, Uncas, Cora, and Magua are all killed, and Hawkeye and Chingachgook go off into the forest, leaving the civilized world behind.

The Noble Savage

Many of the Indian characters portrayed in James Fenimore Cooper's novels were versions of the "noble savage" stereotype of Native Americans. From the very first contact that white Europeans had with indigenous peoples in North and Central America, some Europeans chose to romanticize the people they found living so differently from Europe's "civilized" ways. Europeans recognized that Indians lived without many of the benefits of civilization; they thought that this made the Indians more pure and that the Indians had a more "authentic" relationship with the natural world.

There was another side to this stereotype, of course—the "savage" side.

Europeans felt that the Indians' lack of Christian beliefs and their "primitive" cultural ways made them less than human. Many believed that anything that could be done to convert Indians to white ways was acceptable, and this belief allowed them to inflict incredible brutality and destruction on the Native Americans.

Cooper's treatment of Indian characters revealed both sides of the stereotype. Some of his Indian characters seem to possess real wisdom while others are cruel and barbaric. In the end, however, Cooper failed to present a realistic picture of Native Americans.

Cooper wrote the next Leatherstocking Tale, *The Prairie,* while living with his family in Europe. Having headed westward to the prairie, Natty Bumppo, now in his eighties, once again finds the civilized world overtaking him. Borrowing the plot line from *Mohicans, The Prairie* also features a kidnapped white woman and rival Indian tribes. But the real story here is in the theme: the questioning of the rightness of manifest destiny. From the old scout's point of view, the prairie should be left alone; in fact, at the end of the book the main characters turn back and recross the Mississippi, while Natty is left to die facing the setting sun. Most critics agree that *The Pioneers* and *The Prairie,* in which Natty Bumppo appears in old age, are the strongest of the Leatherstocking Tales.

For more than a decade, Cooper left the Leatherstocking Tales. Two sea novels—*The Red Rover* (1828) and *The Water-Witch* (1830)—allowed Cooper to do the same thing for an ocean setting and sailing as he did for the frontier: make them proper subjects for American literature. But Cooper soon found himself drawn into politics and writing nonfiction. His political essay called *Notions of the Americans* (1828) defended American democracy to the aristocratic-minded British reading public. He also wrote *History of the Navy of the United States* (1839); a book on politics, *The American Democrat* (1838); and several travel books about his experiences in Europe. None of these books appealed much to readers.

Perhaps it is not surprising, then, that Cooper returned to the Leatherstocking saga with *The Pathfinder* and *The Deerslayer*. These two books relate the earliest adventures of Natty's youth, on the trail of the Mingos with his friend Chingachgook. Young Natty is even allowed love interests, though he never considers marriage or settling down. Taken together, the five Leatherstocking books remain the core of Cooper's achievement and are still widely read today.

Cooper's legacy

Cooper continued to write until the very end of his life. Though he continued to earn a living from his writing, he never again felt secure with his American audience. By the early 1850s Cooper's health was failing; he was suffering from a chronic deterioration of his liver. He died one day before his birthday, on September 14, 1851.

Though Cooper's body of work—more than fifty works of fiction and nonfiction—was uneven, his Leatherstocking Tales left an important legacy. They introduced the themes of the frontier, white/Indian conflict, and America's westward expansion as proper subjects for literary works. Perhaps even more importantly, they introduced American readers to seemingly authentic frontier heroes such as Natty Bumppo and began to shape the romantic idea of the American West that influenced many later fictional works about the West. The images Cooper created have lasted to this day, as evidenced by the continued interest in his writings and the frequency with which his stories are adapted for film, television, and radio.

For More Information
Clark, Robert, ed. *James Fenimore Cooper: New Critical Essays*. New York: Vision and Barnes & Noble, 1985.

Darnell, Donald G. *James Fenimore Cooper: Novelist of Manners*. Newark: University of Delaware Press, 1993.

Long, Robert Emmet. *James Fenimore Cooper*. New York: Continuum, 1990.

Railton, Stephen. "James Fenimore Cooper." In *Antebellum Writers in New York and the South,* vol. 3 of the *Dictionary of Literary Biography*, pp. 74–93. Detroit: Gale, 1979.

Ringe, Donald A. *James Fenimore Cooper*. Boston: Twayne, 1988.

Walker, Warren S. *James Fenimore Cooper: An Introduction and Interpretation*. New York: Barnes & Noble, 1962.

Crazy Horse

Born c. 1842
South Dakota
Died September 5, 1877
Fort Robinson, Nebraska

Warrior and tribal leader

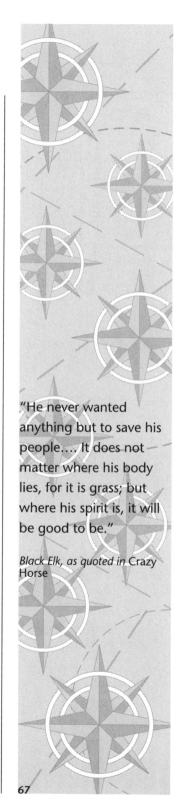

Oglala Sioux warrior Crazy Horse was present at every major battle in the Plains Indians' long war to retain control of their lands in the West. A quiet, distant leader, Crazy Horse was noted for his uncommon bravery. He rose to a position of leadership not only within his own tribe but within the confederacy (loose grouping) of tribes that came together in the 1860s and 1870s to combat the white advance onto Indian lands in present-day South Dakota, Nebraska, Wyoming, and Montana. Crazy Horse led his people to their greatest victory in the Battle of Little Bighorn in 1876. However, within a year of this victory over forces led by General George Armstrong Custer (1839–1876; see entry), the Indian forces were divided and Crazy Horse was dead.

Following a vision

Crazy Horse's name as a child was Horse Stands in Sight, but his friends called him Curly. He was given the name Crazy Horse later in life. Like most Sioux youth, Curly dreamed of the day that he would become a powerful warrior. Among Curly's people, a tribe known as Oglala Sioux, the path to manhood was reached by way of a vision, a powerful waking dream that indicated the path that one's life would follow. Their elders led most young men to their vision, but Curly was not like most young men. He looked different—he had lighter skin and light brown wavy hair—and acted different—he was quieter and less rambunctious than his peers were. Curly would come to his vision in his own way, and the life path that the vision foretold was also quite different.

In 1855, when he was about thirteen years old, Curly rode away from his tribal camp, stripped off his clothes, and prepared to accept his vision. After lying on sharp rocks to stay awake and depriving himself of food and water for three days, Curly finally had his vision. In the vision, described by Judith St. George in *Crazy Horse*, "a man dressed in a plain shirt and buckskin leggings came riding up out of the lake on horseback. He was wearing only one feather in his long, flowing brown hair and he had a small stone tied behind his ear." The dream warrior told Curly never to wear a war headdress, to sprinkle himself and his pony with dust before battle, to paint a single lightning bolt on his face, and never to take the spoils of battle for himself. If he followed this vision, he would be protected from arrows and bullets. The vision also predicted that Curly would meet his death with his arms pinned by one of his own people. Curly had had his vision and was ready to become a man and a warrior.

Curly returned to his tribe triumphant, but his triumph did not last, for his father scolded him for leaving camp on his own and for seeking a vision without the counsel of elders. "You are not yet a man," he told Curly. But the young man felt he was close. With his friends he tested his bravery and his riding skills in small raids on the white travelers who crossed Indian land on a path the Oglala called the Holy Road and the whites called the Oregon Trail (the main route at the time for overland travelers heading west). Although still young, Curly had already learned to hate the white people who took Indian land, disturbed Indian hunting grounds, and made promises that they never kept. Curly felt no shame in stealing horses, food, and supplies from the

white travelers; he considered it fair trade for all that they took from the Indians.

A warrior is born

Though Curly trusted his vision, he was not yet a man in the eyes of his people. Then, when he was thirteen or fourteen, Curly did his people the great service of locating a buffalo herd only two days' travel from the Sioux camp. Allowed to join the band of hunters, Curly showed his bravery by killing two of the great shaggy buffalo on his own. At the tribal dance of celebration, Curly was praised for his contribution to his tribe, a great honor for a Sioux. Around the time he was seventeen Curly took part in his first battle, a fight against the Arapaho Indians to claim hunting lands surrounding the Powder River in eastern Wyoming and Montana. Clad only in a breechcloth (a strip of cloth covering the genitals) and sprinkled with dust, Curly killed two Arapaho and avoided a hail of arrows. Upon Curly's return his father took him aside and granted him a warrior's name, his own name: Curly was now known as Crazy Horse.

Holding back the white tide

Crazy Horse became a warrior and a man at a time of great transition for his tribe. Before the arrival of the white man, the Sioux tribes had ranged widely across the vast Plains, camping where the hunting was good and living lightly off the land. But beginning in the 1840s, the Plains began to see a steady stream of white emigrants crossing the country in search of a better life in Oregon and California. The rush of people crossing Indian land increased dramatically after gold was discovered in California in 1849. Emigrants soon came into conflict with the various tribes who lived along the Oregon Trail, and beginning in 1855, U.S. troops were sent onto the Plains to eliminate the Native Americans' threat to westward expansion. Army forces and Indians soon met in battle. Crazy Horse watched closely the changes sweeping his land. He saw army troops attack defenseless women and children, and he came to believe that the white men had no intention of keeping the treaties they forced the Indians to make.

In 1857 all the Sioux tribes—the Oglala, Brulé, Minneconjou, Sans Arcs, Blackfeet, Two Kettles, and Hunkpapa—met near Bear Butte at the eastern edge of the Black Hills to discuss the white threat. The Sioux feared that the white trespassers would soon try to seize the land the Sioux considered holy, land that was crucial to their cultural and religious lives. Among the chiefs gathered at the meeting were Sitting Bull, the great military, spiritual, and political leader of the Hunkpapa Sioux; Spotted Tail; and Hump, whose life Crazy Horse saved only three years later. Though tribe members agreed on the threat that faced them, they were unable to come to an agreement on how to combat it, and they left the meeting with no clear plan for resisting the white advance.

Clashes between whites and Indians increased on the northern Plains in the years following the Civil War (1861–65; a war fought between the Northern and Southern United States over the issue of slavery). Crazy Horse was among those who refused to back down in the face of a growing army presence in the region. After hundreds of Cheyenne were slaughtered at Sand Creek in 1864, Crazy Horse joined in an attack on the Julesburg stockade in Colorado Territory. Crazy Horse's most notable battle of this period occurred in December 1866, when Captain William J. Fetterman led a band of eighty soldiers out of Fort Kearny and—against orders—beyond sight of the fort. Crazy Horse and a small band of men lured Fetterman's forces ever further from the fort. Suddenly, the remainder of the large force of Native Americans poured down from the surrounding hills, slaughtering Fetterman and all his men. Only twelve Indians lost their lives in this battle that helped convince the army to abandon their positions in Wyoming a few years later.

During the many clashes with white soldiers, Crazy Horse secured his standing among his people not only by demonstrating bravery in battle, but also by constantly looking out for the good of his people. In 1865, at a meeting of all the Oglala Sioux, Crazy Horse was named a "shirt-wearer," or battle leader, a great honor. Unlike the other shirt-wearers, who made fiery speeches and boasted of their exploits in battle, Crazy Horse was reserved, almost shy. He led by example, not by words. Yet he also had a serious weakness. He had long been in love with a woman named Black Buffalo Woman, who was married to another warrior. Crazy Horse's love clouded his commitment to his people, and in 1870 he "stole" Black Buffalo Woman away (though historians believe that Black Buffalo Woman went willingly and in accordance with Indian custom). Her husband, No Water, chased Crazy Horse down and shot him, though not fatally. Crazy Horse was stripped of his status as shirt-wearer, and he struggled to regain the respect of his people. Crazy Horse later married another woman, however, and slowly regained his people's trust.

"This is a good day to die!"

By the late 1860s the Sioux had made life so difficult for whites in the Powder River area that the whites virtually withdrew from the northern Plains. The Fort Laramie Treaty of 1868 called for the closing of military forts along the Bozeman Trail, safeguarded the tribes' absolute and undisturbed use and occupation of reservations, forced out white settlers, and promised punishment for any whites who injured Indians. As part of the agreement, prominent Indian leaders Red Cloud and Spotted Tail led their people to permanent "agencies" (Indian-controlled reservations) south of the Black Hills. But Crazy Horse, refusing to honor a treaty that he believed the whites would not honor, took the position of war chief of the Oglala.

Within six years Crazy Horse's prediction had come true, for after the discovery of gold in the Black Hills in 1874 countless miners and settlers poured into the area, protected by the U.S. Army. The U.S. government attempted to avoid breaking the Fort Laramie Treaty by offering to buy the land from the Indians, but the Sioux refused to sell the land that lay at the center of their religion and was believed to be the home of Wakan Tanka, the Great Spirit. Undeterred, the United States government declared that the Sioux were in violation of the treaty and promptly decreed that all Indians in the region had to report to reservations by January 31, 1876. Those who did not would be killed by the armed forces that were massing nearby.

The various tribes soon realized that a unified military effort was needed to preserve their traditional freedoms. The Cheyenne and Sioux gathered in a great encampment in the Rosebud area of Montana and then moved to the Little Bighorn River. Led by Crazy Horse and Sitting Bull, the Indians showed great courage in a June 17, 1876, clash with soldiers led by General George Crook. Then, on June 25, the Indians' camp on the Little Bighorn was attacked by forces led by General George Custer. Sweeping down on the white soldiers in the new battle formations that Crazy Horse had taught them, the Indians first routed a band of men led by Major Marcus Reno. Then, calling out to his warriors "Hoka hey! It is a good day to fight! It is a good day to die!" Crazy Horse led his warriors in the utter destruction of Custer's band of 225 men. Only about twenty Indian warriors lost their lives, while Custer and all of his troops were killed.

The end of the vision

The great victory at Little Bighorn cheered the Indians and shocked the whites, but the victory was short lived. After the battle the various tribes went their separate ways, and increased pressure from the military drove many of them onto reservations. Crazy Horse continued to raid mining camps in the Black Hills, killing as many of the invading miners as he could find. But after soldiers under the command of Colonel Nelson A. Miles (1839–1925) attacked his village on January 8, 1877, Crazy Horse knew the end was near. Although Crazy Horse and his warriors fought off Miles and his troops, the Indians' camp and supplies were ruined. By spring the great warrior and his one thousand followers faced starvation.

On May 6, 1877, Crazy Horse led hundreds of his people to Fort Robinson to take their place on the Red Cloud Agency. Crazy Horse retained the respect and love of his people, who knew that he had kept them free longer than other Oglala leaders had kept their people free. But, stripped of his horses and his guns, Crazy Horse did not settle easily into life on the agency. He negotiated with the government for his own agency but was faced with the hostility of other Indian leaders who were jealous of the treatment that Crazy Horse received. When Crazy Horse was asked to join the whites in fighting a band of Nez Percé Indians, he replied, according to St. George, "We are tired of war; we came in for peace, but now that the Great Father asks our help, we will go north and fight until there is not a Nez Percé left!" Crazy Horse's words were misinterpreted, however, to suggest that Crazy Horse vowed to fight until there was not a white man left. Panicked, white leaders at Fort Robinson ordered Crazy Horse's arrest.

On September 5, 1877, Crazy Horse arrived at Fort Robinson and was promptly placed under arrest by Indian police, including several of his own warriors. When Crazy Horse learned that he was to be sent to a prison in Florida, he struggled to escape. With Little Big Man pinning Crazy Horse's arms, soldiers stabbed Crazy Horse with their bayonets. Within a matter of hours the great warrior Crazy Horse was dead, and in the way his first vision had predicted.

Much of the life of Crazy Horse is shrouded in mystery. No authentic picture of him is known to exist, and most of what is known about him comes secondhand, through the words and memories of those who knew him. To this day no one knows where his body was buried or the exact date of his birth. Yet he has been memorialized on a U.S. postage stamp and in a nearly six-hundred-foot-high statue that remains under construction on Thunderhead Mountain in South Dakota. He is remembered today as one of the greatest of all Indian leaders, brave, wise, and dedicated to the good of his people.

For More Information

Ambrose, Stephen E. *Crazy Horse and Custer: The Parallel Lives of Two American Warriors*. New York: Doubleday, 1975.

Brown, Vinson. *Crazy Horse, Hoka Hey (It Is a Good Time to Die!)*. Happy Camp, CA: Naturegraph, 1987.

Clark, Robert A. *The Killing of Chief Crazy Horse*. Lincoln: University of Nebraska Press, 1988.

Dugan, Bill. *Crazy Horse*. New York: HarperCollins, 1992.

Freedman, Russell. *The Life and Death of Crazy Horse*. New York: Holiday House, 1996.

Goldman, Martin S. *Crazy Horse: War Chief of the Oglala Sioux*. New York: Franklin Watts, 1996.

Guttmacher, Peter. *Crazy Horse, Sioux War Chief*. New York: Chelsea House, 1994.

Masson, Jean-Robert. *The Great Indian Chiefs: Cochise, Geronimo, Crazy Horse, Sitting Bull*. Translated by Annie Heminway. Hauppage, NY: Barron's, 1994.

Razzi, Jim. *Custer and Crazy Horse: A Story of Two Warriors*. New York: Scholastic, 1989.

St. George, Judith. *Crazy Horse*. New York: G.P. Putnam's Sons, 1994.

George Armstrong Custer

Born December 5, 1839
New Rumley, Ohio
Died June 25, 1876
Montana

U.S. Army officer

Despite his early achievements as the "Boy General," the flamboyant George Armstrong Custer is most remembered for his death.

George Armstrong Custer made a name for himself early. As the youngest general in the Union army during the Civil War (1861–65; a war fought between the Northern and Southern United States over the issue of slavery), he achieved fame as the "Boy General." Custer coveted such fame. He dressed to be noticed, with elaborate uniforms, sometimes made of velvet, and long, curly golden locks. Indians identified him as "Long Hair." Newspapers eagerly reported on his life and adventures. The flamboyant Custer's early fame was well grounded by his abilities in the field, however. He earned his reputation as "the best Cavalry General in the Army," according to Jeffry D. Wert in *Custer: The Controversial Life of George Armstrong Custer.*

Despite his impressive achievements, Custer is most remembered for his dramatic death. In 1876 he led the charge at the battle against the northern Plains Indians at Little Bighorn. In a hard-fought battle, his forces were slaughtered. The Indians had rallied to defeat one of America's most recognized war heroes. Controversy about Custer's last command continues: Some historians portray him as a frontier hero who died at his post; others, Wert observes, consider Custer as "the singular symbol

George Armstrong Custer.
(Reproduced from the Collections of the Library of Congress.)

of the nation's guilt over its sad history of continental conquest." In either case, Custer's abysmal failure at Little Bighorn overshadows his excellence as a Civil War general.

Private life of a soldier

Custer was born in New Rumley, Ohio, on December 5, 1839. He grew up in Monroe, Michigan. He knew from an early age that he wanted to be a soldier, and a year after graduating from high school he won an appointment to West Point Academy. Despite his keen interest in the military, Custer spent his time at West Point on the verge of being expelled for poor academic performance, cheating, and dangerous pranks. He graduated at the bottom of his class.

Gettysburg heroism

After his graduation from West Point, Custer excelled as a soldier in some of the more crucial battles of the Civil War. Under the command of General Alfred Pleasonton, Custer showed cool steadiness in combat and demonstrated inspiring leadership. At Pleasonton's urging, Custer was jumped four ranks—from captain to brigadier general—on the eve of the battle of Gettysburg. During this decisive battle, Custer's volunteer regiment of Michigan cavalry charged Jeb Stuart's Confederate cavalry and, for the first time in the war, sent Stuart into retreat. This clash was one of the turning points of the Civil War. Another victory against Jeb Stuart in late 1863 cemented Custer's reputation as one of the best Union cavalrymen.

Custer's victories won him early career advancement but also inspired his own high regard for his abilities. As biographer Robert Utley notes:

> "Custer's luck" became his hallmark, a phenomenon for incredulous wonder by friends and observers, an article of faith in his self-appraisal. He came genuinely to believe himself fated to win regardless of the risks.

> The press seized on Custer as a "Boy General" and lauded his exploits, his elaborate style of dress, and his flowing golden curls. Custer's fame grew to such an extent that people would stop him on the street. His overwhelming popularity was enjoyed by few other military officers.

In 1864 Custer married his sweetheart, Elizabeth "Libbie" Clift Bacon. Libbie would remain his steadfast companion, following him throughout his military campaigns. On the few occasions that they were separated during their marriage, the couple wrote almost daily letters to each other. Although Elizabeth would die more than fifty years after her husband, she never remarried. Instead she devoted herself to Custer's memory and promoted him as an American hero, writing three books about his exploits.

Under General Philip Sheridan (1831–1888), Custer quickly impressed his new superior with victories at the battles of Winchester and Cedar Creek in late 1864. As a reward, Sheridan granted Custer command of a division. As the Civil War continued, Custer had more success in battle. In addition, on April 9, 1865, by being in the right place at the right time, Custer happened to be the Union officer who received the news of General Lee's wish to surrender to General Ulysses Grant. Custer's military skill and evident luck built his reputation as one of the Union heroes of the Civil War.

Peacetime troubles

After the glory and excitement of war, Custer found it difficult to deal with the boring daily routine of peacetime. He knew how to rally men for battle, but he lacked the finesse required to inspire peacetime troops. He was also criticized for being a harsh disciplinarian. While on a command in Texas, Custer ordered the heads of misbehaving soldiers to be shaved and ordered deserters to be shot without a trial. Moreover, his habit of promoting friends and family members made fellow officers angry.

To make matters worse, Custer's rank was reduced to that of captain in the rapidly shrinking peacetime army. The prospects for promotion seemed to disappear. Custer resigned his command on January 31, 1866, and left Texas for New Orleans, where he briefly entered politics. After months of uncertainty about his future, Custer was offered the post of lieutenant colonel of the Seventh Cavalry.

Returning to the army in the summer of 1866, Custer prepared to join his troops in Kansas to guard settlements

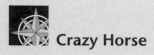

Crazy Horse

Oglala Sioux warrior Crazy Horse (1842–1877; see main entry) led the Sioux to their greatest victory in the Battle of Little Bighorn in 1876. A quiet, distant leader, Crazy Horse was noted for his uncommon bravery and rose to a position of leadership not only within his own people but within the confederacy of tribes that came together in the 1860s and 1870s to combat the white advance onto Indian lands in present-day South Dakota, Nebraska, Wyoming, and Montana.

Crazy Horse had predicted the battle over the Black Hills. Consequently, he prepared his warriors for battle with the whites. When General George Custer attacked the Indian encampment at Little Bighorn on June 25, 1876, Crazy Horse and his men were ready. Sweeping down on the white soldiers in the new battle formations that Crazy Horse had taught them, the Indians first routed a band of men led by Major Marcus Reno. Then, calling out to his warriors "Hoka hey! It is a good day to fight! It is a good day to die!" Crazy Horse led his warriors in the utter destruction of Custer's band of 225 men. Only about twenty Indian warriors lost their lives, while Custer and all of his troops were killed. However, the U.S. military intensified their efforts to fight the Native American groups in the area. Within a year of the Indians' Little Bighorn victory over forces led by General George Armstrong Custer, the Indian forces were divided. Crazy Horse was killed by Indian police while being held at Fort Robinson, Nebraska, on September 5, 1877.

against Indian attack. However, his style of command continued to offend his men; in addition, his good luck in battle was gone. He led a disastrous campaign against the Sioux, which led to desertions among his soldiers. When he left his post to greet his wife in the middle of another campaign, Custer was court-martialed for absence without leave and "conduct to the prejudice of good order and military discipline," according to Wert. Found guilty on both charges, he could have been ruined permanently, but thanks to General Philip Sheridan, he was reinstated in 1868.

The Indian Wars

Under pressure from settlers and railroaders to eliminate Indians from the Great Plains, the army had adopted a

"total warfare" policy against the Indians. Custer was placed in charge of patrolling part of Kansas and began to relentlessly pursue Indian groups. In the winter of 1868, he came upon a Cheyenne village on the Washita River. He attacked at once. In this surprise attack Custer's forces wiped out the warriors, captured a large number of women and children, massacred all the Indians' horses, and destroyed winter food supplies. However, Custer had not bothered to make a full survey of the surrounding area and did not know that large numbers of Kiowas and Arapahos were camped just downstream. One of his officers, Major Joel Elliott, and a detachment of nineteen men, were ambushed by warriors from these villages and wiped out. It was the only blemish on a battle that brought Custer and the Seventh Cavalry national fame as Indian fighters.

In 1867 Custer started writing adventure stories for magazines. He thrived as a writer and "dashed off" pages, according to his wife. The true stories he wrote for *Galaxy* magazine were published as his autobiography, *My Life on the*

George Armstrong Custer's troops attacking a Cheyenne village along the Washita River.
(Archive Photos, Inc. Reproduced by permission.)

Plains, in 1874. Custer was a natural showman, and accompanied Buffalo Bill as a guide to Grand Duke Alexis of Russia on an 1871 buffalo hunt. As a military officer, he skirmished with Indians throughout the early 1870s, chasing the northern Plains Indians across the vast grasslands.

Battle of Little Bighorn

With the discovery of gold in the Black Hills, the United States wanted the land opened to white settlement. A treaty had already granted the land to the Sioux and the Indians, who considered the land sacred and refused to sign a new agreement. Military might was the only way to secure the land. At a White House meeting on November 3, 1875, President Ulysses S. Grant (1822–1885) and high-ranking army officials "'contrived' a war against the Sioux," according to Wert.

Custer's last campaign was a part of this strategy. From Fort Lincoln, Dakota Territory, he took command of the Seventh Cavalry. He prepared for the aggressive campaign like "a boy with a new red sled," as one private observed, according to Wert. Wert also notes that as the cavalry prepared for departure, an eyewitness declared that "probably never had a more eager command started for hostile Indians."

In Custer's experience with the northern Plains Indians over the years, the Indians usually scattered at the first sight of army troops. Unknown to Custer, the Indians were prepared to make a stand this time. An unprecedented concentration of Teton Sioux and northern Cheyennes— approximately seven thousand men—had gathered to fight near the Little Bighorn River. Yet the numbers of Indians did not tell the whole story. "Never before or after were the northern Plains tribes better prepared for war," maintains Robert M. Utley. "They were numerous, united, confident, superbly led, emotionally charged to defend their homeland and freedom."

On June 25, 1876, Custer's scouts caught sight of a huge Indian encampment. Fearing that the enemy might be fleeing, Custer decided—just as he had at Washita—to attack at once, confident that his outnumbered men would prevail without difficulty. He split his command and sent three

companies to surround the Indians. Instead of fleeing, the Indians attacked "like bees swarming out of a hive," one Lakota Indian observed, according to Wert. The Seventh Cavalry was soon overrun, and all 225 of the men who had joined Custer were killed. Custer himself, America's greatest Indian fighter, also was dead.

Horrified by the massacre, the army retaliated against the Sioux. Throughout the following winter, under the brutal and efficient Colonel Nelson Miles, the Sioux were hunted, their villages burned down, food supplies destroyed, and women and children killed. In the spring of 1877, the battered Sioux surrendered and the war came to an end.

Custer had sustained the worst loss in the history of the U.S. Army. Controversy about the battle has hardly subsided, even after many years. To some, Custer is a martyr to duty and country. To others, Custer is the symbol of Americans' vicious treatment of Indians.

For More Information

Bailey, John W. *Pacifying the Plains: General Alfred Terry and the Decline of the Sioux: 1866–1890*. Westport, CT: Greenwood, 1979.

Deloria, Vine, Jr. *Custer Died for Your Sins: An Indian Manifesto*. New York: Macmillan, 1969.

Howard, James. *The Warrior Who Killed Custer: The Personal Narrative of Chief Joseph White Bull*. Lincoln: University of Nebraska Press, 1968.

Monaghan, Jay. *Custer: The Life of General George Armstrong Custer*. Boston: Little, Brown, 1959.

Utley, Robert M. *Cavalier in Buckskin: George Armstrong Custer and the Western Military Frontier*. Norman: University of Oklahoma Press, 1988.

Van de Water, Frederic. *Glory Hunter: A Life of General Custer*. New York: Bobbs-Merrill, 1934.

Wert, Jeffry D. *Custer: The Controversial Life of George Armstrong Custer*. New York: Simon & Schuster, 1996.

Wyatt Earp

Born March 19, 1848
Monmouth, Illinois
Died January 13, 1929
Los Angeles, California

Lawman, gambler

Wyatt Earp was one of the legendary lawmen of the Old West. Though he was a sheriff or marshal in several western towns, he is best known for his role in the famous gunfight at the O.K. Corral in Tombstone, Arizona. Like many western heroes and villains, Earp's life has become the stuff of myth, and has been distorted and misreported so frequently that it is difficult to sort out truth from falsehood. It is clear, however, that his bravery and skill made him one of the most respected and feared lawmen in the West.

Early years

Wyatt Berry Stapp Earp was born in Monmouth, Illinois, on March 19, 1848. The third son of Nicholas and Virginia Earp, Wyatt had four brothers—James, Virgil, Warren, and Morgan—who also later enjoyed some fame for their exploits in the West. The Earp boys spent most of their youth in Illinois and Iowa. Earp's father and two older brothers fought for the Union in the Civil War (1861–65; a war fought between the Northern and Southern United States over the issue of

"He had killed only when he saw no other choice, and his victims had been criminals who deserved bullets, not sympathy. He believed, as strongly as a man can believe, that he had done everything he could to avoid killing."

Carl R. Green and William R. Sanford in Wyatt Earp

Wyatt Earp.
(The Corbis Corporation. Reproduced by permission.)

83

slavery). Earp too tried to enlist but was sent home by his father. As the end of the Civil War approached, the boys moved west with their parents to San Bernardino, California, where, according to biographer Casey Tefertiller, "Wyatt learned to hate plowing, hoeing, and just about everything else connected with farming.... [T]he teenaged Wyatt knew it was time to leave farming and find another way to make a living."

For a time, Wyatt worked as a stagecoach driver making runs from San Bernardino to Los Angeles and across the desert to Prescott, Arizona. In 1868, he and his brother Virgil handled mule teams grading the railroad bed for the Union Pacific Railroad. A smart and enterprising young man, Wyatt soon bought his own mule team for grading and hired himself out to the railroad, earning himself twenty-five hundred dollars. Wyatt and Virgil then rejoined the rest of the Earp family, who had returned to Illinois. Wyatt soon relocated to Lamar, Missouri, where he married his first wife, Urilla Sutherland. In February 1870, just one month after his marriage, Earp won an election for the position of town constable—his first job as an officer of the law and his only elected post. But Wyatt didn't stay long in Lamar. When Urilla died of typhoid fever (a deadly and contagious disease), the disheartened Earp became involved in a scandal. He was suspected of stealing public funds and was charged with horse theft (neither charge has ever been proven, and historians know little about the details). Earp eventually left town under a cloud of suspicion over the charges.

Cow town lawman

According to Tefertiller, "Earp followed his year of misfortune with a period of adventure, serving as a hunter for a government surveying crew one season and a buffalo hunter another." During this period a new phenomenon—the cattle drive—was transforming Kansas. Thousands of cattle from Texas were driven northward to the rail lines that had just been extended westward into Kansas. The cowboys who led the cattle drives were transforming small Kansas towns into hotbeds of gambling, prostitution, and lawbreaking. Wyatt Earp, a steady man who believed in the law, soon found a place in these cow towns.

Wyatt's first taste of cow town peacekeeping came when he helped settle a dispute between the Ellsworth, Kansas, town marshal and a group of rowdy Texans who were preparing to shoot up the town. Though the facts of this encounter are disputed, Earp's reputation as a peacekeeper was strong enough to earn him a job as a police officer in Wichita, Kansas, a town with a reputation for wildness nearly unmatched in a state full of wild towns. Earp worked in Wichita from 1874 to 1876. He had to strike a delicate balance between scaring off the truly dangerous criminals and helping the town win the business of the mere rowdies. Earp, who was more inclined to settle disputes with words or fists than with bullets, proved skilled at the job. He also performed the less glamorous tasks of the policeman—sweeping streets, scaring off wild dogs, and inspecting chimneys.

Wyatt Earp as a young lawman in the West.
(Archive Photos, Inc. Reproduced by permission.)

In 1876, Earp left Wichita to become the chief deputy of Dodge City, Kansas, where two other well-known lawmen, Jim Masterson and Bartholomew "Bat" Masterson, worked as his aides. During his first year in Dodge City there were only two killings, down from seventy in the year before his arrival. But when the cattle season ended Earp grew bored with his job and looked elsewhere for excitement. He thought he had found that excitement when he left for the gold rush in the Black Hills of Dakota Territory in 1877, but he soon discovered that the area had been mined to exhaustion and there was little gold left. Earp didn't mind; he made a small fortune selling firewood to the other miners in the region. When he returned to Dodge City in 1878, Earp wore a badge as the town's assistant marshal (1878–79), and he soon ran into Mattie Blaylock, who would later become his second wife, and John "Doc" Holliday (1851–1887), a famous gunman who would become his lifelong friend.

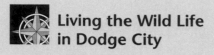

Living the Wild Life in Dodge City

In April of 1876, a reporter for the *Atchison Daily Champion* (Kansas) penned the following poem about the wild cow town that was Dodge City, Kansas:

Did you ever hear of Dodge City,

Where nearly every house is a shanty,

And the roughs sing this queer little ditty

"Take a hand pard? —quarter ante."

Where killing a man is no sin,

And stealings are branded as jokes.

Where the principal commerce is gin,

And the law is but a terrible hoax.

Poem quoted in Tefertiller, Wyatt Earp: The Life Behind the Legend

Tombstone is the wildest of the Wild West

In 1877, a prospector named Edward Schieffelin found silver in a deserted part of the territory of Arizona, and before too long the rush of silver seekers had turned the area into a boomtown. Schieffelin named the town Tombstone, for a friend had warned him that a tombstone was what he would find there. Instead, Schieffelin got rich off the silver he discovered, and the town soon filled with money-hungry miners, con men, gamblers, and gunfighters. Far from civilization, Tombstone became a haven for outlaws and the symbol for the Wild West.

Always one to seek out adventure, Wyatt arrived in Tombstone in December of 1879, accompanied by his wife, Mattie, and his brothers James, Morgan, Virgil, and Warren. Within a year Virgil Earp had been appointed town marshal, and Wyatt sometimes helped out as a deputy—that is, when he wasn't winning money at the gambling tables of the Oriental Saloon, where he also worked as a guard. The Earp brothers soon began to feud with a gang of outlaws led by Joseph Isiah "Ike" Clanton. The Earps didn't like the Clantons—Ike and his younger brother Billy—or the McLaury brothers—Tom and Frank—who rustled cattle and robbed stagecoaches in the area. The Clantons and McLaurys saw the Earps as a threat to their livelihood. Everybody in town soon knew that these men were headed toward a showdown.

The gunfight at O.K. Corral

The gunfight at O.K. Corral—now a legendary Western conflict—occurred when the lawmen and the outlaws finally met for a showdown in October of 1881. First, Frank

McLaury challenged Morgan Earp to a gunfight, but Earp declined. Then the Earps' friend, Doc Holliday, got into an argument with Ike Clanton in a saloon on the afternoon of October 25, 1881—but neither man resorted to violence. Still seething, Ike Clanton waved a gun in town and made threats against the Earps and Holliday. Sensing trouble, Virgil Earp deputized his brothers Wyatt and Morgan, as well as Doc Holliday, and the men arrested Clanton for carrying guns within the city limits. Clanton was fined and released, while outside the courthouse Wyatt Earp solved an argument with Tom McLaury by "buffaloing" him—smacking him on the side of the head with his pistol.

Still, the Clantons and McLaurys were not ready to give up. Later in the day, they gathered near a horse stable known as the O.K. Corral. The Earp brothers and Doc Holliday, who had heard rumors that the outlaws were planning revenge, approached a vacant lot on Frémont Street, where the outlaws awaited them. There the enemies stood, face to face, just feet apart, each waiting for the other to make the first move. Then—suddenly—gunfire spewed from the pistols and rifles of the armed men. Within a matter of minutes, Frank and Tom McLaury and nineteen-year-old Billy Clanton were dead, and every one of the lawmen was injured except for Wyatt Earp. Ike Clanton escaped without harm when he ran for the safety of a nearby building. This short, brutal gunfight has gone down in history as the gunfight at O.K. Corral.

Beyond O.K.

Though the Earps and Holliday had rid Tombstone of three outlaws, some in town felt that the lawmen had committed outright murder. Town sheriff John E. Behan agreed, and he issued warrants for the arrest of Wyatt Earp and Doc Holliday. Though the charges against the men were eventually dismissed, they kept the men from being heroes. Virgil Earp was dismissed from his job as town marshal for his part in the killings and was criticized for having deputized his brothers to come to his aid.

The Earps' violent encounters did not end with the gunfight at O.K. Corral. Just one month later, Virgil was ambushed and shot on his way into the Oriental Saloon by an unidentified gunman; he was disabled for life. The next March, Morgan was shot and killed. Wyatt blamed the Clanton gang for the violence and vowed that he would have his revenge. Eventually, Wyatt and Holliday hunted down and murdered several of the men they thought were responsible for the shootings. After killing Frank Stillwell, whom he blamed for Morgan's death, Wyatt told his lawyer, according to biographers Carl R. Green and William R. Sanford, "I let him have both barrels. I have no regrets. I know I got the man who killed Morg."

Branded as a murderer, Wyatt stayed on the run, living for brief periods of time in Colorado, Idaho, Arizona, and Alaska. Though not a great deal is known about his life during this time, historians believe that he gambled, sold real estate, and raised racehorses. In 1888, after Mattie Earp died, Earp married his longtime girlfriend Josephine Sarah Marcus. The aging gambler and lawman eventually settled in California, where he died on January 13, 1929, at the age of eighty—having outlived every one of his four brothers.

A lawman's legacy

Wyatt Earp became a legend during his own lifetime, and he was portrayed both as a hero and a murderer in the many accounts of his life. According to Tefertiller, "Other men had killed and left their pasts behind, but controversy followed Wyatt like a detective in a pulp novel. He could run fast and far, but he could never escape from Tombstone and the five months when his actions stirred the conscience of a nation." His life has since been discussed in numerous biographies and a number of feature films, including *Frontier Marshal* (1939), *Law and Order* (1953—starring Ronald Reagan as Wyatt Earp), *Wichita* (1955), *Sunset* (1988), *Tombstone* (1993), and *Wyatt Earp* (1994). Wyatt Earp, a stern, complex, and brave man, has thus come to symbolize the figure of the sheriff in the Old West.

For More Information

Books

Barra, Allen. *Inventing Wyatt Earp: His Life and Many Legends.* New York: Carrol & Graf, 1998.

Bell, Bob Boze. *The Illustrated Life and Times of Wyatt Earp*. Phoenix, AZ: Boze Books, 1993.

Erwin, Richard E. *The Truth about Wyatt Earp*. Carpinteria, CA: O.K. Press, 1992.

Green, Carl R., and William R. Sanford. *Wyatt Earp*. Hillside, NJ: Enslow, 1992.

Lake, Stuart. *The Life and Times of Wyatt Earp*. Boston: Houghton Mifflin, 1956.

Marks, Paula. *And Die in the West—the Story of the O.K. Corral Gunfight*. New York: William Morrow, 1989.

Nash, Jay Robert. *Bloodletters and Badmen*. New York: M. Evans, 1973.

Rosa, Joseph. *The Taming of the West: Age of the Gunfighter*. New York: Smithmark, 1993.

Ross, Stewart. *Fact or Fiction: Bandits & Outlaws*. Surrey, Brookfield, CT: Copper Beech Books, 1995.

Tefertiller, Casey. *Wyatt Earp: The Life Behind the Legend*. New York: John Wiley and Sons, 1997.

Wukovits, John. *The Gunslingers*. Broomall, PA: Chelsea House, 1997.

Web Sites

Wyatt Earp Historical Homepage. [Online] http://www.techline.com/~nicks/earp.htm (accessed April 12, 2000).

Thomas "Broken Hand" Fitzpatrick

Born c. 1799
County Cavan, Ireland
Died February 7, 1854
Washington, D.C.

Trapper, guide, government agent

Thomas "Broken Hand" Fitzpatrick was not your ordinary mountain man. Like his peers—the famous mountain men Jim Bridger (1804–1881; see entry), Jedediah Smith (1799–1831), Kit Carson (1809–1868; see entry), and a few others—Fitzpatrick was a veteran trapper, an able explorer, and a seasoned and brave Indian fighter. Along with these men, Fitzpatrick blazed the way for the settlement of the vast lands west of the Mississippi River and helped guide important expeditions across the torturous Rocky Mountains. Unlike the others, however, Fitzpatrick was an educated and ambitious man who late in life established a distinguished reputation as a government agent to the Plains Indians. Fitzpatrick was largely responsible for the Fort Laramie Treaty of 1851, a short-lived but important peace treaty between the United States and the many tribes living in the West.

Little is known about Fitzpatrick's early life. He was born in County Cavan, Ireland, into a Catholic family of eight children, and must have received some formal education, for he later proved to be a skilled writer. By the age of seventeen he had come to the United States and seems to

Thomas Fitzpatrick was a prominent trapper and explorer who helped blaze the trails that allowed settlers to cross the difficult Rocky Mountains. He was also a seasoned guide who helped lead some of the most important mapping and military expeditions of the 1830s and 1840s.

Thomas "Broken Hand" Fitzpatrick.

have spent several years doing various jobs in the Midwest. By 1823 found himself on the verge of a great adventure, for he had signed on to join one of William Henry Ashley's fur trading expeditions that was leaving St. Louis and venturing into the nearly uncharted American interior.

First expedition

Ashley's expedition introduced Fitzpatrick to the hard life men faced in the West. The men had to push, pull, and drag their boats up the Missouri River, all the while looking out for hostile Indians. Along the way they met a band of Arikara Indians in a fierce battle that left twelve dead and as many wounded. Unable to proceed upriver, Ashley sent a party of men—including Fitzpatrick—to discover an overland route to the rich fur-trapping grounds in the Rocky Mountains.

Fitzpatrick was second in command to Jedediah Smith on what would become a historic expedition. The party crossed the wide plains of present-day South Dakota and Wyoming, and though they kept peace with the Indians they met, Jedediah Smith was badly mauled by a gigantic grizzly bear, leaving Fitzpatrick in charge. Winter set in and travel became more difficult, but still the explorers kept on, until one day in March 1824 they realized that the streams they encountered were no longer flowing east but were now flowing west. The men had discovered the long-sought South Pass through the Rocky Mountains. "Little did these hardy pioneers dream that they were marking a trail destined to be, for nearly half a century, the most important route to the Pacific," writes Fitzpatrick biographer LeRoy Hafen in *Broken Hand: The Life of Thomas Fitzpatrick, Mountain Man, Guide and Indian Agent.* More importantly for Fitzpatrick and the others, they had discovered some of the richest beaver-trapping country in the West. When they returned east in the fall of 1824 the men were laden with furs—and Fitzpatrick was a confirmed mountain man.

Life as a fur trapper

For the next dozen years, Fitzpatrick enjoyed the life of a fur trapper in the Rocky Mountain West. Working in small parties, fur trappers searched throughout the region for untrapped streams. When they found such streams they set up camp and sought to catch as many beaver as they could to supply the demand for beaver fur in the east and in Europe. They endured the harsh mountain winters hunkered down in the small cabins they built, and they looked forward to the annual summer Rendezvous, a great meeting of trappers and traders from throughout the West. The Rendezvous was the social event of the season, providing ample entertainment and allowing the trappers to trade their furs for guns, clothes, or other supplies.

By 1830 Fitzpatrick had joined with Jim Bridger, Milton Sublette, and several others to form the Rocky Mountain Fur Company; according to Hafen, Fitzpatrick was the "brains of the outfit." Though the partners hoped that their company would allow them to extract more profit from their labors, their timing was not the best. Fur trapping in the West was becoming very competitive, with several American and British companies sending trappers into the region. (Much of the country was jointly claimed by England and the United States, so the trappers were competing not only for fur but to establish their country's claim to the land.) By 1834 the partners had dissolved the Rocky Mountain Fur Company. Fitzpatrick continued to trap for a few more years, and it was during this time that he earned the nickname "Broken Hand." While out trapping alone, Fitzpatrick was chased by a band of fierce Blackfeet Indians. Trapped on the edge of a high river bluff, he urged his horse to jump. Fitzpatrick survived the leap, though his horse didn't, and he promptly prepared to fire on the Indians—only to shoot a hole in his left wrist. He eventually scared off the Indians, but his hand was maimed for life.

Trusted guide to Whitman and Spalding

In May of 1836 Fitzpatrick signed on as a guide for an expedition headed west to Oregon. This famous missionary party was led by Dr. Marcus Whitman and the Reverend H. H. Spalding, and included their wives, who would soon become the first white women to cross the Continental Divide (see Narcissa Prentiss Whitman entry). The party followed a route along the north bank of the Platte River that would later be-

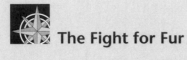

The Fight for Fur

In the 1820s, when fur trappers first began extensive trapping in the western half of the present-day United States, most of the fur trappers shared information and were glad to give their fellow trappers a hand. French-Canadian, American, and English trappers all got along fairly well, for there seemed to be more beaver than the men could ever hope to trap. By the 1830s, however, conditions had changed dramatically. Competition had heated up between the British Hudson's Bay Company, Fitzpatrick's Rocky Mountain Fur Company, John Jacob Astor's American Fur Company, and several other smaller companies. More and more men seemed to be chasing fewer and fewer beaver. Friendly relations among trappers soon broke down.

Fitzpatrick, Bridger, and the experienced members of the Rocky Mountain Fur Company were often trailed by less experienced trappers, who "stole" the territory that the experienced men had discovered. According to Joe Meek, one of Fitzpatrick's men and quoted in Hafen, "They tampered with the trappers, and ferreted out the secret of their next rendezvous; they followed on their trail, making them pilots to the trapping grounds…. In this way grew up that fierce conflict of interests, which made it 'as much as his life was worth' for a trapper to suffer himself to be inveigled [coaxed] into the service of a rival company." When novice fur trapper Zenas Leonard met up with Fitzpatrick in 1831, he found the seasoned trapper less than helpful, as he remembered in *Adventures of Zenas Leonard Fur Trader:*

> He was an old hand at the business and we expected to obtain some useful information from him, but we were disappointed. The selfishness of man is often disgraceful to human nature; and I never saw more striking evidence of this fact, than was presented in the conduct of this man Fitzpatrick. Notwithstanding we had treated him with great friendship and hospitality, merely because we were to engage in the same business with him, which he knew we never could exhaust or even impair—he refused to give us any information whatever, and appeared to treat us as intruders.

Leonard was wrong about one thing: the fur trade could be exhausted, as most trappers discovered by the late 1830s. Diminishing demand for beaver furs soon ended the fur trade altogether.

come famous as the Mormon Trail, so named because it was the route on which Mormon religious leader Brigham Young (1801–1877; see entry) led his followers to the Great Salt Lake.

Fitzpatrick was soon serving as a guide to a number of historic expeditions into the West. It was a job for which he was well suited, for he had as good a knowledge of the western lands as any man and had proven himself a dedicated and loyal guide. His good relations with many western tribes proved invaluable to the several parties he led along the Oregon Trail. Fitzpatrick knew how to tread the fine line between respecting the Indians' claim to the land and giving in to their demands and threats.

In 1843 Fitzpatrick signed on as the guide to John Charles Frémont's (1813–1890; see entry) second expedition to the West. More than a guide, Fitzpatrick actually commanded one section of the traveling party, which often split into separate groups to explore alternate routes. After mapping the territory along the Oregon Trail all the way to The Dalles in present-day Oregon, the party headed south along the eastern side of the coastal mountains, finally crossing a high snowy pass (elevation 9,338 feet) of the Sierra Nevada Mountains into California in late February 1844. From California the expedition crossed present-day Nevada and Utah on their long way back to St. Louis, which they reached on August 7, 1844. It had been an expedition of nearly three thousand miles, and Fitzpatrick had proven himself one of the best guides in the land.

For the next several years Fitzpatrick continued to serve his country as a guide for several military expeditions. He first accompanied Colonel Stephen Watts Kearny on an expedition to South Pass and back that was intended to scare the Indians from interfering with the ever-increasing traffic on the Oregon Trail. Then he joined Lieutenant J. W. Abert on an expedition to survey the no-man's-land of eastern New Mexico, northern Texas, and western Arkansas. Upon the outbreak of the Mexican-American War (1846–48; a conflict over the position of the southern border of Texas), Fitzpatrick served as a guide on several missions into New Mexico, but by this time his heart was set on a new career: he was to serve as an agent to the Indians living on the vast plains between the Mississippi River and the Rocky Mountains.

Becomes an Indian agent

On December 1, 1846, Fitzpatrick began his service as Indian agent (a government official in charge of protecting Indians on a reservation and distributing government aid to them). He had good experience in dealing with the many western tribes, and he hoped to develop a way for whites and Indians to live peaceably together. Fitzpatrick believed that Indians should receive justice—by which he meant compensation for the lands that were taken from them—and that they should be taught the skills they would need to survive alongside the white race that would surely continue to spread across the continent. Fitzpatrick thought that the Indians' future lay in learning to farm like the white man. He also believed that Indians who would not give up their warlike ways should be punished, severely if need be. With these policies in mind Fitzpatrick worked diligently to bring about the peace treaty that was signed at Fort Laramie (in present-day Wyoming) in 1851.

Called by Fitzpatrick, legions of Indians began to travel to Fort Laramie in the summer of 1851. Some estimates suggest that as many as sixty thousand Native American from dozens of tribes camped near the fort, though a more conservative estimate places the number at ten thousand. The Plains Indians—the Cheyennes, Arapahoes, and Sioux—arrived first and were soon joined by their enemies from the mountains, the Shoshone (or Snakes) and Crows. Beginning on September 8, the whites and Indians talked peace for eight days. On September 16 they signed a treaty that allowed the United States to build roads and military posts in Indian country, fixed the boundaries for the various tribes, set punishments for attacks committed by whites and Indians, and promised a payment of fifty thousand dollars in goods to the Indians each year for fifty years. Fitzpatrick's vision of peaceful coexistence had triumphed—at least for the moment.

But the peace was not to last. The Indians soon forgot their peace resolutions and launched attacks on the whites, who were crossing the land in ever-increasing numbers and killing off the buffalo on which the Indians depended. Worse for Fitzpatrick, the U.S. Senate refused to endorse fifty years of payments and asked Fitzpatrick to return to the Indians with the message that they would receive payments for only fifteen years. Fitzpatrick continued his work as an Indian agent, but it became increasingly clear that the great conflict between whites and Indians must resolve itself in violence. For his part, Fitzpatrick died peacefully far from the mountains that he loved. He succumbed to pneumonia and died in his hotel room in Washington, D.C., on February 7, 1854.

Thomas "Broken Hand" Fitzpatrick made three distinct contributions to the settling of the West. First, he was a prominent trapper and explorer who helped blaze the trails that allowed settlers to cross the difficult Rocky Mountains. Later he was a seasoned guide who helped lead some of the most important mapping and military expeditions of the 1830s and 1840s. Finally, he served his country in the difficult role of Indian agent, managing to press the needs of his nation while honoring the culture of the Indians that he admired.

For More Information

Garst, Shannon. *Broken-Hand Fitzpatrick, Greatest of Mountain Men.* New York: J. Messner, 1961.

Hafen, LeRoy R. *Broken Hand: The Life of Thomas Fitzpatrick, Mountain Man, Guide and Indian Agent.* 1973. Reprint. Lincoln: University of Nebraska Press, 1981.

Leonard, Zenas. *Adventures of Zenas Leonard Fur Trader.* Edited by John C. Ewers. Norman: University of Oklahoma Press, 1959.

John Charles Frémont

Born January 21, 1813
Savannah, Georgia
Died July 13, 1890
New York, New York

Explorer, military leader, politician

ohn Charles Frémont, known popularly as "The Pathfinder," was responsible for leading some of the greatest mapping expeditions of the nineteenth century. Covering more ground than the famous Lewis and Clark expedition (see Lewis and Clark entry), and reporting on his discoveries in far greater detail, Frémont's various expeditions west of the Mississippi River offered the American public a detailed view of lands that were then largely unknown. His reports helped fuel the national fever known as "manifest destiny" (the belief that the United States was destined to stretch all the way to the Pacific Ocean) and encouraged many to settle in the West. Frémont himself was a charismatic and controversial figure who wrote of his explorations with great flair, though he was often criticized—and once nearly sentenced to prison—for some of his questionable decisions.

"Frémont was required to work long hours in difficult wilderness conditions, yet he found his labors exhilarating and described the job as 'a kind of picnic with work enough to give it zest.'"

Edward D. Harris, in John Charles Frémont and the Great Western Reconnaissance

John Charles Frémont.
(Archive Photos, Inc. Reproduced by permission.)

Humble beginnings

Frémont was born on January 21, 1813, in Savannah, Georgia, to Anne Pryor and her lover Charles Frémon. Young

Charley—as Frémont was called—grew up poor. Even as a child Frémont had a quick wit and a love of adventure. In his teens, Frémont (who added the *t* to his name at age twenty-three to sound more American) was employed by a Charleston lawyer who provided the boy with a good education. Frémont excelled at his studies and entered Charleston College when he was just sixteen. He was expelled from school after being distracted from his studies by a love affair. Frémont taught for a time and then jumped at the chance to have his first real adventure sailing aboard the warship *Natchez* on a tour of the coast of South America.

Birth of a surveyor

Frémont returned from his sailing trip in 1835 and went to work with a team that surveyed a proposed railway route between Charleston, South Carolina, and Cincinnati, Ohio. According to Edward D. Harris, author of *John Charles Frémont and the Great Western Reconnaissance,* "Frémont was required to work long hours in difficult wilderness conditions, yet he found his labors exhilarating and described the job as 'a kind of picnic with work enough to give it zest.'" He had found his career. Frémont joined the Army Corps of Topographical Engineers as a second lieutenant in 1838 and was assigned to a team reporting to famed scientist and explorer Joseph Nicolas Nicollet. The team was directed to map the region between the upper Mississippi and Missouri Rivers (most of present-day Minnesota, Iowa, South Dakota, and North Dakota).

Frémont's enthusiasm for exploring soon brought him to the attention of Senator Thomas Hart Benton of Missouri. An influential antislavery senator, Benton believed that the United States had the divine right to expand its influence throughout North America. In Frémont he saw someone who might venture into the wilderness beyond the Great Plains and bring back the maps and the detailed descriptions of the landscape that would make settlement possible. Frémont warmed to Benton's plans—and to Benton's young, beautiful daughter, Jessie. Though Jessie's parents hoped that their daughter would marry an influential politician, Jessie and Frémont fell deeply in love and eloped (ran away to get mar-

ried without her parents' consent) in 1841. The family soon welcomed their new son-in-law. Benton became one of Frémont's biggest supporters in the years to come and gave Frémont political advantage. But Jessie was by far Frémont's biggest supporter; without her Frémont could not have written his required reports. Jessie took Frémont's disorganized notes and thoughts and shaped them into a coherent story.

John Charles Frémont and his expedition planting a flag atop a peak in the Rocky Mountains in 1842. *(The Corbis Corporation. Reproduced by permission.)*

Western expeditions

In the spring of 1842 Frémont prepared to lead his first expedition for the Army Corps of Topographical Engineers. His goal was to map the first leg of the Oregon Trail (one of the main routes used to travel west, leaving from various points in Missouri). Frémont's party was to map the route from Westport, Missouri (present-day Kansas City), to South Pass in present-day Wyoming. The best-known and most helpful member of this exploring party was Kit Carson

(1809–1868; see entry), a renowned guide and mountain man. Carson was so highly valued as a guide that he was paid an extravagant salary of one hundred dollars a month. Despite his enthusiasm, Frémont was not known as an especially skilled mountain man. He hired experienced and talented trail guides to help ensure the success (and survival) of his expeditions.

The party reached South Pass on August 8, 1842, but Frémont—longing for more adventure—was determined to scale the highest peak in the Wind River Range. In a death-defying ascent, Frémont and several of his party reached the 13,300-foot summit. With the help of his wife Jessie, Frémont recorded this and his other adventures and discoveries in his *Report of an Exploration of the Country Lying Between the Missouri River and the Rocky Mountains on the Line of the Kansas and Great Platte Rivers*. The report was widely read by those eager to learn about the West and helped make Frémont something of a national hero.

Frémont's next expedition—his most famous—called for him to map the country along the Oregon Trail all the way to the Pacific Ocean. The trip would take him beyond the boundaries of the United States and into Oregon Country, which was partially occupied by the British. Frémont's goal was to pave the way for this great territory to become part of the United States. Frémont's forty-man party left Westport, Missouri, in early June 1843, with Thomas "Broken Hand" Fitzpatrick (c. 1799–1854; see entry) acting as the guide. On their long and wandering journey the party found time to survey the northern shores of the Great Salt Lake (in present-day Utah); the report on the survey encouraged Brigham Young (1801–1877; see entry) to lead the Mormons to settle there four years later. Frémont's party traveled north to the Snake River and then to the Columbia River, reaching the British outpost of Fort Vancouver in early November 1843. Though Fort Vancouver was Frémont's official destination, following orders was not in his nature, so he decided to continue on.

Remembering Kit Carson's stories about the beauty of California, Frémont prepared to lead his expedition south along the east side of the coastal mountain range (in the north the range is called the Cascades, but in the south it is called the Sierra Nevadas) in late November. Despite the warnings from

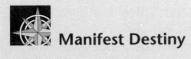

Manifest Destiny

By the 1840s, very few Americans questioned whether the United States should be expanding into the lands west of the Mississippi River; they only asked how that expansion would occur. As Mexico and the United States argued over the borders of the Republic of Texas, formerly part of the nation of Mexico, indignant Americans proclaimed their nation's natural right to control the breadth of the continent. Most Americans assumed without question that their nation would eventually extend from the Atlantic to the Pacific Ocean, while some even imagined that the United States would control all of North and South America. In 1845, as war with Mexico loomed, John L. O'Sullivan, editor of *The United States Magazine and Democratic Review,* defined this faith in American expansion as the nation's "manifest destiny." The idea of manifest destiny implied that Americans had the God-given right to acquire and populate the territories stretching west to the Pacific Ocean. This idea has since been criticized as an excuse for the bold land grabs and the slaughter of Indians that characterized expansion. However, those who believed in it thought they were demonstrating the virtues of a nation founded on political liberty, individual economic opportunity, and Christian civilization. Senator Thomas Hart Benton was among many who believed that John Charles Frémont's mapping expeditions into the American West would pave the way for Americans to claim the continent as their own.

many Native Americans that the mountains were impassable in the winter, Frémont pushed his men up and over the Sierra Nevada Mountains and they reached the Sacramento River in California on March 4, 1844. Frémont's party stopped for a short while at John Sutter's fort (see John Sutter entry) in the Sacramento Valley, which would become famous a few years later as the home of the California gold rush. Frémont then led his men into southern California, east across the Mojave Desert, over the Rocky Mountains in Colorado. Continuing eastward, the party reached St. Louis on August 6, 1844.

Frémont's report of his expedition caused quite a stir when it was presented to Congress on March 1, 1845. Filled with scientific information, maps, drawings, and advice to settlers, the report was most notable for Frémont's enthusiastic narrative of the adventures the party had encountered. The report sold thousands of copies and made Frémont and his wife real celebrities. Everywhere he went crowds gathered to see him. In St. Louis in the spring of 1845, writes Harris, "his fame was now so great that each time he ventured out in public he was mobbed by men seeking a place on his new expedition."

The Bear Flag Revolt

Frémont's charge for his 1845 expedition was to survey the lands along the Arkansas and Red Rivers in present-day Oklahoma and Texas. But Frémont once again had his own ideas. After quickly surveying those rivers, he and his party of sixty men headed due west, across the Rocky Mountains, south of the Great Salt Lake, and into California, which was still a Mexican territory. Frémont later claimed that he was authorized by the U.S. government to travel to California, though no records of this authorization exist. The presence of this large party of well-armed Americans alarmed the Mexican governor of California, and he ordered Frémont to leave. Frémont led his party north to Oregon Territory but returned to California in June 1846. Historians have debated whether Frémont was authorized by the U.S. government or acting on his own when he returned to California; most believe he was acting on his own. Frémont then led a group of American settlers in the Mexican territory in what became known as the Bear Flag Revolt against Mexican rule.

When Mexico and the United States officially went to war on July 19, 1846 (mainly over their clash of interests in Texas), U.S. Navy commodore Robert Stockton placed Frémont in charge of American forces in California, and Frémont aided the American victory over the Mexicans there. Later, Stockton even appointed Frémont governor of California, and Frémont held this post for more than a month. But Frémont's leadership was soon questioned when army general Stephen Kearny, an old enemy of Frémont, arrived to take charge of the American forces in California. Kearny charged that Stockton had had no authority to empower Frémont and that Frémont had directly defied the orders of a superior officer (Frémont had been ordered to turn over control in the territory to Kearny, but he had refused). Frémont had received orders from Washington, D.C., to return with Kearny, and on the return journey Kearny announced that Frémont was under arrest for mutiny.

Frémont was later convicted of mutiny and disobedience at a court-martial and dismissed from the army, though the military court asked the president, James K. Polk (1795–1849), to lessen the sentence, which he did. Outraged over the charges and his court-martial, Frémont resigned from the army in 1848. Though Frémont's reputation was tarnished, many felt that the charges had political overtones and continued to revere Frémont.

Final adventures

Though he no longer served as an army expedition leader, Frémont was not ready to stop exploring. In 1848 he led a private expedition in search of a railroad route across present-day southern Colorado. Determined to prove that the route could be crossed in the winter, Frémont led his party to disaster. Trapped in the snow-covered mountains, eleven members of the party died, and some may have resorted to cannibalism (eating human flesh) to survive.

Frémont survived the disastrous expedition and returned to California to find that gold discoveries on land he owned there had made him a wealthy man. When California attained statehood in 1850, Frémont served as one of its first senators, and he created quite a stir with his strong antislavery speeches. In fact, his support of abolition cost him the next election. In 1853 Frémont set off on his final expedition. Traveling across the San Juan Mountains in southern Utah during the winter without an experienced guide, Fré-

John C. Frémont became something of a celebrity when the report of his western expeditions was published. *(The Corbis Corporation. Reproduced by permission.)*

mont's party struggled against near starvation and frostbite before they made their way out of the mountains.

In 1856 the newly formed Republican political party was looking for a strong antislavery candidate with a national reputation to run for president. Frémont accepted the party's nomination, though he lost the election to Democrat James Buchanan. When the Civil War (1861–65; a war fought between the Northern and Southern United States over the issue of slavery) broke out, President Abraham Lincoln (1809–1865) named Frémont commander of the Department of the West. Frémont declared martial law (military rule) and issued an order freeing the slaves in Missouri. These actions exceeded Frémont's authority and caused Lincoln to relieve Frémont of his command. Given command of forces in Kentucky, Frémont soon found himself outclassed by Confederate general Thomas "Stonewall" Jackson and was again relieved of command.

Frémont's postwar years were neither happy nor terribly successful. He attempted several failed business projects before being made governor of Arizona Territory in 1878. When it became clear that he was using government money for personal expenses, he was asked to resign this post. In his later years his wife Jessie supported the family with her writing. Just before Frémont died in New York on July 13, 1890, Congress awarded him a pension (a sum of money to be paid regularly).

Frémont's reputation has long been clouded. By his rivals he was seen as a reckless adventurer whose first priority was to build his reputation. To the mountain men whose skills allowed Frémont to build his reputation as an explorer Frémont was an Eastern dandy. Quoted in Harris's *John Charles Frémont,* mountain man Joseph Walker, who was with Frémont on his third expedition, said of him, "Frémont morally and physically was the most complete coward I ever knew, and if it were not casting an unmerited reproach on the sex I would say that he was more timid than a woman. An explorer! I knew more of the unexplored region 15 years before he set foot on it than he does today." Despite these criticisms, there is no doubt that Frémont's expeditions were key factors in the opening of the Far West in the late 1840s and 1850s. At the very least, Frémont's colorful reports stir enthusiasm for the West and encouraged emigrants to leave their homes for a new life in the West.

For More Information

Egan, Ferol. *Frémont, Explorer for a Restless Nation.* New York: Doubleday, 1977.

Goff, John S. *John C. Frémont.* Cave Creek, AZ: Black Mountain Press, 1993.

Harris, Edward D. *John Charles Frémont and the Great Western Reconnaissance.* New York: Chelsea House, 1990.

Nevins, Allen. *Frémont, Pathmarker of the West.* New York: Harper & Brothers, 1939. Reprint. Lincoln: University of Nebraska Press, 1992.

Rolle, Andrew. *John Charles Frémont: Character as Destiny.* Norman: University of Oklahoma Press, 1991.

Sanford, William R., and Carl R. Green. *John C. Frémont: Soldier and Pathfinder.* Springfield, NJ: Enslow, 1996.

Geronimo

Born June 1829
No-doyohn Cañon, Arizona
Died February 17, 1909
Fort Sill, Oklahoma

Warrior and tribal leader

The world has come to recognize Geronimo as one of history's great warriors. Leading small bands of Apache on bloody raids, Geronimo struck fear into the hearts of early settlers of New Mexico and Arizona. His ability to disappear into the dusty landscape proved frustrating to the U.S. troops who pursued him throughout the arid region. When he finally surrendered in 1889, Geronimo was the last renegade of the Chiricahua Apache. His final surrender marked the ending of Indians' real threat to white settlers of the Southwest. The story of Geronimo's life is one of the most recounted tales in Native American history—despite the fact that little is known about Geronimo's personality or his day-to-day experiences.

"He stood erect as a mountain pine, while every outline of his symmetrical form indicated strength and endurance.... His proud and graceful posture combined to create in him the model of an Apache war-chief."

John Clum, the only Indian agent to capture Geronimo, as quoted in Geronimo and the Struggle for Apache Freedom

Geronimo.
(Photograph by Ben Wittick. Reproduced from the Collections of the Library of Congress.)

Early years

Geronimo related that he was born in June 1829 in No-doyohn Cañon, Arizona, but many historians claim Geronimo was born in 1827. Geronimo was given the name Goyathlay (also spelled Goyahkla; which means "One Who Yawns") at birth and was called this until his late teens. Goyathlay's grandfather was the chief of a Chiricahua Apache tribe: Goyathlay's father was not a chief because he had joined his wife's tribe of Bedonkohe Apache, thereby losing his right to rule by heredity. Mangas Coloradas succeeded Goyathlay's grandfather as chief of the Chiricahua Apaches, a position Goyathlay might have held otherwise.

At the age of seventeen, sometime around the year 1846, Goyathlay was invited to join the council of warriors, signifying that he was now considered a man in the tribe and not a boy. As a member of the council, he was eligible to fight in battle and to marry. Goyathlay gave many ponies to the father of a young woman named Alope, and she became his wife. In his lifetime, Goyathlay married about eight times. His many children from these marriages would not live easy lives. Four of his children were killed by Mexicans, and four were imprisoned by the U.S. government.

Renamed Geronimo

Intermittent warfare broke out between Mexican settlers and the various bands of Apache in the mid-1800s. Conflict was not new to the Apache. Centuries before, the Spanish conquistadors had eagerly ensnared the Indians in order to sell them on the lucrative slave market. The Apaches—unlike other, more subdued Indian tribes—had responded with swift counterattacks before retreating into the harsh mountain terrain, which was unsuitable for farming; thereafter, the Apaches' economic structure grew dependent on raiding settled communities. Following the Mexican-American War (1846–48)—in which the United States acquired most of present-day Arizona and New Mexico, California, Nevada, Utah, Texas, and parts of Wyoming and Colorado—the Americans pledged to prevent Apaches from raiding across the border into Mexico. But this was a difficult policy to implement, as the Apaches could not relinquish a pattern of raiding that had sustained them for centuries.

In 1858 a group of Apaches was attacked near Janos, Chihuahua, by a mixed group of Mexican troops and settlers. Goyathlay's mother, wife, and three children were killed. After the death of his family, Goyathlay sat alone in the mountains weeping for his loss. As he grieved he heard his name called four times by spirits, after which he was told that he could never be killed by a bullet and that the spirits would always guide his arrows. Armed with his new power, Goyathlay began a personal crusade for the revenge of his family that would not end for more than thirty years. Though he could not bring his family back, Goyathlay claimed in his autobiography that he "could rejoice in this revenge."

Goyathlay was given the name "Geronimo" during his first fight after the spirits spoke to him. Mexican troops involved in the Janos massacre were stationed at the small town of Arispe in Sonora, Mexico, and they met the Apache war party outside of town in the summer of 1859. Goyathlay led the two-hour fight, and when it was finished, the Apaches were in command of the field. Impressed by Goyathlay's bravery, the Mexicans called him "Geronimo." Some suggest that the name is a Mexican mispronunciation of Goyathlay. Others speculate that the troops that day might have named the Apache war leader for Saint Jerome, the fiery fourth-century saint depicted in Christian art as a lion. Indeed, Geronimo's ferocity in battle became so legendary that Americans would later shout his name as a battle cry. After the Apache victory at Arispe, Geronimo led almost yearly raids against the Mexicans.

White settlements on Apache land

Around 1851, Geronimo heard about some white men coming to measure land to the south of his homeland. These men, led by John Russell Bartlett, were surveying the land to try to figure out a new boundary between Mexico and the United States. Accompanied by other warriors, Geronimo went to visit them. While not understanding each other's language and lacking an interpreter, the two groups still made a treaty with one another promising to be brothers. After this group of surveyors left, the Apaches soon discovered miners combing the Indian hunting grounds for precious minerals. Apaches raided the miners' camps and stole their mules to show their anger over the invasion of Apache lands. Apaches thought gold was a symbol of the sun and sacred to their god, Usen, and they resented the miners coming to take it away.

During the 1860s, whites advanced into the West and onto Apache land. Geronimo led many raids against white settlements and immigrant trains, terrorizing those who wished to settle in the region. U.S. soldiers were soon sent to protect the white settlers. In an effort to stop the fighting, U.S. officers invited the Apache leaders to hold a conference at Apache Pass (Fort Bowie) in 1863. There, treacherous soldiers massacred many of the Apaches. Further trouble erupted, and the Apaches renounced their friendship with the white men, vowing never again to trust the U.S. troops.

By 1871 Congress had passed a measure to fund the confinement of Apaches from Arizona and New Mexico to reservations. In 1872 President Ulysses S. Grant (1822–1885) sent General Oliver O. Howard (1830–1909) to Arizona to make peace with the Apaches. Geronimo claimed to have traveled to Apache Pass to make a treaty with the general. In Geronimo's view, General Howard kept his word with the Apaches and treated them as if they were brothers; he claimed he could have lived in peace forever with him. "If there is any pure honest white man in the United States Army, that man is General Howard," Geronimo recalled later, according to *Geronimo: Apache Freedom Fighter*.

But peace did not last long. Even though Geronimo was ordered by military authorities to remain on the San Carlos Reservation, he managed to escape in 1875. For two years, Geronimo lived with a small band of followers, stealing Mexican cattle and horses and selling them in New Mexico. Meanwhile, the new Indian agent (a government official in charge of protecting Indians on a reservation and distributing government aid to them), John Clum, blamed every raid in the Southwest on the renegade Geronimo. Clum succeeded in capturing Geronimo in 1877 and kept him in prison for four months. A new Indian agent was appointed, and he freed Geronimo, who was now in his late forties.

Geronimo tried to live as a farmer on the reservation, but he and his people were not given enough rations. The Apache resolved to break out of the reservation again in 1881. Geronimo and a small band of followers left the reservation, raiding in Mexico and the Southwest for food and supplies. While in the Sierra Madre mountain range, leading one of the bands on a raiding spree, Geronimo and his warriors were surrounded by U.S. general George H. Crook's troops and forced to surrender to government authorities in 1883.

Geronimo was kept a prisoner under chains for four months and then transferred to San Carlos. He lived there peacefully until the summer of 1885, when a rumor surfaced that officers were planning to imprison Apache leaders.

A life on the run

Fearing for their safety, the Indian leaders held a council meeting and decided that they would leave the reservation; Geronimo believed it would be better to die on the warpath than to be killed in prison. With 250 Apache followers, Geronimo and Whoa led the Apaches through Apache Pass, where they met with soldiers in battle. Heading toward Old Mexico, they again encountered soldiers on the second day and fought well into the night. The soldiers were unaccustomed to fighting on the rough terrain, and the Apaches were well equipped with arms and supplies that they had accumulated while liv-

Geronimo surrendered to U.S. troops three times and was either released or escaped custody each time. His fourth surrender, to General Nelson A. Miles in 1886, was his last.
(The Corbis Corporation. Reproduced by permission.)

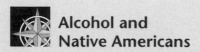

Alcohol and Native Americans

The Apaches had a powerful desire for alcohol but a particularly difficult time handling it. For centuries, the Apaches drank *tizwin,* a fermented corn drink. Angie Debo notes in *Geronimo: The Man, His Time, His Place* that although the drink had a "relatively low alcoholic content," the "Apaches were efficient drinkers." She adds that "after a preliminary fast they achieved a calculated debauch that threw the whole band into disorder." The resulting unruly behavior caused Indian agents (government officials in charge of protecting Indians on a reservation and distributing government aid to them) to ban *tizwin* on the reservation. Rules against drinking angered the Apache and influenced many to leave the reservation. Although Indians eventually returned to the reservations, alcohol continued to be a persistent problem for them. Some reservations continue to ban alcohol into the twenty-first century. Many scientific studies have pondered the problem of alcoholism among Native Americans. Peter Cooper Mancall explores the relation between alcohol and Indians in *Deadly Medicine: Indians and Alcohol in Early America.* "Alcohol abuse has killed and impoverished American Indians since the 17th century, when European settlers began trading rum for furs," writes Mancall. Indian deaths related to alcohol are four times higher than for the general population in the United States, according to Mancall.

ing on the reservation. After this battle, the Apaches were able to flee south to Casa Grande and camp in the Sierra de Sahuaripa Mountains. Geronimo claimed that the Apaches roamed the area for one year and then returned to San Carlos, taking with them their cattle and horses. Upon their return to the reservation, General Crook ignored Geronimo's pleas and confiscated all the livestock that the Apaches had obtained rightfully from the Mexicans. Once again, the white men had cheated Geronimo.

Upset with the decision, Geronimo undertook plans to travel to Fort Apache. Upon instructions from General Crook, officers and soldiers were told to arrest Geronimo—and to kill him if he resisted. Informed of Crook's plans, Geronimo prepared to head south to Old Mexico with about four hundred Apache. But while the Apache were camping in the mountains west of Casa Grande, they were surprised by government troops. Geronimo recounted that one boy was killed and nearly all of the women and children were captured. Geronimo and the others took refuge in the foothills of the Sierra Madres, but they were soon attacked again by a very large army of Mexican troops. Meanwhile, the U.S. Army also continued their efforts to rout the Indians. The Apache were weary from the fighting when Geronimo and his men decided to surrender to General Crook and a party of about two thousand soldiers (some say five thousand). But as the soldiers prepared to return the Indians to their reservation, Geronimo sensed

treachery and escaped with forty others back into the mountains of Mexico. As a result of Geronimo's escape, General Crook resigned and was replaced by General Nelson A. Miles. General Miles would pursue Geronimo like no other.

Determined to capture and secure Geronimo under government control, General Miles ordered U.S. troops to trail the Apaches. Though they stayed ahead of the troops,

Geronimo and General Crook in 1886, near Tombstone, Arizona.
(The Corbis Corporation. Reproduced by permission.)

the Apaches feared that if they returned to the reservation they would be put in prison and killed; and if they stayed in Mexico, soldiers would continue to fight them. Hemmed in on all sides, Geronimo surrendered, for the last time, to General Miles in a canyon near Fronteras in Sonora, Mexico, on September 4, 1886. Geronimo told Miles that "this is the fourth time I have surrendered." Miles replied, "I think it is the last," according to Miles's *Personal Recollections*. Geronimo did not know that this was the beginning of his life as a prisoner of war.

Prisoner of war

Instead of being killed as he had feared, Geronimo became a prisoner of war. After his final surrender, Geronimo and his followers were shipped by train to San Antonio, Texas, where they were imprisoned. Shortly thereafter, Geronimo and his band were moved to Fort Pickens in Pensacola, Florida. The Florida climate was devastating to the Apache; many died of tuberculosis and other diseases. Geronimo and other Apache leaders pleaded with the government to allow them to return to their homelands, but to no avail. Other tribes heard the Apache's pleas. In 1894, the Kiowa and Comanches, both former Apache enemies, invited the Apache to live with them on their reservation near Fort Sill, Oklahoma. Geronimo spent the remainder of his life at Fort Sill growing watermelons. When the government agents let him leave the reservation, the once ferocious warrior supplemented his income by peddling his signature and coat buttons to curious onlookers at fairs and exhibitions like Buffalo Bill's Wild West Show in Buffalo, New York; Omaha, Nebraska; and St. Louis, Missouri.

In February 1909, with a belly full of whiskey, Geronimo fell from his horse and spent the night sprawled in damp weeds. He contracted pneumonia and died a few days later on February 17, 1909. At the time of his death, Geronimo was still listed as a prisoner of war. Although Geronimo did not succeed in his attempts to return his people to their homelands, he had spent his life trying. Geronimo had fought against enormous odds to save his people, and he refused for thirty years to obey the commands of his white oppressors.

During his numerous battles, Geronimo suffered seven serious injuries, reinforcing his notion that no bullet could kill him. In 1913, Geronimo's people were permitted to return to Apacheria to live quietly with the Mescalero Indians in New Mexico.

For More Information

Barrett, S. M. *Geronimo's Story of His Life*. New York: Duffield and Company, 1906.

Debo, Angie. *Geronimo: The Man, His Time, His Place*. Norman: University of Oklahoma Press, 1976.

Hermann, Spring. *Geronimo: Apache Freedom Fighter*. Springfield, NJ: Enslow Publishers, 1997.

Kent, Zachary. *The Story of Geronimo*. Chicago: Children's Press, 1989.

Mancall, Peter C.*Deadly Medicine: Indians and Alcohol in Early America*. Ithaca, NY: Cornell University Press, 1995.

Miles, Nelson. *Personal Recollections*. New York: Werner, 1897.

Shorto, Russell. *Geronimo and the Struggle for Apache Freedom*. Englewood Cliffs, NJ: Silver Burdett Press, 1989.

Wyatt, Edgar. *Geronimo: The Last Apache War Chief*. New York: McGraw-Hill, 1952.

Mifflin Wistar Gibbs

Born April 17, 1823
Philadelphia, Pennsylvania
Died July 11, 1915
Little Rock, Arkansas

Abolitionist, pioneer, businessman,
lawyer, elected official, college president

Mifflin Wistar Gibbs was a pioneer in every sense of the word. In the 1850s he was among the many pioneers who set out for California in search of riches during the gold rush. Gibbs found not riches but racism, and he was forced to make his way not as a miner but as a shopkeeper. Refusing to accept the limits placed on him by racism, Gibbs became a pioneer for his race. He campaigned against discrimination in California before moving to Canada. In the 1870s he returned to the United States and began an illustrious career as a politician and public servant. He was the first black elected a municipal judge in the United States, and he received several federal appointments, eventually becoming consul in Madagascar. His autobiography, *Shadow and Light,* published in 1902, helped publicize his story of achievement to the world.

> "Labor to make yourself as indispensable as possible in all your relations with the dominant race, and color will cut less figure in your upward grade."

Mifflin Wistar Gibbs.

From stable boy to abolitionist

Mifflin Wistar Gibbs was born in Philadelphia on April 17, 1823, to Jonathan Clarkson Gibbs, a Methodist minister, and Maria Jackson Gibbs. Gibbs's father died shortly after Mifflin's eighth birthday, and the boy was put out to work as a stable boy for three dollars a month. He worked at a series of similar jobs until he was sixteen, when he was apprenticed to carpenter James Gibbons, a former slave who had bought his freedom. Under Gibbons, Gibbs learned a skill that would serve him well in life. He helped Gibbons build several black churches in the Philadelphia area in the 1840s. During his apprenticeship, Gibbs studied in his free time and also joined a local black literary society, the Philomatheon Institute. At the institute he met some of Philadelphia's leading black citizens and began to speak out against slavery in the South.

After finishing his apprenticeship, Gibbs won a place for himself in Philadelphia as an abolitionist (a vocal opponent of slavery) and a builder. He was an active member of the Underground Railroad, a network which helped runaway slaves reach safety in the North and Canada, and was a member of a committee that petitioned (presented a formal request of citizens to) the Pennsylvania legislature to give blacks the right to vote. After the National Antislavery Convention held in Philadelphia in 1849, Frederick Douglass, a former slave and leading black abolitionist, invited Gibbs to accompany him on a speaking tour in western New York, Ohio, and Pennsylvania. Gibbs had just completed the tour and returned to Rochester, New York, when word of the gold rush in California lured him westward.

Gold rush racism

Gibbs made his way to California in 1850 by boat. He first traveled south along the Atlantic Coast, then crossed the Isthmus of Panama before taking a steamship north to San Francisco. San Francisco was a bustling town, the harbor crowded with ships and the city sprawling with the influx of miners bound for the goldfields. Gibbs quickly found work as a carpenter, but just as quickly found himself out of work when white carpenters refused to work alongside an African American. For a time Gibbs worked shining shoes and doing other menial jobs, but he was too ambitious to be satisfied with such work for long. He had saved enough money by 1852 to form, along with fellow black Philadelphian Peter Lester, the Pioneer Boot and Shoe Emporium. For several years their business prospered, but all was not well in California.

Though many blacks traveled to the West because they believed that they might escape the racism and ill treatment that they received in the East, they were often disappointed. As whites poured into California, they created laws similar to those they had made in the East; in April 1850, for example, a state law barred nonwhites from testifying in court in any case involving a white person. Gibbs soon felt the sting of this law firsthand, when a disgruntled customer beat Lester right in front of him. Because resisting the assault would have meant death and because the black businessmen could find no help in the courts, they were helpless. Gibbs joined other area blacks in 1851 to draw up the first black protest, which was published in one of the leading papers. Gibbs also participated in state political conventions in 1854, 1855, and 1857, where he protested the treatment of blacks in California.

His stay in San Francisco was not entirely negative, however. Gibbs was an active member of the San Francisco Atheneum, the intellectual center for blacks in the city, and with other members of the group he established the state of California's first black newspaper, the *Mirror of the Times*, in 1856. Moreover, he had succeeded in building a fairly successful business that was supported by many members of the community. By 1858, however, Gibbs had grown tired enough of discrimination in California that he jumped at the opportunity to travel to the city of Victoria, on the British colony of Vancouver Island (which later became part of the Canadian province of British Columbia).

Success in Canada

With his partner Lester, Gibbs bought some cheap land in Victoria. The city was attractive for several reasons: because the territorial governor was sympathetic to blacks, there was little discrimination, and a new gold rush brought people and trade into the city. The black community in Victoria eventually grew to nearly eight hundred people. Gibbs's various business enterprises soon made him a wealthy man, and—after applying for British citizenship—he became one of the city's leading citizens. In 1859 Gibbs traveled back to the United States to marry Maria A. Alexander; the couple would have five children together. In 1861 Gibbs helped form a black militia for defense of the city, and in 1866 he was elect-

Blacks in the West

To many white Americans, the West was a land of opportunity. White pioneers traveled westward on frontier trails to claim cheap land and build farms, and white fortune hunters took to the goldfields of California and elsewhere to strike it rich. Such opportunities were also open to some black Americans, and many took advantage of them. Black cowboy Nat Love (1854–1921) and mountain man Jim Beckwourth (c. 1800–1866; see entry), who entered the West when it was still "young" (not yet civilized), found that there were few limits placed on their ambition. Both Love and Beckwourth became famous for their respective achievements. Other blacks who moved onto the frontier in the early days of settlement often enjoyed access to land and business opportunities. But as more white people poured into the West, the opportunities for blacks declined.

In the nineteenth century the majority of Americans believed that blacks were inferior to whites. They supported policies and laws that deprived black people of the rights—such as voting, legal protection, and economic access—that were available to white people. This was especially true in the South, where the institution of slavery had made blacks the property of whites. As western towns and cities grew, many of them instituted the same racist laws that had existed in the South. These laws allowed for discrimination and violence against black people. While anti-black discrimination in the West was never as bad as it was in the South and East, the West was hardly a land of opportunity for black Americans. Sadly, it was not until the Civil Rights movement of the 1960s that blacks would demand and gain their full civil rights and equal protection under the law. Mifflin Gibbs achieved a great deal, thanks in part to the openness of the West, but an intelligent, ambitious man like Gibbs, and many others like him, could have achieved much more if they had not been limited by racism.

ed to the town council. His status in the city was further enhanced in 1867, when he and some associates received a charter to build a railroad to a coal mine north of the city. Despite all his successes, however, Gibbs felt that his economic prospects were limited. Gibbs thought that since the Civil War (1861–65; a war between the Northern and Southern United States over the issue of slavery) was over and slavery had ended, perhaps it would be possible for a black man to succeed in the United States.

Successful lawyer and politician

Going west was an experience that changed many Americans in the nineteenth century; the opportunities available in the West—including the opportunity to fail—helped school pioneers in the qualities that were needed for success. Not every pioneer learned from that schooling, but for Gibbs, his experiences in the West prepared him well for the career that would follow. Gibbs returned to the United States a different man than the one who had left nearly twenty years earlier. A young and relatively inexperienced man when he left, he had now run several successful businesses, learned the byways of politics, and studied law with a British lawyer in Victoria. After studying law at Oberlin College in Ohio, Gibbs set out to establish a career in the South, where he felt that his skills as a lawyer could best benefit his people.

By 1871 Gibbs had settled in Little Rock, Arkansas, and by 1872 he had opened his own law office with partner Lloyd G. Wheeler. He found himself immersed in the tumultuous world of Republican Party politics. Gibbs was named Pulaski County attorney in 1873, a post he soon resigned to become a municipal judge, the first African American to be elected to such a position in the United States. Gibbs left office after he was on the losing side of a small-scale civil war among political factions, but he remained influential in Republican politics. In 1876 he traveled to the national party convention as a delegate, helping to elect Rutherford B. Hayes to the presidency.

In the coming years, Gibbs would serve the Republican presidential administrations in a variety of ways. (At the time, Republicans defended the rights of African Americans.) Beginning in 1877 he served as the register in the U.S. Land Office in Little Rock, where he oversaw decisions about federal land sales in a region that was still relatively underpopulated. Gibbs reached the pinnacle of his political career in 1897 when he was named U.S. consul (a diplomatic office) to the African country of Madagascar. Thus for over twenty years Gibbs loyally served the only political party that defended the rights of black people.

Gibbs retired from public service in 1901 but continued to pursue a variety of business interests in Arkansas. He served as president of the Capital City Savings Bank, was a partner in the Little Rock Electric Light Company, and participated in a variety of business and real estate ventures in the state. Moreover, he continued to travel widely and lecture on the possibilities available to black people. In 1902 Gibbs published his autobiography, *Shadow and Light*. Second in prominence only to Booker T. Washington's famous autobiography, *Shadow and Light* argued that blacks could achieve success in America if they worked hard and applied themselves to jobs in industry and agriculture. It was an optimistic message offered by a man whose own success provided a real example of what blacks might achieve. Gibbs died on July 11, 1915, at the age of ninety-two.

For More Information

Dillard, Tom W., ed. Introduction to *Shadow and Light,* by Mifflin Wistar Gibbs. Lincoln: University of Nebraska Press, 1995.

Gibbs, Mifflin Wistar. *Shadow and Light.* 1902. Reprint. New York: Arno Press and the New York Times, 1968.

Lapp, Rudolph M. *Blacks in Gold Rush California.* New Haven, CT: Yale University Press, 1977.

Logan, Rayford W., and Michael R. Winston, eds. *Dictionary of American Negro Autobiography.* New York: Norton, 1982.

Simmons, William J. *Men of Mark.* Cleveland, OH: Geo. M. Rewell, 1887.

Winks, Robin W. *The Blacks in Canada.* New Haven, CT: Yale University Press, 1971.

Woodson, Carter G. "The Gibbs Family."*Negro History Bulletin* (October 1947): 312–22.

James J. Hill

Born September 16, 1838
Wellington, Ontario, Canada
Died May 29, 1916
St. Paul, Minnesota

Railroad builder, financier, and founder of the Great Northern Railway

James J. Hill was a powerful business tycoon who established an extensive railroad empire that connected rail lines, farms, mines, and communities into a lucrative network of trade. His first rail network, the Saint Paul, Minneapolis, and Manitoba Railway, linked wheat producers throughout the thriving northern states and gave Hill the economic clout to pursue his dream: the creation of his own transcontinental rail line. In 1889 that dream was realized with the Great Northern Railway, which stretched from Minneapolis across the northernmost parts of the United States to Seattle, a prime port on the Pacific Ocean. The Great Northern Railway was not the first transcontinental railroad but according to many historians and business experts it was by far the best. More than one hundred years after the creation of this rail line, *Trains Magazine* named Hill the most influential figure in American railroading.

Hill was "the railroad-building genius who opened up the great northwestern wilderness."

Obituary, World's Work, July 16, 1916, p. 243.

A comfortable Canadian childhood

Born September 16, 1838, in Wellington, Ontario, Canada, James Hill (he added the middle initial *J* later in life)

James J. Hill.
(Archive Photos, Inc. Reproduced by permission.)

came from a long line of James Hills who traced their ancestry through Ireland and back to Scotland. As a boy James loved to hunt and fish with his younger brother Alexander. While hunting one day with a bow and arrow, James's bow snapped, and the wayward arrow dislocated his eyeball from its socket. A local doctor managed to reattach Hill's eye in the socket, but James would never see more than dark shades out of this eye. Hill attended a nearby Quaker academy from age eleven to fourteen and enjoyed a strong friendship with his Quaker schoolmaster, William Weatherald, until the end of his life. With a Baptist father, a Methodist mother, and a Quaker mentor, Hill gained a deep appreciation for religious values, though he never showed a strong commitment to organized religion as an adult.

Like many youths during that time, Hill came to admire the French general Napoleon Bonaparte and aspired to one day ruling an empire of his own. He even gave himself a middle name, Jerome, in honor of Napoleon's brother. According to biographer Michael P. Malone, Hill "talked all his life of his youthful idea of building a fleet of steamboats on the Ganges and other legendary rivers; like Alexander the Great or Charles 'Chinese' Gordon, he hoped to find his destiny in the fabled lands of the East." One day Hill would build an empire almost as great as his dreams.

Tough times as a young adult

Hill's life changed dramatically in 1852 with the death of his father. After this traumatic event, Hill was forced to leave school and become a clerk at a general store in the growing town of Rockwood. He excelled at this job, quickly learning the ways of business and finance. As he neared the age of eighteen, he prepared to leave home and find his way in the world. Biographer Malone recounts how Hill decided to move to the United States:

> An itinerant trader from Saint Paul, Minnesota, took a liking to [Hill] after he had voluntarily watered the man's horse. Handing him a tattered copy of a New York newspaper captioned "Splendid Chances for Young Men in the West," the trader said, "Go out there, young man—that's the place for you." Jim carried the copy around, reading and rereading it, until it fell to pieces, and now he finally focused his dreams of adventure on a real decision.

In the winter of 1856, Hill left Ontario with his life savings: six hundred dollars. He traveled first to the East Coast of the United States, visiting New York City, Philadelphia, and cities in the South before arriving in St. Paul, in the territory of Minnesota. Situated on the Minnesota River, the city was quickly becoming a center for milling locally grown wheat into flour. The friendly, hardworking Hill soon found work on the docks of St. Paul, and he learned about shipping a variety of products in and out of the thriving city.

A born entrepreneur

"If ever there was a born entrepreneur," writes Malone, "it was Jim Hill—highly intelligent, highly motivated, highly acquisitive—and it was only a matter of time before he went into business on his own." He started by delivering wood, horse feed, and coal to local markets; with the help of friends, his business quickly expanded to ship a wide variety of goods to points north of St. Paul from a growing cluster of warehouses and transfer facilities. Befriending prominent businessmen and investors and gaining a reputation for hard work and integrity—as well as a quick temper—Hill quickly became one of St. Paul's leading businessmen. On August 19, 1867, Hill married Mary Mehegan; over the years the couple would have ten children (one of whom died) and build a sizable mansion in one of the best neighborhoods of St. Paul. By the 1870s, James J. Hill had made a fortune—but he was far from satisfied.

Minnesota railroads

By the late 1870s, Hill set his sights on a failing local railroad, the Saint Paul and Pacific (SP&P), and hoped to make it the base of his transportation empire. The SP&P connected several towns along the fertile Red River Valley and ended in St. Paul. Hill envisioned the future value in an agricultural region served by the railroad. He hoped that with proper management the SP&P could dominate trade and shipping in the area. In partnership with several investors, Hill took over the SP&P in 1878. Not only did these men receive the tracks and trains of the railway; they also gained control of a variety of potential assets, including millions of acres of land that the government had granted to the railway's founders. If immigration and farming increased as Hill and his partners hoped, they could sell this land to settlers and make even more money.

Hill and his partners soon turned the SP&P, which they renamed the Saint Paul, Minneapolis, and Manitoba Railway, into a transportation powerhouse. By purchasing additional rail lines (some of which continued to operate independently, but under Hill's supervision) and building some of the best quality railroads in the United States, the partners brought a new level of quality to American railroading. While other railways concentrated on quickly stretching rail lines across vast distances, the Manitoba—the name the railroad system was known by—built rail networks that looked like a tree. The base of the railroad was its strong trunk lines, which could carry vast amounts of goods to the major markets, but the Manitoba also had many branch lines to serve the agricultural communities that the railway itself helped build. By providing roads of commerce linking small towns to larger markets, the railroads breathed life into small towns across the region. The Manitoba was efficient in that it offered quick service and fair rates; it was powerful in that it dominated local real estates sales and exercised a distinct influence on local politics. By the 1880s it dominated trade and shipping throughout the rich agricultural lands of Minnesota, and it quickly expanded into the Dakotas.

Dreams of a powerful empire

As the Manitoba railroad system grew, observers noted Hill's knowledge of and control over every aspect of the railway. Traveling ceaselessly to the railway's many stations and construction sites, Hill astonished his employees by addressing them by name and suggesting how they might correct problems they encountered. He demanded a great deal from his employees and was a difficult person to work for. He was known to shout and throw objects when he grew angry. Moreover, Malone asserts that Hill banned coffee breaks among office employees and once fired a stationmaster because he did not like the man's name—Spittles.

It wasn't long before Hill began to plan the expansion of the railroad westward. He was not the first to dream of a transcontinental railroad. In fact, by the 1880s several railroads already spanned the continent, including the Northern Pacific and the Union Pacific. According to Hill, the problem with these railroads was that they had been built too quickly and with too little concern for developing the land they crossed. These railways needed frequent repairs, charged high rates, and were owned by poorly managed companies that were deep in debt. But because these railroads crossed the continent, only they could provide service to American traders who wanted to sell their goods throughout the United States and the world. If Hill wanted his railway to be a part of the growing empire of national and international trade, he realized that it would have to have access to the Pacific Ocean.

The railroads cross the prairies

In the early 1880s, the Manitoba began to build an extensive network of rail lines throughout the northeastern section of what was then Dakota Territory, thus paving the way for the settlement and development of the region. Minot, North Dakota—named after one of Hill's engineers— became a northern boomtown and provided the jumping-off point for the railway's westward expansion. Early in 1887, after receiving federal approval for land use and assistance in renegotiating access to Indian lands, the Manitoba embarked on the single most concentrated period of railroad construction in its history. Their goal was to cross 640 miles of prairie from Minot to Helena, in present-day Montana. Beginning in late spring, Hill's workers moved 9.7 million cubic feet of earth and more than 32,000 cubic yards of rock. Once they hit their stride they were building several miles of railroad a day. By mid-November the railroad crews had made it to Helena in one of the most astonishing feats of construction in American history. The Manitoba could now provide service to the flourishing mining industries of Montana.

By 1889 Hill had acquired interests in several railroad companies throughout the region. He had different levels of control in the various companies. Around this time he reorganized his growing railroad interests into one company, the Great Northern Railway Company. While Hill had been the driving force in each of the railways he had served, with the consolidation of the railroads under Great Northern he became the undisputed leader. Hill's first job as president of the Great Northern was to plan a railway route from Montana across the Rocky Mountains and the Cascade Range and on to the Pacific Ocean. In the West, Hill built his railway in the same way he did in the Midwest: he gave life to the region's economy—based on mining and logging—by providing an efficient way of shipping goods across the continent.

The railroads cross the mountains

For his western railroad, which was to be called the Great Northern like its parent company, Hill needed a low, easy route over the mountains that lay between the Plains and the Pacific Ocean. Unlike the railroads to the south that had to cross one mountain range, the Great Northern had to cross two mountain ranges. Luckily, Hill had the services of John F. Stevens, a college-educated and highly skilled engineer who also happened to be a seasoned woodsman and explorer.

In the midst of a blizzard in December 1889, Stevens left his Indian guide and trudged through the snow and minus-forty-degree temperatures to discover Marias Pass, which at 5,214 foot elevation was the lowest pass over the northern Rockies. This discovery pleased Hill, for it allowed the railroad to proceed directly west from Grand Forks to Minot in present-day North Dakota, and then to Havre and to Marias Pass in present-day northwestern Montana. "The resulting avoidance of grades and curvature spelled out once again the torah of [Hill's] credo," writes Malone, "a highly efficient, low-cost line that could, better than any competitor, carry long-distance cargoes of heavy tonnage." The railway construction across Marias Pass and into the Flathead Lake region of Montana was completed by 1891. From there the railroad advanced to the rail hub of Spokane in Washington Territory.

In order to reach Seattle there was another mountain range to cross. The Cascade Range posed profound challenges for railway engineers. Unlike the Rockies, which start from a high plateau, the Cascades soar to towering peaks virtually from sea level. Engineers had to figure out how to lift their lines from sea level to pass level and back in just over one hundred miles. Stevens found the best possible place for the crossing at the 4,061-foot pass that now bears his name, Stevens Pass. Though it was the best, it was far from perfect. While he would have liked to tunnel through the mountain, Stevens was forced to recommend that the only way to cross the pass was to construct what was, in Malone's words, "undeniably every railroad man's nightmare: a horribly costly series of switchbacks." A switchback is a zigzag pattern of rails that allows a train to climb a steep incline more easily than if it were to head directly up the incline. Under the most difficult of conditions the track was laid, and the last spike was driven on Hill's transcontinental railway on January 6, 1893.

Empire builder

Hill's railroad was a prime example of American industry. While the rival railroads were poorly built and deeply in debt, the rails of the Great Northern Railway were of sound construction and the company was undeniably healthy and prosperous. All across the country, from the grain-growing Plains to the Montana mines to the rich timber stands of western Washington, the Great Northern Railway invested money and branch lines in the communities it serviced.

While Hill boasted of the improvements that his railroad brought to previously remote territories, his critics charged that every action of the railroad was designed to enrich Hill, his partners, and their investors. From the rates they charged to the land they sold and the towns they built, Hill and company extracted a profit. Hill, it was true, grew fabulously wealthy. According to Malone, "his fortune, which had stood at $9.6 million in 1890, rose to $12 million in 1895 and was approaching $20 million by the turn of the nineteenth century. Thus, in an age when a millionaire was truly wealthy, Jim Hill became a true *multi*millionaire, in fact one of America's most wealthy and powerful men."

Managing an empire

Hill managed his empire in the same way he built it— by insisting on efficiency, sometimes ruthlessly seizing on business opportunities, and remaining dedicated to his grand vision of empire. Unwilling to relax and enjoy the fruits of his labor, Hill continued to seek challenges after his railway reached the Pacific. Hill's companies invested heavily and quite profitably in the Lake Superior iron ore region of northeastern Minnesota and northern Wisconsin and Michigan. He continued to expand his rail system, building branch lines and incorporating smaller rail lines into his network.

Although he faced political resistance and intense competition from railroad rival Edward H. Harriman, Hill—with the support of financier J. P. Morgan—gained control of his old rival, the Northern Pacific Railroad, by 1899. Then in 1900 Hill added another gem to his collection of railroads when he acquired the Chicago, Burlington, and Quincy Railroad. This last acquisition gave Hill unprecedented control of shipping from the Great Lakes westward to the Pacific, allowing him to dominate nearly the entire northern half of the United States. At the turn of the century Hill was not only one of the most powerful men in his region, but also one of the most powerful in the world.

Hill remained president of the Great Northern company until 1907, when he handed over the reigns to his son, Louis. In his semiretirement, Hill enjoyed the company of his many children and grandchildren, collected art, and engaged in philanthropy. By the spring of 1916, he was bedridden; in late May he lapsed into a coma. Hill died on May 29, 1916, surrounded by all his children but one. On the day of his funeral, every train on the "Hill lines" came to a halt for five minutes to honor the passing of the great "Empire Builder." His legacy can still be seen today in the Burlington Northern Railway, which continues to haul freight over many of the same routes that Hill pioneered.

For More Information

Hidy, Ralph W., and others. *The Great Northern Railway: A History.* Boston: Harvard Business School Press, 1988.

Malone, Michael P. *James J. Hill: Empire builder of the Northwest.* Norman: University of Oklahoma Press, 1996.

Martin, Albro. *James J. Hill and the Opening of the Northwest.* New York: Oxford University Press, 1976.

Martin, Albro. *Railroads Triumphant: The Growth, Rejection, and Rebirth of a Vital American Force.* New York: Oxford University Press, 1992.

Pyle, Joseph G. *The Life of James J. Hill.* 2 vols. New York: Doubleday-Page, 1916–17.

Stover, John F. *The Life and Decline of the American Railroad.* New York: Oxford University Press, 1970.

Yenne, Bill. *The History of the Burlington Northern.* New York: Brompton Books, 1991.

Andrew Jackson

Born March 15, 1767
Waxhaw Settlement, South Carolina
Died June 8, 1845
Nashville, Tennessee

United States president, congressman, general, governor, judge

F ew individuals played as crucial a role in the early westward expansion of the United States as Andrew Jackson. As a military leader, Jackson led his ragtag band of soldiers to victories over several tribes and scored a decisive victory over the British in the Battle of New Orleans during the War of 1812 (1812–14; a conflict between the British and the Americans over the control of the western reaches of the United States and over shipping rights in the Atlantic Ocean). Made famous by his military victories, Jackson went on to become the seventh president of the United States. As president, Jackson oversaw the large-scale removal of native peoples from the eastern United States. Most historians view Jackson's "Indian Removal" policies as a shameful episode in America's past, but in its time the policy was welcomed by many.

Hardscrabble beginnings

Andrew Jackson's parents were among the thousands of Irish immigrants arriving in the United States in the early 1700s. The Jacksons built a small cabin and settled in a valley

"I thank God that my life has been spent in a land of liberty and that he has given me a heart to love my country with the affection of a son. And filled with gratitude for your constant and unwavering kindness, I bid you a last and affectionate farewell."

From Jackson's farewell address to the American people, March 4, 1837

Andrew Jackson.
(Reproduced from the Collections of the Library of Congress.)

in the Appalachian Mountains of South Carolina, about 160 miles northwest of Charleston. The couple was expecting their third son when Andrew Jackson senior died (of unknown causes); that son, named Andrew Jackson after his father, was born on March 15, 1767. Unable to care for the family on her own, Jackson's mother moved in with her sister and her large family, who lived nearby.

Jackson's mother, Elizabeth Hutchinson, was a pious woman who wanted her son to become a Presbyterian minister. But from an early age, Jackson had other ideas. Though his mother sent him to decent schools, Jackson proved better at fighting than he did at school. He gathered only a basic knowledge of history, geography, and literature, and never learned to spell correctly or write a proper sentence. But he excelled at footraces, jumping matches, and wrestling, and became known as a fierce competitor.

Jackson was gripped with the excitement that swept the colonies at the beginning of the American Revolution in 1776. By 1780, when the war reached South Carolina, thirteen-year-old Jackson signed on as an orderly to Colonel William Richardson Davie. The British captured Jackson and his brother after a minor battle. When Jackson refused to clean the muddy boots of a British officer, the man slashed him with a sword, leaving lifetime gashes on Jackson's forehead and left hand. But Jackson was lucky, for he was the only member of his family to survive the war: His oldest brother, Hugh, died in an early battle; Robert succumbed to smallpox he had encountered in the British prison camp; and his mother died of cholera while tending to sick soldiers in Charleston. At age fourteen, Andrew Jackson was an orphan.

Frontier lawyer and politician

Jackson lived for a time with a cousin and then an uncle, but mostly he spent his time with a group of troublemaking boys in Charleston. According to biographer Milton Meltzer, writing in *Andrew Jackson and His America,* "They were a wild lot: nothing interested them but drinking, gambling, cockfighting, and brawling. Andy took to that life happily." In 1782, near the end of the Revolutionary War, Jackson left Charleston for Waxhaw, South Carolina. There he attended and then taught school—even though he was still a teenager. Finally, in 1784, he decided to study law under a prominent attorney named Spruce MaCay in Salisbury, North Carolina. Jackson passed the bar exam (a qualifying exam for lawyers) in 1786, but he made more of an impression with his wild ways than with his skills as a lawyer. Finally, in October 1788, Jackson decided to begin anew in the frontier town of Nashville, in what would become Tennessee. Jackson made a name for himself prosecuting debtors and handling land claims for investors. He made a small fortune as well, and when his clients couldn't pay in cash he accepted land, slaves, and livestock as payment.

In August 1791, Jackson married the dark-eyed, dark-haired Rachel Donelson Robards, daughter of a prominent landowner. From the beginning the couple was mired in scandal, for Rachel had not legally divorced her first husband when she married Jackson. Three years later they had to remarry to put a stop to the charges of bigamy and adultery leveled against them. The scandal of their first improper marriage would come back to haunt them when Jackson ran for president.

When Tennessee became America's sixteenth state in 1796, it sent Andrew Jackson as its representative to the U.S. House of Representatives. Jackson was elected to fill his state's U.S. Senate seat the following year, but he was out of his depth among the educated and distinguished members of the Senate. Writes his biographer Robert Remini, "He had assumed responsibilities far beyond his reach, and he virtually made a fool of himself." Jackson returned to the friendlier arena of Tennessee politics in 1798 and was soon appointed judge of the state's superior court. One man described Jackson's decisions as "short, untechnical, unlearned, sometimes ungrammatical, and generally right." Jackson served as a judge for six years before leaving in 1804 to tend to his growing business enterprises, his plantation, boatbuilding, horse breeding, and the selling of slaves.

Despite his high standing in Tennessee politics, Jackson remained as much a hell-raiser as he had been in his early teens. In 1803, he traded shots with Tennessee governor John Sevier in the streets of Knoxville when the governor slandered Jackson's wife. Neither man was hurt in this encounter or in their subsequent duel. In 1806 Jackson dueled again with noted shooter Charles Dickinson; Jackson came out on top, killing his opponent, but he carried his enemy's bullet in his chest for the rest of his life. In 1813, in a gunfight with a former soldier, Jesse Benton, who had insulted him, Jackson nearly lost an arm; these bullets remained in his body for twenty years. Jackson often chose violence as the easiest way to solve his problems.

Military heroics

On the strength of his political reputation—and in spite of his total lack of military experience—Jackson was commissioned major general of the Tennessee militia in April 1803. For years he saw no action, but when the War of 1812 (1812-14) pitted the United States against British and Indian forces on the western frontier, Jackson was eager to lead his men against their enemies. Jackson first earned his reputation as a fierce Indian fighter in September 1813 when he and his men slaughtered 186 Creek warriors who had attacked Fort Mims; the soldiers killed all the women and children traveling with the warriors as well. In March 1814 Jackson scored an even greater victory, killing nine hundred Creek warriors and taking three hundred prisoners at a battle near Horseshoe Bend on Alabama's Tallapoosa River. This battle ended Indian resistance in the region and made Jackson a hero.

Jackson's greatest heroics in the War of 1812, however, came at the Battle of New Orleans. Jackson had learned that the British forces led by Sir Edward Pakenham were preparing to capture the city of New Orleans and thus gain control of the Mississippi River and cripple American trade. After easily defeating a tiny American naval fleet, Pakenham's force of seventy-five hundred men marched on the city on January 8, 1815. Awaiting him were Jackson's forces, a motley

A crowd gathered in and around the White House to celebrate Andrew Jackson's inauguration. *(Reproduced from the Collections of the Library of Congress.)*

assortment of Tennesseeans, New Orleans gentlemen, Choctaw Indians, free blacks, and a band of pirates led by the Laffite brothers. The strategically placed U.S. forces rained bullets on the British, killing two thousand soldiers in less than an hour and losing only a few lives themselves. The battle secured the Mississippi Valley, made a hero of Andrew Jackson, and sparked a wave of pride among American citizens. Ironically, the battle should never have been fought, for the treaty that ended the war—the Treaty of Ghent—had already been signed. Because news traveled slowly, neither force knew of the treaty.

Jackson's victory in New Orleans made him a national hero. He was honored with a congressional gold medal and President James Madison (1751–1836) said, according to biographer Alice Osinski, "History records no example of such a glorious victory, obtained with so little bloodshed on the part of the victorious." Jackson soon returned to the field of battle when he traveled south to settle conflicts between Seminole

Jackson on Indian Removal

As part of his first address to Congress after being elected president in 1828, Jackson offered these views about the government's policy toward Indians living in the United States:

> Our conduct toward these people is deeply interesting to our national character. Their present condition, contrasted with what they once were, makes a most powerful appeal to our sympathies. Our ancestors found them the uncontrolled possessors of these vast regions. By persuasion and force they have been made to retire from river to river and from mountain to mountain, until some of the tribes have become extinct and others have left but remnants to preserve for a while their once terrible names. Surrounded by the whites with their arts of civilization, which by destroying the resources of the savage doom him to weakness and decay, the fate of the Mohegan, the Narragansett, and the Delaware is fast overtaking the Choctaw, the Cherokee, and the Creek. That this fate surely awaits them if they remain within the limits of the States does not admit of a doubt. Humanity and national honor demand that every effort should be made to avert so great a calamity. It is too late to inquire whether it was just in the United States to include them and their territory within the bounds of new States, whose limits they could control. That step can not be retraced. A State can not be dismembered by Congress or restricted in the exercise of her constitutional power. But the people of those States and of every State, actuated by feelings of justice and a regard for our national honor, submit to you the interesting question whether something can not be done, consistently with the rights of the States, to preserve this much-injured race.
>
> As a means of effecting this end I suggest for your consideration the propriety

Indians and white settlements near the northern border of the Spanish territory of Florida. Whites insisted on their right to settle and hunt on Seminole land, and the Seminoles were quick to defend themselves by attacking white settlements. Invading Florida in the spring of 1818, Jackson engaged in search-and-destroy missions. Jackson's forces captured the towns of St. Mark's and Pensacola and executed two British citizens for inciting Indian attacks. Jackson's controversial actions ran counter to War Department orders—which restricted American advances onto Spanish territory—but helped end Spanish control of the region. By destabilizing the region, he helped convince the Spanish that it was no longer in their interest to protect the distant territory; by 1819 Spain sold Florida to the United States for five million dollars. For a short time, Jackson served as governor of the Florida Territory.

of setting apart an ample district west of the Mississippi, and without the limits of any State or Territory now formed, to be guaranteed to the Indian tribes as long as they shall occupy it, each tribe having a distinct control over the portion designated for its use. There they may be secured in the enjoyment of governments of their own choice, subject to no other control from the United States than such as may be necessary to preserve peace on the frontier and between the several tribes. There the benevolent may endeavor to teach them the arts of civilization, and, by promoting union and harmony among them, to raise up an interesting commonwealth, destined to perpetuate the race and to attest the humanity and justice of this Government.

This emigration should be voluntary, for it would be as cruel as unjust to compel the aborigines to abandon the graves of their fathers and seek a home in a distant land. But they should be distinctly informed that if they remain within the limits of the States they must be subject to their laws. In return for their obedience as individuals they will without doubt be protected in the enjoyment of those possessions which they have improved by their industry. But it seems to me visionary to suppose that in this state of things claims can be allowed on tracts of country on which they have neither dwelt nor made improvements, merely because they have seen them from the mountain or passed them in the chase. Submitting to the laws of the States, and receiving, like other citizens, protection in their persons and property, they will ere long become merged in the mass of our population.

Source: Richardson, James D., comp. "First Annual Message to Congress." Messages and Papers of the Presidents. 2:456–59. From American Journey Online: The Native American Experience. Woodbridge, CT: Primary Source Media, 1999.

In 1824, Jackson decided to run for president. Former president Thomas Jefferson (1743–1826) made no secret of his fear of an Andrew Jackson in the White House: "He is one of the most unfit men I know for such a place." But the nation was changing, as more citizens desired someone in office who would represent their needs. In the election of 1824, Jackson received more popular votes than either of his opponents. However, he lost the presidency when he failed to win a majority of votes in the electoral college, and the House of Representatives chose John Quincy Adams (1767–1848) as president. Calling Adams's election part of a "corrupt bargain," Jackson and his backers charged that house members led by Henry Clay (1777–1852) had cut a deal to make Adams president. (Clay was made secretary of state in return for getting his supporters in the House to vote for Adams.) Jackson vowed that he would win the next time.

The people's president

For the next four years, Jackson dedicated himself to winning the presidency. Promising to "purify the Departments" and "reform the government," he appealed to the common man in a way that no presidential candidate had before. In the election, he won a clear majority in both popular (647,276 to 508,064) and electoral (178 to 83) votes. It was a great triumph, but sadly it was colored by tragedy, for Jackson lost his beloved wife, Rachel, who died of a heart attack on December 22, just weeks before his inauguration. Jackson blamed her death on his political enemies, who had made an issue of their first illegal marriage and defamed her character.

Jackson took office amid the biggest and wildest party ever to hit the nation's young capital. He had invited "the people" to his inaugural ball, and the people had come, crashing into the White House, breaking the fine china, spilling liquor on the fine carpets, and plundering the house for souvenirs. This party, and the presidency itself, reflected Jackson's personality. Unwilling to appoint distinguished politicians to public office, Jackson instead began the tradition of placing allies and friends in key federal offices. Known as the "spoils system," this tradition has been followed by nearly every president since. Jackson felt that it was time for the government to reflect the will of the people, and he believed that every citizen was capable of government service. The general public knew only one major political figure in Jackson's cabinet—Secretary of State Martin Van Buren.

Jackson proudly used his executive veto power when he thought it would best express the will of the people. Several of his vetoes were designed to limit the power of the federal government: In 1830 he vetoed the Maysville Road bill because he thought that states should build their own roads, and in 1832 he vetoed the recharter of the Bank of the United States. Jackson did not like the Bank of the United States, which he felt only served the needs of the very rich. His veto of the bill, which had easily passed both houses, demonstrated his popular appeal:

The rich and powerful too often bend the acts of government to their selfish purposes. [W]hen laws undertake to add . . . artificial distinctions, to grant titles, gratuities, and exclusive privileges, to make the rich richer and the potent more powerful, the humble members of society—the farmers, mechanics, and laborers—who have neither the time nor the means of securing like favors to themselves, have a right to complain of the injustice of their government.

Indian Removal

Among Jackson's more controversial policies as president was his call for the removal of Indians beyond the limits of white settlement. In his first address to Congress as president, Jackson asked: "What good man would prefer a country covered with forests and ranged by a few thousand savages to our extensive Republic, studded with cities, towns, and prosperous farms, embellished with all the improvements which art can devise or industry execute, occupied by more than 12,000,000 happy people, and filled with all the blessings of liberty, civilization, and religion?" Jackson believed that the massive transfer of Native Americans beyond the Mississippi River was ultimately the most humane policy the United States could undertake. He signed the Indian Removal Act of 1830, which called for the removal—voluntary or forced—of all Indians to lands west of the Mississippi. The Indian Territory that was defined by Congress covered parts of the present-day states of Oklahoma, Nebraska, and Kansas.

In addition to the Indian Removal Act, Jackson signed over ninety resettlement treaties with various tribes. Jackson promised the Indians, as quoted in Osinski's *Andrew Jackson,* that "their white brethren will not trouble them ... and they can live upon [their land], they and all their children as long as grass grows or water runs in peace and plenty." Jackson told Congress, however, that "whenever the safety, interest or defense of the country" was at stake, Congress could "occupy and possess any part of Indian territory." As a result of Jackson's policies, thousands of Indians were forced to migrate along a trail that led from their ancestral lands to the western lands set aside for them. Many Indians faced disease and death on these terrible journeys.

Jackson did not run for president after his second term. In one of his last official acts before leaving office in

1837, Jackson recognized the independence of the Republic of Texas, thus setting the stage for the Mexican-American War (1846–48; a war fought over the position of the southern border of Texas) and the eventual admission of Texas into the Union. Jackson faced his share of difficulties as president: he faced down South Carolina's threat to secede from the Union and weathered the financial tumult that he caused by closing the Bank of the United States. Still, he left office loved by many Americans and is remembered to this day as one of the nation's strongest presidents. Jackson retired to the Hermitage, his plantation in Tennessee, where he rode his horses and kept up an active correspondence on public affairs. He died quietly at his home on June 8, 1845.

For More Information

Brown, Dee. *Andrew Jackson and the Battle of New Orleans*. New York: Putnam, 1972.

Coit, Margaret L. *Andrew Jackson*. Boston: Houghton Mifflin, 1965.

Collier, Christopher, and James Lincoln Collier. *Andrew Jackson's America, 1824–1850*. New York: Benchmark Books, 1999.

Gutman, William. *Andrew Jackson and the New Populism*. New York: Barron's Education Series, 1987.

Hilton, Suzanne. *The World of Young Andrew Jackson*. New York: Walker & Company, 1988.

Judson, Andrew. *Andrew Jackson*. Springfield, NJ: Enslow Publishers, 1997.

Meltzer, Milton. *Andrew Jackson and His America*. New York: F. Watts, 1993.

Osinski, Alice. *Andrew Jackson*. Encyclopedia of Presidents Series. Chicago: Children's Press, 1987.

Remini, Robert V. *Andrew Jackson*. New York: Harper Perennial, 1999.

Viola, Herman J. *Andrew Jackson*. New York: Chelsea House, 1986.

Jesse James

Born September 5, 1847
Clay County, Missouri
Died April 3, 1882
St. Joseph, Missouri

Robber, murderer

To some, Jesse James was a hero, a brave defender of the South who stole from the rich and gave to the poor. To others, he was a worthless criminal, a cold-blooded murderer interested only in himself. The facts seem to show that Jesse James was a criminal, but as with many western figures the facts don't tell the whole story. For Jesse James was more than a person, he was a legend, a modern day Robin Hood, and his exploits were popularized in fiction and song, and later in movies.

A preacher's son

Had he followed in his parents' footsteps, Jesse James would have been a religious man and an upright citizen. His mother, Zerelda Cole, left a Catholic convent when she was just sixteen to marry a well-educated Baptist minister named Robert James. The couple left Kentucky in the early 1840s to start a small farm in Clay County, Missouri, about twenty miles northwest of Kansas City. Robert became a pastor at New Hope Baptist Church and helped found William Jewell College in nearby Liberty, Missouri. Their first son, Alexander

"When these guys wanted money, they went in daylight to [take] their money. No one would dare shoot when they robbed a bank…. The James boys were liked by the poor and God knows there was plenty of us and the law made no serious effort to get them."

L. A. Sherman, as quoted in Jesse James by Theodore Miller

Jesse James.
(The Granger Collection, New York. Reproduced by permission.)

Franklin James (known as Frank), was born in 1843; their second son, Jesse Woodson James, was born on September 5, 1847. Despite the difference in their ages, the boys would stick together for much of their lives.

Robert James was caught up in the gold rush fever that swept the nation in 1849 and 1850, and he left his family in 1850 to try his luck in the California goldfields. He would never return, for he died of pneumonia before striking it rich. Zerelda remarried, divorced, and remarried again to a doctor named Reuben Samuel. She continued her boys' religious upbringing, but they were soon drawn away from religion and toward the tumult and violence of the conflict that became the American Civil War (1861–65; a war fought between the Northern and Southern United States over the issue of slavery).

Schooled in violence

Western Missouri and Kansas were battlefields for the powerfully charged pro- and antislavery sentiments that fueled sectional conflict in the years leading up to the Civil War. The 1854 Kansas-Nebraska Act had ruled that residents of Kansas and Nebraska could decide for themselves whether they would be slave or free states. Hoping to sway public opinion, slave owners from Missouri (known as "Bushwhackers") clashed with antislavery factions from Kansas (known as "Red Legs" or "Jayhawkers") in battles that earned Kansas the nickname "Bloody Kansas." When Kansas joined the Union as a free state in 1861—the same year the Civil War started—the battles grew ever more heated.

It was only natural for the James brothers to back the Confederacy (the Southern states that broke away from the Union in 1860 and 1861), for their family owned slaves themselves. During the Civil War both Frank and Jesse took part in bloody raids on Union sympathizers. Frank joined with guerrilla leader William Clarke Quantrill in a violent raid on Lawrence, Kansas, on August 20, 1863, and Jesse sided with a band of raiders led by one of Quantrill's lieutenants, "Bloody Bill" Anderson.

By his eighteenth birthday, Jesse had become an expert marksman and horseback rider and an experienced fighter. A series of raids conducted in 1864 and 1865 gave Jesse James a thorough education in violence and murder.

From soldier to criminal

When Confederate general Robert E. Lee surrendered to Union forces on April 9, 1865, to end the Civil War, Jesse James was one of thousands of Confederate soldiers who headed home to an uncertain future. On his way home, James was shot in the chest by Union soldiers. It took him months to recover; during his convalescence he fell in love with his cousin, Zerelda, whom he later married, and nursed his hatred of all things related to the North. With his brother Frank, his cousin Cole Younger, and others, Jesse began to plot how to use their skills as guerrilla soldiers to wage their own war on enemies of the South—and line their pockets in the process.

Jesse James as a young outlaw.

On the morning of February 13, 1866, the James brothers began their long and illustrious career as bank robbers. A gang of ten men entered the town of Liberty, Missouri. Four men went inside the Clay County Savings and Loan Bank, while six others waited outside. After shooting and killing one man, the gang made off with over sixty thousand dollars in bonds and currency. Though Jesse was probably not along on this first heist, it is believed that he helped plan it.

For the next ten years, the James boys and their cousins, the Younger brothers—Cole, James, John, and Robert—were the central figures in a criminal gang that made off with hundreds of thousands of dollars in stolen goods. They soon developed a successful formula for their bank robberies, planning carefully and attacking suddenly and violently. After each robbery the gang disappeared, returning to their quiet home lives as farmers and living off the money

Jesse James, the Song

Jesse James became a popular hero thanks to the efforts of those who wrote fanciful stories, repeated tall tales, and sang songs such as the one below. This song has been attributed to Billy Gashade, though its authorship is uncertain.

Jesse James

1) Went down to the station, not many days ago,
   Did something I'll never do again,
   I got down on my knees and delivered up the keys
   To Frank and his brother, Jesse James.

   CHORUS 1:
   Poor Jesse, good-bye, Jesse,
   Farewell, Jesse James,
   Robert Ford caught his eye and he shot him on the sly,
   And he laid poor Jesse down to die.

2) O Jesse was a man and friend to the poor,
   He would never see a man suffer pain,
   But with his brother Frank, he robbed the Chicago Bank,
   And he stopped the Glendale train.

   (CHORUS 1)

3) O the people in the west, when they heard of Jesse's death,
   They wondered how he came to die.

they stole. In their career, the gang robbed banks in seven states: Arkansas, Iowa, Kentucky, Minnesota, Missouri, Texas, and West Virginia.

The James gang robbed their first train in 1873. Loosening a rail at a curve in the tracks, the robbers forced the train to stop and robbed it at gunpoint, making off with just two thousand dollars. Later train robberies were more lucrative. In 1875, for example, the James brothers and seven others robbed the Missouri-Pacific Express train of seventy-five thousand dollars.

It was Ford's pistol ball brought him tumbling from the wall,
And it laid poor Jesse down to die.

> CHORUS 2:
> O Jesse leaves a wife, she's a mourner all her life,
> And the children, they were brave,
> But the dirty little coward, he shot Mister Howard,
> And he laid poor Jesse in his grave.

4) Now Jesse goes to rest with his hands upon his breast,
And the devil will be upon his knees,
He was born one day in the county of Clay,
And he came from a solitary race.

> (CHORUS 1 and 2)

5) This song it was made by Billy Gashade,
As soon as the news did arrive,
He said there was no man with the law in his hand
Who could take Jesse James when alive

> (CHORUS 1 and 2)

From American Journey Online: The Westward Expansion. *Woodbridge, CT: Primary Source Media, 1999.*

The legend begins

Newspapers reporting on the exploits of the gang often marveled at the bravery and audacity of these thieves who had the nerve to rob banks and trains in broad daylight, but it took a journalist named John Newman Edwards to make a hero of Jesse James and his cohorts. "In the *Kansas City Times*," writes Roger A. Bruns, author of *Jesse James: Legendary Outlaw*, Edwards "compared the perpetrators of the [September 1872 robbery of the Kansas City Fair] with ancient legendary figures like King Arthur and his Knights of the Round Table." Edwards admitted that the James gang committed crimes, but he called them daring, noble crimes, committed against the evil Northerners "who had treated the people of the Confederacy so viciously," writes Bruns. In the many articles that Edwards wrote about James, he consistently praised the outlaw's valor, his kindness to the weak and poor, and his defense of the South.

Once the gang moved on to train robberies, the national press began to report on their actions, and readers across the nation became familiar with the names of these prominent outlaws. Many of these stories took their cue from Edwards's reporting and portrayed the gang members as noble heroes acting on principle. Before long the stories about James and his gang bore little resemblance to the facts. Contrary to the evidence, James was presented as a modern-day Robin Hood who robbed from the rich and gave to the poor. It was written that he never robbed Southerners—but in truth he did. The stories may not have been true, but they sold the magazines and dime novels that were snatched up eagerly by readers. Jesse James and his men had become legends in their own time.

Bank robbing is a dangerous business

The James gang had years of bank-robbing experience under their belt when they decided to rob the bank in the peaceful farming community of Northfield, Minnesota, on September 7, 1876. But this robbery was doomed from the start. The bank employees told the bandits that they couldn't open the safe (though it was actually already open), and a vigilant citizen, realizing what was taking place, alerted people milling about in town. Soon a number of Northfield's citizens had taken up guns, and gang members Bill Chadwell and Clell Miller were shot dead in the street. The gang panicked, a gunfight ensued, and the gang barely escaped. Every one of the Younger brothers was injured, and the gang was on the run. (Two of Northfield's citizens had been killed as well.) A posse (a group of citizens summoned to aid in law enforcement) set out after the gang and eventually captured Jim and Cole Younger and sent them to prison. Clearly, the James gang was not invulnerable.

Jesse James lay low following the Northfield disaster. He and his family stayed at their home near Nashville, Ten-

Cover of a 1938 dime novel about Jesse James. Jesse James became a legend in his own time through glamorized versions of his exploits published in newspapers. That legend continued to interest readers long after the outlaw's death.
(*The Corbis Corporation. Reproduced by permission.*)

nessee, and Jesse took the name John Howard. In Tennessee Jesse and his wife had several children. But in 1879 James's money began to run out, and he moved his family back to Missouri. It was not long before he, Frank, and a new gang of robbers and horse thieves staged their next heist. Attacking a train near Glendale, Missouri, on October 8, 1879, the robbers nabbed thousands of dollars (some sources say six thousand dollars, while others say thirty-five thousand dollars). Though they stuck together through two years of robbery and murder, this second James gang soon found themselves hounded by police and private detectives. It didn't help that the newspapers that had once celebrated their exploits now portrayed the

James brothers as the ruthless killers that they probably always had been. Lacking the strong family bonds of the earlier gang, this second James gang fought among themselves over the loot they had stolen. And they betrayed one another.

Shot in the back

Two of the gang members, brothers Charles and Robert Ford, never liked Jesse James and often argued with him. So when Missouri governor Thomas T. Crittenden offered a ten-thousand-dollar reward for the capture and conviction of Jesse James, the Fords began plotting. On April 3, 1882, the Fords met Jesse at his home in St. Joseph, Missouri. The men sat around the breakfast table planning their next robbery when Jesse stood up to straighten a picture on the wall. Bob Ford pulled a gun and shot him in the back of the head, killing him instantly.

The Ford brothers were quickly convicted of murder and sentenced to die, but Governor Crittenden just as quickly issued a pardon that spared their lives. Some claimed that the governor had plotted with Robert Ford to murder James, but the charges were never proven. Perhaps fearing that he too would be murdered, Frank James soon turned himself in to authorities, claiming that he was tired of being hunted by the law. James was tried but never convicted of bank robbery and murder, and he died in 1915 at the age of seventy-two.

The legend of Jesse James continued to grow after his death. Just after his death someone composed a song telling of his exploits (see box on p. 148), and a St. Joseph, Missouri, opera house staged a drama about his life. For a small fee James's mother told stories about her sons or produced a few stones from Jesse's grave site. Banks erected plaques noting that they had been robbed by the great Jesse James. But it was in the dime novel (a short, inexpensive book) that James gained his greatest fame. "In the dime novels," writes Bruns, "James became a national hero. Americans got to know him as a misunderstood trailblazer who was done in by treachery. He was portrayed as an heroic bad man of the plains, who stole horses, robbed stages, trains, and banks, mostly for honor and pride, not for money." In just two years (between 1901 and 1903), the Street and Smith publishing house sold six million copies of more than one hundred different Jesse James novels. Later, movies repeated the myths first spread in the dime novels.

The legend of Jesse James is largely a myth, for there is little real evidence of noble behavior on his part, only stories and rumors and tall tales that grow ever taller with each telling. This lack of agreement between myth and reality is part of what makes Jesse James the characteristic western hero that he is. From the time that white men first confronted the American West, they have pursued dreams—of a Northwest Passage, of gold, of rich agricultural land—across the vast and often forbidding landscape. And they have needed heroes who seem large enough, brave enough, and violent enough to tame it. For better or worse, Jesse James is one such hero.

For More Information

Books

Baldwin, Margaret, and Pat O'Brien. *Wanted, Frank and Jesse James: The Real Story.* New York: J. Messner, 1981.

Bold, Christine. *Selling the Wild West: Popular Western Fiction, 1860–1960.* Bloomington: Indiana University Press, 1987.

Bruns, Roger A. *The Bandit Kings: From Jesse James to Pretty Boy Floyd.* New York: Crown, 1995.

Bruns, Roger A. *Jesse James: Legendary Outlaw.* Springfield, NJ: Enslow Publishers, 1998.

Miller, Theodore. *Jesse James.* Englewood Cliffs, NJ: Prentice-Hall, 1976.

Rosa, Joseph G. *The Gunfighter: Man or Myth?* Norman: University of Oklahoma Press, 1969.

Settle, William A. *Jesse James Was His Name.* Lincoln: University of Nebraska Press, 1966.

Slotkin, Richard. *Gunfighter Nation: The Myth of the Frontier in Twentieth-Century America.* New York: HarperPerennial, 1992.

Steele, Philip W. *The Many Faces of Jesse James.* Gretna, LA: Pelican Publishing Company, 1995.

Stiles, T. J. *Jesse James.* New York: Chelsea House, 1994.

Web Sites

"The James-Younger Gang: Come Ride with Us." [Online] http://www3.islandnet.com/~the-gang/index.html (accessed April 15, 2000).

Meriwether Lewis

Born August 18, 1774
Albemarle County, Virginia
Died October 11, 1809
Tennessee

William Clark

Born August 1, 1770
Caroline County, Virginia
Died September 1, 1838
St. Louis, Missouri

Explorers

Between 1804 and 1806, Meriwether Lewis and William Clark led the most famous expedition in American history. They were the first Americans to record the riches of the continent's interior. Publication of the expedition's discoveries provided vital information to those who followed in their footsteps, and it stirred the imaginations of people living in the East. Lewis and Clark's discoveries whet the nation's appetite for information about the West.

Lewis and Clark's discoveries whet the nation's appetite for information about the West.

Friends on the frontier

Meriwether Lewis was born in Albemarle County, Virginia, on August 18, 1774. Lewis's father was killed in the Revolutionary War (1776–83), when Lewis was five years old. Lewis finished his formal schooling at the age of eighteen and became a Virginia gentleman farmer. In 1794 he joined militia volunteers to help put down the Whiskey Rebellion in Pennsylvania. Farmers there turned their grain into distilled spirits, such as whiskey, which was easier to transport to markets in the East than the grain itself was. The Pennsylvania farmers

led the rebellion to oppose a tax on whiskey that they felt was unfair. Lewis answered President George Washington's call for militia volunteers to help end the rebellion. Lewis found that he quite enjoyed a soldier's life and joined the U.S. Army.

While on frontier duty, Lewis became acquainted with William Clark, who was commanding a special company of sharpshooters to which Lewis was transferred. Clark was born on August 1, 1770, in Caroline County, Virginia, but he had developed a keen sense of the western frontier at an early age. At age fourteen, he had moved with his family to Kentucky where they were among the earliest settlers. Clark and Lewis quickly became friends.

Meriwether Lewis.
(Reproduced from the Collections of the Library of Congress.)

Aiding a president

After service on the Mississippi River, Lewis was asked by Thomas Jefferson—an old friend of Lewis's family and then president of the United States—to become Jefferson's White House secretary (this position is comparable to the White House chief of staff today). Lewis held the position from 1801 to 1803. As secretary, Lewis learned of Jefferson's dream of sending an expedition to find a waterway connecting the Atlantic Ocean and the Pacific Ocean. A route had already been established from the Atlantic Ocean west to St. Louis in present-day Missouri. Jefferson hoped for a route that would allow ships to continue west from St. Louis, across the continent to the Pacific Ocean. When Jefferson offered Lewis leadership of the expedition, Lewis accepted, choosing thirty-two-year-old Clark as his coleader. Although the War Department commissioned Clark as a second lieutenant of artillery, Lewis designated Clark's rank as captain. The complementary skills of the two men allowed them to share the leadership of the voyage well.

Jefferson's instructions for the expedition were to find "the most direct and practicable water communication across the continent for the purposes of commerce." A waterway to the Pacific was only part of Jefferson's interest in the expedition. He also wanted to know everything about the land and people that made up the western portion of the continent. To prepare for the desired scientific investigations, Lewis went to Philadelphia, Pennsylvania, for several weeks to study botany and astronomy. Clark prepared for the trip by recruiting and training men in military drills and building boats. In 1803, Lewis spent the winter with Clark near St. Louis in present-day Missouri, where he gathered information from fur traders who were familiar with the upper reaches of the Missouri River.

William Clark.
(Archive Photos, Inc. Reproduced by permission.)

Setting out for the unknown

The expedition set out on May 14, 1804. A total of forty-five men traveled in three boats. Of these, twenty-nine men were to travel all the way to the Pacific, while the others were to turn back at approximately the halfway point. The first part of the journey up the Missouri River was through well-traveled country. In late July, a little beyond the mouth of the Platte River, the expedition met members of the Oto and Missouri tribes and informed them that their territory had been taken over by the United States. The party was threatened only once on its way west—on September 25 near present-day Pierre, South Dakota, by a group of Teton Sioux. The expedition countered with a show of force and then spoke to the Native Americans in a friendly manner, and a confrontation was avoided. In October the expedition stopped near present-day Bismarck, North Dakota, to spend the winter with the Mandan Indians. The territory of the Mandans was the farthest point about which the Americans

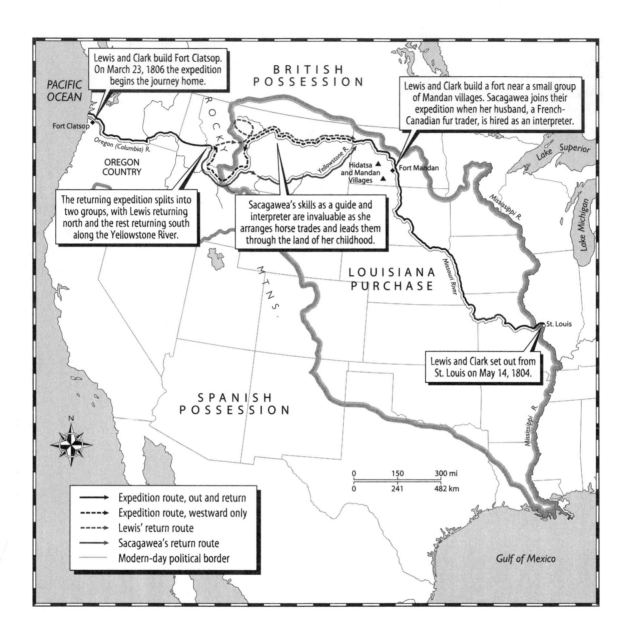

The Lewis and Clark
Expedition left St. Louis,
Missouri, in May 1804 and
arrived on the coast of
Oregon Territory in the
winter of 1805. *(Map by XNR
Productions, Inc. Reproduced by
permission of The Gale Group.)*

had any definite knowledge. The Americans built a small fort
near the Mandan village and spent five months there, sixteen
hundred miles from St. Louis.

In the spring of 1805, thirteen men from the expedition headed back to St. Louis. The rest of the men set out on
April 7, 1805, this time into unknown country. Clark wrote in

his journal: "I could not but esteem this moment of my departure as among the most happy of my life." They reached the junction of the Missouri and the Yellowstone Rivers (in what is now Montana) on April 25.

Along this stretch of the trip, Clark usually took charge of managing the canoes, while Lewis, accompanied by his big Newfoundland dog, Seaman, kept to the shore, exploring, hunting, and gathering specimens. On June 3, 1805, they reached a place where "the river split in two." Lewis followed the northern fork for a while, which he decided was not the main course. He named it the Marias River, in honor of his cousin, Maria Wood. He then turned around and caught up with Clark.

By August the party was still in present-day Montana on the eastern side of the Rocky Mountains. The Missouri River had dwindled to a series of shallow tributaries, which Lewis's canoes could not negotiate. Luckily, Lewis had hired Toussaint Charbonneau as an interpreter-guide. Though Charbonneau was nearly worthless, his wife, Sacajawea, was the sister of the chief of the Shoshone Indians that lived in this area, and she helped the expedition obtain the horses it needed to cross the Rocky Mountains. Once across, the explorers drifted in new canoes down the Clearwater and Snake Rivers and continued down the Columbia River toward the Pacific Ocean. Along the way they bartered for food with the Native Americans, but by that time they had very little left to trade, so they often offered entertainment in exchange for food. One of the men played his violin while a servant named York danced, and Lewis showed off his watch, telescope, and compass. After carrying their boats and equipment overland around Cascade Falls on November 2, they found that the river was subject to tidal flows and knew that they must be close to the Pacific. They got their first view of the ocean on November 7, 1805. Winter quarters were built south of the mouth of the Columbia, not far from present-day Astoria, Oregon; they named Fort Clatsop in honor of a nearby Clatsop tribe. It was a difficult winter, as it rained nearly every day and food was rather scarce. The group was anxious to begin the trip home.

Homeward bound

On March 23, 1806, they began the homeward trek. Rowing upstream on the Columbia, they had difficulty getting food. When they reached the Clearwater River they recovered horses they had left behind. When the group reached Travelers' Rest Creek, near present-day Lolo, Montana, Lewis and Clark split their party in two so they could explore even more of the West on their way home. Lewis's party of nine planned to explore the Marias River. Clark divided his group of twenty-two, sending one group down the Missouri River and the other, including himself, overland to the Yellowstone River, where they would then paddle downriver and back to the Missouri.

Lewis's party had a skirmish with some Blackfeet Indians, who did not respond well to the Americans. The Blackfeet were not interested in ruining their business connections with the Canadians to trade with the Americans. Lewis's acknowledgment of his friendship with the Nez Percé and Shoshone tribes, which were enemies of the Blackfeet, only added to their problems. At night, Blackfeet warriors attacked the explorers, and in the struggle the Lewis party killed two Blackfeet. This was the only time members of the expedition killed Native Americans. Lewis and his party quickly made their way out of Blackfoot territory and back toward the Missouri River, where they met up again with Clark's party.

The party reached the Mandan villages on August 14, 1806, and persuaded Chief Big White to come with them back to Washington, D.C. They returned to St. Louis on September 23, 1806. "We were met by all the village," wrote Clark, "and received a hearty welcome from its inhabitants." From St. Louis, Lewis and Clark traveled on to Washington to report personally to the president.

Life after the expedition

The expedition had been a great success. Both Lewis and Clark were awarded large land grants in the West. In 1806, Lewis was appointed governor of the Louisiana Territory. He resigned his army commission, but before going to St. Louis to take office, he tried to finish editing his journals of the exploration for publication. Even though he delayed his trip for almost one year, Lewis was unable to complete the journals. On a trip to Washington, D.C., in 1809 to carry out some official business, Lewis stopped in an isolated cabin in

Sacajawea's Son

Sacajawea was the teenage wife of one of Lewis and Clark's interpreters, Toussaint Charbonneau. She proved more valuable as an interpreter and guide than her husband did. On February 11, 1805, while traveling with the expedition, Sacajawea gave birth to a son, who was named Jean Baptiste but affectionately called "Pomp." The baby boy traveled with the expedition, and William Clark grew fond of the boy. As the expedition was returning home, Clark saw an unusual rock formation along the Yellowstone River. On July 25, 1806, Clark climbed it and named it "Pompy's Tower." The rock is now called Pompeys Pillar.

When the expedition returned to the Mandan villages, Clark offered to take the little boy east and raise him. But Pomp was not yet weaned. Later Clark wrote the following letter to Charbonneau, reiterating his desire to raise Charbonneau's son:

> As to your little Son (my boy Pomp) you well know my fondness for him and my anxiety to take and raise him as my own child. I once more tell you if you will bring your son Baptiest [sic] to me I will educate him and treat him as my own child—I do not forget the promis [sic] which I made to you and Shall now repeat [sic] them that you may be certain—

> Charbono, if you wish to live with the white people, and will come to me, I will give you a piece of land and furnish you with horses, cows, & hogs...Wishing you and your family great suckcess [sic] & with anxious expectations of seeing my little dancing boy Baptiest I shall remain your friend.

In 1809, Charbonneau and Sacajawea visited St. Louis with Jean Baptiste. Charbonneau attempted to work 320 acres he was granted for service on the expedition, but soon found himself ill suited for the job. On March 26, 1811, he transferred his land title to Clark for one hundred dollars and prepared to return home. In April, he and Sacajawea left their son in Clark's charge.

Clark adopted the boy and educated him at the best schools on the East Coast. When he was eighteen, Pomp met a German prince who was traveling in the United States, went back to Europe with him, and spent six years touring the continent. He returned to the United States and became an important fur dealer and guide. He moved to California (which was at the time still Mexican territory) and became the alcalde (judge) of San Luis Rey in 1847. While trying to strike it rich mining for gold, he died in 1866 of pneumonia.

Tennessee to spend the night. The next day he was found dead with a gunshot wound in his head. It was never clear what happened, but there is evidence that Lewis, who was subject to depressive moods, shot himself. When Jefferson heard of Lewis's death, he accepted the theory of suicide that

The Lewis and Clark expedition greeting a group of Native Americans.
(The Corbis Corporation. Reproduced by permission.)

was suggested by those who found his body. But a strong minority, then and later, felt that Lewis had been murdered, for murders were common on this particular trail at the time.

After the expedition, Clark entered the fur-trading business and became a partner in William Henry Ashley's Missouri Fur Company. On March 12, 1807, Jefferson appointed him brigadier general of militia and Indian agent for Upper Louisiana Territory. In 1813 he was appointed governor of Missouri Territory and continued in the position until Missouri earned statehood in 1821. Having a longtime interest in Indian culture, he accepted a position as superintendent of Indian Affairs in 1822 and served in this capacity for the remainder of his life. He died of natural causes in St. Louis, September 1, 1838.

For More Information

Ambrose, Stephen E. *Undaunted Courage: Meriwether Lewis, Thomas Jefferson, and the Opening of the American West.* New York: Simon and Schuster, 1996.

Blumberg, Rhoda. *The Incredible Journey of Lewis and Clark.* New York: Lothrop, Lee & Shepard Books, 1987.

Brown, Marion Marsh. *Sacajawea: Indian Interpreter to Lewis and Clark.* Chicago: Childrens Press, 1988.

Cavan, Seamus. *Lewis and Clark and the Route to the Pacific.* New York: Chelsea House, 1991.

De Voto, Bernard, ed. *The Journals of Lewis and Clark.* Houghton Mifflin, Boston: 1953.

Edward, Judith. *Lewis and Clark's Journey of Discovery in American History.* Springfield, NJ: Enslow, 1999.

Fitz-Gerald, Christine Maloney. *Meriwether Lewis and William Clark.* Chicago: Childrens Press, 1991.

Hall, Eleanor J. *The Lewis and Clark Expedition.* San Diego, CA: Lucent Books, 1996.

Jackson, Donald, ed. *Letters of the Lewis and Clark Expedition with Related Documents.* Urbana: University of Illinois Press, 1962.

Kozar, Richard. *Lewis and Clark.* Philadelphia: Chelsea House, 1999.

Lewis, Meriwether, and William Clark. *History of the Expedition Under the Command of Captains Lewis and Clark.* 3 vols. Edited by Elliott Coues. New York: Allerton Book Co., 1922.

Peters, Arthur King. *Seven Trails West.* New York: Abbeville Press, 1996.

Petersen, David, and Mark Coburn. *Meriwether Lewis and William Clark: Soldiers, Explorers, and Partners in History.* Chicago: Childrens Press, 1988.

Raphael, Elaine, and Don Bolognese. *Sacagawea: The Journey West.* New York: Scholastic, 1994.

St. George, Judith. *Sacagawea.* New York: Putnam, 1997.

Annie Oakley

Born August 13, 1860
Darke County, Ohio
Died November 3, 1926
Greenville, Ohio

Sharpshooter, entertainer

A nnie Oakley was one of the best sharpshooters of her time. In fact, her ability with guns seemed magical to many fans. A small woman—five feet tall, one hundred pounds—she could handle several heavy rifles at one time to shoot down flying glass balls. From thirty feet, her bullet could split a playing card—held with the thin side facing her—in two. She could shoot a moving target behind her back while looking at the reflection in a knife blade. Speeding around an arena on horseback or on a bicycle, Oakley could hit targets. She performed her feats in stage shows around the world, but her real fame came from her performances in Buffalo Bill's Wild West Show. As a part of the notorious Wild West Show, she became renowned as a western hero even though she had never lived in the West.

Difficult early years

Born Phoebe Anne Moses (her last name has also been recorded as Mosey, Mauzy, or Mozee) in rural Ohio in 1860, Oakley lived in poverty and suffered much hardship early in

"The largest share of applause was bestowed on Annie Oakley, a young girl whose proficiency with shotgun and rifle seems almost miraculous."

London (Ontario) Free Press. *September 2, 1885.*

Annie Oakley.
(AP/Wide World Photos, Inc. Reproduced by permission.)

life. When young Oakley was five, her father became an invalid after being caught in a winter blizzard; he died a year later at the age of thirty-three. Oakley's mother struggled to take care of her eight children. Oakley helped feed the family by catching quail and grouse in cornstalk traps. "Somehow we managed to struggle along for several years," Oakley is quoted as saying in Glenda Riley's *The Life and Legend of Annie Oakley*. To get even more food for her family, Oakley took her father's rifle from the mantel and went hunting. She shot a squirrel in the head on her first shot. The kickback of the gun—which she said she had filled with an amount of gunpowder large enough "to kill a buffalo"—gave her a black eye and a broken nose. Yet Oakley didn't mind her injuries because her family could eat squirrel stew that night.

Despite Annie's help, her mother was unable to take care of all the children. At age eight Oakley was sent to live in nearby Greenville with Samuel C. and Nancy Ann Edington, who ran the Darke County Infirmary (poorhouse). While with the Edingtons, Oakley learned some valuable domestic skills; she worked and was able to send some money home to her mother. Soon, however, she was hired from the infirmary by a farming family who treated her cruelly, beat her, and failed to pay her. After two years of this torture, Oakley ran away to her mother. Still too poor to care for her daughter, Oakley's mother again sent the girl to the Edingtons' poorhouse. Several years later, Oakley's mother remarried, and Oakley went to live on her mother and stepfather's meager farm. Hoping to help her poor family pay their mortgage, Oakley became a professional hunter. She was very successful at hunting, and the birds she killed were welcomed by hotel kitchens as far away as Cincinnati. Hotel guests never complained of bird shot in their meals, because Oakley always hit the birds in the head. After age ten, Oakley proudly proclaimed "[I] never had a nickel in my pocket that I didn't earn," according to Jean Flynn in *Annie Oakley: Legendary Sharpshooter*. Oakley's hunting went so well that she earned enough to pay off her family's mortgage.

Wins shooting contest

Although Oakley had succeeded in getting her family out of debt, she still couldn't read. Oakley's mother sent her

Annie Oakley performing in the Wild West Show. Shooting glass balls while she stood on the back of a galloping horse was Oakley's specialty.
(The Corbis Corporation. Reproduced by permission.)

to live with Annie's older sister Lydia in 1876. Lydia lived in Cincinnati, where Annie could attend school. Oakley enjoyed visiting the shooting galleries in Cincinnati. One day, while Oakley was easily hitting several of the targets at one booth, a man noticed her skill and asked her if she'd like to make some money using a gun. The man arranged a shooting match between Oakley and Frank Butler, a traveling marksman. The purse was one hundred dollars, more than some people made in a year at the time. She and Butler shot at clay pigeons as these targets were thrown into the air. Oakley hit twenty-five and Butler twenty-four; she won the match as well as Butler's heart. The two wrote letters to each other regularly after the match, and according to most sources they were married one year later. Some historians contend that Oakley and Butler lived together for a time before marrying.

In Frank Butler, Oakley had found an excellent shooting partner, an enthusiastic promoter of her abilities, a great friend, and someone to teach her to read. In the beginning of their marriage, Oakley traveled with her husband's show but watched him perform from backstage. Oakley got her first chance in the spotlight in 1882 when Frank's regular partner took ill. Oakley delighted crowds with her performance, and Butler made her his regular partner. Oakley took the stage name Annie Oakley, and the couple performed throughout the Midwest.

Joins Buffalo Bill's Wild West Show

Not long after she began performing with Butler, Oakley was approached by Lewis Sells, owner of what he called "The Biggest of all Big Shows," the Sells Brothers Circus. Sells wanted Oakley to shoot targets from the back of a galloping horse in his circus. Butler became Oakley's manager rather than her performing partner, and Oakley was billed as a world champion markswoman. Believing that her skills could be better appreciated in a western-themed show, Butler and Oakley approached William "Buffalo Bill" Cody (1846–1917; see entry) about a position for her in Buffalo Bill's Wild West Show. After Annie impressed Buffalo Bill Cody's partner at her audition, Cody allowed her to join the show for a three-day trial. Cody was astounded by "Missie," as he called Oakley, and she joined the show full-time in 1884. She performed with the show for the next seventeen years, the longest tenure of any of the show's performers.

For her act, Oakley wore handmade western costumes and a cowboy hat with a silver star pinned to it. During her ten-minute act, she galloped on a horse while shooting at glass balls that Butler tossed into the air. She jumped across a table to grab a second gun to shoot clay targets. She shot two targets at once while holding two guns and shot her gun upside down. To add theatrics to her performance, Oakley did a quick kick when she hit her target; when she missed (usually

An Indian Princess

In 1884 the powerful Sioux chief Sitting Bull was touring St. Paul, Minnesota; his Indian agent (the government official in charge of the Indian reservation where Sitting Bull lived with his people) had hoped that the chief would learn to appreciate white civilization and persuade his people to live more like whites. Sitting Bull sat still and expressionless through his tours of local businesses and a school, but he came to life when he saw Annie Oakley perform in Buffalo Bill's Wild West Show. He nicknamed Oakley "Wan-tan-yeya Ci-sci-la," which translated to "Little Sure Shot." He was so fond of Oakley that he insisted on adopting her as a daughter and presented her with his ceremonial headdress. As Glenda Riley notes in *The Life and Legend of Annie Oakley,* Oakley at first considered the adoption "just a lark." Keen to publicize her as a western woman, Oakley's husband and manager, Frank Butler, used the adoption to enhance Oakley's western image. In 1885, however, Sitting Bull joined the Wild West Show; he and Oakley became great friends. When he left the show later that year, she started a correspondence with him. Oakley would later regard her adoption by Sitting Bull as an honor. He too valued his friendship with Oakley and even willed all of his belongings to her. Oakley was outspoken in her disgust at Sitting Bull's murder in 1890. "Had he been a white man someone would have been hung for his murder," she wrote, according to Riley.

on purpose), she stamped the ground or pouted and shot off Butler's hat. She ended her act with a fancy sideways kick as she ran off the stage.

A "true" western heroine

Though the Buffalo Bill show billed Oakley as "the little girl of the Western plains," she had never lived in the West, having only crossed the Mississippi River to perform with the Sells Brothers Circus. Nevertheless, marksmanship was a skill required in the West, and Oakley's ability to entertain with guns fit in perfectly with Cody's show. At a time before radio, television, or movies, Buffalo Bill's Wild West Show did more to create the myth of the West than any other form of entertainment did. The show's poster promised to provide the viewer with three hours of western "scenes that have cost thousands their lives to view" and offered a romanticized version of life in the West. On a ten-acre show lot, the Wild West Show featured Indian attacks, cowboys on bucking broncos, stagecoaches, cattle drives, and dramatizations of a Pony Express ride and the Battle of Little Bighorn. Though the cast included real western heroes and villains—including outlaw Doc Middleton and army scout Buffalo Bill Cody, who himself bore 193 bullet and arrow scars from his western adventures—the show invented a dynamic, thrilling past for each of the performers. Oakley never denied her childhood in Ohio, but audiences soon came to regard her as a "true" westerner. Newspapers reported that she was "a credit to the 'glorious country' beyond the Rockies" and detailed her hunts in the "high western mountains," according to Riley. Other papers praised her hand-sewn costumes as "that of the real wild West" and remarked that she spoke with a "western" accent, notes Riley.

The Wild West Show was so popular by 1887 that Queen Victoria requested that the show perform at her jubilee, which celebrated her fifty-year anniversary as ruler of Britain. At the performance, Grand Duke Michael of Russia challenged Oakley to a shooting match; she won easily, and Prince Edward presented her with a medal of victory. English newspapers called her "Annie Oakley of the magic gun," according to Walter Havighurst in *Annie Oakley of the Wild West*. Her popularity in Europe soared, and she left the Wild West Show to begin her own European and American tour. In 1889, Oakley rejoined Buffalo Bill's Wild West Show and traveled with the show to England, and then to France, Spain, Italy, Austria, and Germany. Commenting on the show's Western authenticity, Frederic Remington wrote in *Harper's Weekly* in the late 1880s that "One should no longer ride the deserts of Texas or the rugged uplands of Wyoming to see the Indians and the pioneers, but should go to London."

Oakley performed with the Wild West Show until 1901. After seventeen years and 170,000 miles of travel, she had only missed four performances due to a brief sickness. Though a serious train accident in that same year partially paralyzed her, she continued working as a traveling markswoman for the next twenty years. She also starred in a play, *The Western Girl*, in 1902 and entertained American troops abroad during World War I (1914–18). When not traveling, she taught women in Pinehurst, North Carolina, to shoot rifles.

In addition to her commitment to her job, Oakley was greatly concerned about the welfare of others. Throughout her life, she displayed deep compassion for orphaned children. Oakley's success as an entertainer earned her and Butler a small fortune, but the couple was frugal. Instead of splurging on themselves, the Butlers supported eighteen orphan girls and paid for their education. At the end of her life, Oakley melted down all her gold medals, sold the metal, and donated the money to a home for children. Oakley's grandniece reported that "the last days of [Oakley's] life were spent in wrapping packages for friends all over the world ... she forgot no one," according to Riley. Oakley died November 3, 1926. Butler died eighteen days later.

For More Information

Flynn, Jean. *Annie Oakley: Legendary Sharpshooter*. Springfield, NJ: Enslow Publishers, 1998.

Havighurst, Walter. *Annie Oakley of the Wild West*. New York: Macmillan, 1954.

Quackenbush, Robert. *Who's That Girl with the Gun? A Story of Annie Oakley*. New York: Prentice-Hall Books for Young Readers, 1987.

Riley, Glenda. *The Life and Legend of Annie Oakley*. Norman: University of Oklahoma Press, 1994.

Spinner, Stephanie. *Little Sure Shot: The Story of Annie Oakley*. New York: Random House, 1993.

Benjamin "Pap" Singleton

Born c. 1809
Nashville, Tennessee
Died 1892
St. Louis, Missouri

Leader of "Kansas Exodus"
and racial unity activist

Benjamin "Pap" Singleton was an African American man who played an important part in the massive emigration of ex-slaves from the South to the West. Although he was not the single source of inspiration for the black exodus from the South, Singleton did play a significant role in helping blacks escape the oppressive social climate of the South following the Civil War (1861–65; a war fought between the Northern and Southern United States over the issue of slavery) and find greater opportunities in the West.

Little documentation of Singleton's life

As is true with many ex-slaves, there are precious few documents recording Singleton's life. Other than a record of his birth in 1809, little is known about him prior to the great exodus of blacks from Tennessee to Kansas, which occurred when Singleton was in his seventies. It is known that as a slave he was sold to various owners in the Gulf States (Louisiana, Mississippi, and Texas), but he escaped several times. He fled to Canada and Detroit, Michigan, but returned

"I am the whole cause of the Kansas immigration!"

Benjamin "Pap" Singleton
(Reproduced from the collection of the Kansas State Historical Society.)

to Tennessee after the Civil War. There is evidence that Singleton spent most of his life working as a cabinetmaker in Edgefield, Tennessee, near Nashville.

When President Abraham Lincoln (1809–1865) issued the Emancipation Proclamation on January 1, 1863, blacks in the South were legally freed from slavery. This began a chain of events that would eventually lead to a great migration of blacks from the southern states to the western frontier. Although free, blacks had a very difficult time earning a living in southern states because of severe discrimination and limited opportunities available to minorities. Moreover, whites and blacks vied for the precious, fertile southern land. The South struggled to adjust to changing political and social circumstances, particularly the demise of slavery. Some whites told blacks that the Emancipation Proclamation would be voided and that blacks would be returned to slavery. White landowners sometimes refused to pay blacks for their labor until a year had passed. This practice trapped blacks in unfair labor agreements and made them like indentured servants. As freed blacks tried to secure land for themselves, many became discouraged by the lack of opportunity in the South and hoped for more independent, prosperous lives.

Land for his people

In 1869 Singleton organized the Tennessee Real Estate and Homestead Association in hopes of helping blacks acquire and settle land in the South. When this venture proved unsuccessful—mainly because whites refused to sell productive land to blacks at fair prices—Singleton began giving speeches promoting the idea that migration out of the South was the best way for blacks to prosper. In the West, he reasoned, blacks would be treated more fairly. Western laws favored equal opportunity and land was abundant there. Singleton imagined self-sufficient black communities where African Americans could live free from the oppression they faced in the South. Singleton and others felt that if blacks owned businesses and participated in social institutions, there would be more opportunities for the entire black population to prosper. Singleton looked to Kansas for better opportunities.

The welfare of the black community was foremost in Singleton's mind. He took his leadership role seriously, believing himself to be an instrument of God. In his testimony before the Select Committee of the United States Senate to Investigate the Causes of the Removal of the Negroes from the Southern States to the Northern States in 1880, Singleton explained that "I have taken my people out in the roads and in the dark places, and looked to the stars of heaven and prayed for the Southern man to turn his heart." However, when the whites did not "turn" their hearts, Singleton vigorously promoted the idea of an exodus. "[W]e are going to learn the South a lesson," he added, according to Nell Irvin Painter in *Exodusters.* In 1873 Singleton's first trip attracted more than three hundred blacks, who followed Singleton to Cherokee County, where the emigrants bought about one thousand acres of land.

Buoyed by the success of the first trip, Singleton and his associates formed the Edgefield Real Estate and Homestead Association by 1874 to further promote the migration of blacks westward. In 1876 Singleton began investigating the possibility of a mass emigration. In a letter to the governor of Kansas quoted in Painter's *Exodusters,* Singleton asked whether blacks could purchase land over a period of time because many could not afford to buy land immediately.

During the following two years, Singleton worked diligently to promote migration to Kansas. In 1877, he traveled there to inspect possible locations for settlement and ran a notice in the Nashville newspaper describing his

 ## Nicodemus, Kansas

Nicodemus (located along U.S. Route 24, two miles west of the Rooks-Graham county line) was the most famous black community and the last surviving colony founded by the Exodusters. The name "Nicodemus" came from a slave who, according to legend, predicted the coming of the Civil War.

Established in 1877–1878, Nicodemus was home to seven hundred African Americans by 1880, and the population continued to grow until 1910. In the beginning, settlers lived in dugouts or sod houses and shared three horses to break the frontier soil. One man even used a cow to pull his plow. The best times in Nicodemus came in the mid-1880s, when plentiful rain provided lush crops and rumors of a potential railroad station circulated. The community held special celebrations on Emancipation Day. Each summer, a square mile of land contained a jubilant carnival with sports and games. The Nicodemus Blues became one of the first black baseball teams in 1907, and the great black baseball player Satchell Paige was a member of the team for a while. Nicodemus became a national historic landmark in 1976, a tribute to its black homesteaders.

A frontier family in front of their sod house in Nicodemus, Kansas. Sod houses were much more practical to build in parts of the frontier that didn't have much timber available.
(Denver Public Library-Wester Collection. Reproduced by permission.)

willingness to discuss opportunities in Kansas real estate. At meetings sponsored by the Edgefield Real Estate and Homestead Association, Singleton urged his audience to start "looking after the interest of our downtrodden race," according to Painter. By 1878 Singleton established a second colony at Dunlap in Morris County, Kansas. He printed handbills reading "Ho for Kansas!" that announced the departure dates of the expeditions to Kansas. The association held festivals and picnics to promote migration. Between 1877 and 1879, the group led more than twenty thousand blacks to Kansas.

Ho for Kansas!

Kansas was the most popular destination for blacks leaving the South. Between 1879 and 1881 approximately sixty thousand blacks migrated to Kansas in search of social and economic freedom The most well-known settlement of

blacks in Kansas was Nicodemus, a colony established through Singleton's efforts. Settled by emigrants from Kentucky in 1877 and 1878, Nicodemus grew to a population of seven hundred people by 1880. Other black settlements included some in Hodgeman, Barton, Rice, and Marion Counties. By 1879 these black communities were thriving, and the black population in the southern states was sufficiently primed for a mass migration. "Come West, Come to Kansas," newspapers urged. The *Colored Citizen* printed advice columns detailing how and where to settle in Kansas. Many papers printed the following article, quoted in Painter's *Exodusters*:

> One thousand Negroes will emigrate this season from Hinds and Madison counties, Miss., to Kansas. We hope they will better their condition, and send back so favorable a report from the "land of promise" that thousands will be induced to follow them; and the emigration will go on till the whites will have a numerical majority in every county in Mississippi.

African American emigrants en route to Kansas. Thousands of blacks moved from the South to Kansas in 1879, seeking better opportunities in the West. *(Reproduced from the Collections of the Library of Congress.)*

The Great Exodus

Though migration had been steady since the early 1870s, the Kansas Fever Exodus of 1879 was the largest single movement of blacks. Thousands of emigrants moved to Kansas seeking their fortune and escaping oppression. A black Texan named C. P. Hicks best described why African Americans were determined to leave the South in his letter to Governor St. John of Texas in 1879. Quoted in *Exodusters*, the letter reads as follows:

> There are no words which can fully express or explain the real condition of my people throughout the south, nor how deeply and keenly they feel the necessity of fleeing from the wrath and long pent-up hatred of their old masters which they feel assured will ere long burst loose like the pent-up fires of a volcano and crush them if they remain here many years longer.

However, no one could pin down the exact reasons for the "simultaneous stampede," as the *Chicago Tribune* called it. "It is one of those cases where the whole thing seemed to be in the air, a kind of migratory epidemic."

Father of the exodus?

Singleton is credited with bringing thousands of blacks to Kansas during the late 1800s and is often referred to as the "Father of the Colored Exodus." Claiming responsibility for the mass migration, Singleton announced in the senate hearing in 1880, as quoted in *Exodusters*: "Right emphatically, I tell you to-day, I woke up the millions right through me! The great God of glory has worked in me. I have had open air interviews with the living spirit of God for my people; and we are going to leave the South."

However, Singleton was not the only catalyst for the migration. Henry Adams, a thirty-six-year-old ex-slave, garnered recognition as another leader of the exodus. Though Adams is often given as much credit as Singleton, the two never met or corresponded. S. A. McClure, A. W. McConnell, and W. A. Sizemore also worked with Singleton to inspire and escort blacks to Kansas. In addition to these men, countless others also promoted the idea of emigration. Rumors spread throughout the black community of free transportation to Kansas and free supplies for Kansas land. Blacks organized conventions to discuss the opportunities in Kansas and sent delegates to investigate the details of the journey.

The social climate of the South also helped promote the idea of emigration. When federal troops withdrew from the South in 1877, Reconstruction (1865–77; the period after the Civil War when the federal government controlled the South before readmitting it to the Union) officially ended. Blacks then faced racial oppression in the South through segregation laws and the terrorist activities of groups like the Ku Klux Klan.

Activist slows down

From mid-1879 to 1880, Singleton settled at his colony at Dunlap. The *Topeka Daily Blade* quoted Singleton as saying "I am now getting too old, and I think it would be better to send some one more competent that is identified with the emigration," according to Painter. Though Singleton reduced the number of settlers he personally conducted to Kansas, he remained dedicated to his mission to help his people and retained his passion for the movement.

Singleton forms more organizations to help blacks

By 1881, Singleton had organized the United Colored Links, a group interested in uniting colored people for the purpose of improving their lives. However, the United Colored Links disbanded after their first convention. Frustrated by the failure of the group to unite under a common cause, Singleton decided to rally them again. According to Painter, Singleton announced in the *North Topeka Times* in 1883 that he had been "instructed by the spirit of the 'Lord' to call his people together to unite them from their divided condition." As he aged, he participated in more organizations that encouraged the migration of blacks out of the South. In 1883, Singleton founded the Chief League, which encouraged blacks to move to the island of Cyprus in the Mediterranean Sea. Later, in 1885, he formed the Trans-Atlantic Society, which encouraged blacks to return to their ancestral homeland in Africa. By 1887 the group disbanded. Singleton died in St. Louis in 1892.

Although Singleton's work attracted much attention, the effect on the regional distribution of the total black population was minor. When the Emancipation Proclamation was signed, less than 8 percent of all blacks lived in the Northeast or Midwest. After the Civil War, the black population in the Northeast fell slightly, while the percentage rose in the Midwest. By 1900, the U.S. Census reported that 90 percent of all blacks remained in the South.

Kansas did not turn out to be the land of opportunity many had hoped for. The influx of so many blacks strained the state's resources in the mid-1880s, and some of the black communities developed into little more than refugee camps. Yet by 1900 blacks in Kansas were generally better off than those in the South. Blacks enjoyed more freedoms in the West. However, they discovered that nowhere in the United States could blacks escape racism. In cities, schools were racially segregated, and some white Kansans resented the increasing population of blacks in the state. Nevertheless, many of the Exodusters succeeded in finding a place where they could live more freely than they had in the South.

For More Information

Entz, Gary R. "Image and Reality on the Kansas Prairie: 'Pap' Singleton's Cherokee County Colony." *Kansas History* (Summer 1996): 124–39.

Fleming, Walter L. "'Pap' Singleton, the Moses of the Colored Exodus." *American Journal of Sociology* (July 1909): 61–8.

Garvin, Roy. "Benjamin, or 'Pap,' Singleton and His Followers." *Journal of Negro History* (January 1948): 7–23.

Higgins, Billy D. "Negro Thought and the Exodus of 1879." *Phylon* (Spring 1971): 39–52.

Painter, Nell Irvin. *Exodusters: Black Migration to Kansas after Reconstruction.* New York: Knopf, 1977.

Schlissel, Lillian. *Black Frontiers: A History of African American Heroes in the Old West.* New York: Simon and Schuster Books for Young Readers, 1995.

Van Deusen, John G. "The Exodusters of 1879." *Journal of Negro History* (April 1936): 111–29.

Belle Starr

Born February 5, 1848
Carthage, Missouri
Died February 3, 1889
Near King Creek, Indian Territory

Rancher and cattle rustler

Belle Starr, known also as the Bandit Queen, lived an exciting and interesting life, but her flamboyant personality fostered many untrue stories of her escapades in Texas.

Known as the Bandit Queen, Belle Starr is one of the most famous characters to come out of the Old West. Describing her as a female Robin Hood, stories recounted how she stole from the rich to give to the poor. Her flamboyant personality fostered exciting stories of her escapades in Texas. She reportedly rode through Dallas whooping and shooting her twin pistols, gave birth to the daughter of famous bandit Cole Younger, married her second husband on horseback while riding away from her disapproving parents, escaped from every jail she was put in, and led several outlaw gangs. Exciting though these tales may be, they are not entirely true. Like the lives of many western heroes and outlaws, an embellished version of Belle Starr's life has become a western legend.

Belle Starr: fact or fiction?

At the time of Starr's death, magazines and dime novels had become very popular, mainly because they printed stories of great adventure on the American frontier. The exploits of real-life frontiersmen were especially popular. Tales

Belle Starr.
(The Granger Collection, New York. Reproduced by permission.)

of frontiersmen Daniel Boone (1734–1820; see entry) and Kit Carson (1809–1868; see entry)—as well as outlaws Jesse James (1847–1882; see entry) and Billy the Kid—excited the imaginations of eager readers. Featuring gunfights, evil villains, and damsels in distress, the thrilling stories were often embellished and exaggerated to make them even more compelling to readers.

In Starr's case, a dime novel popularized a false—but thrilling—version of her life. When Richard K. Fox, a publisher of dime novels, read Starr's *New York Times* obituary, he dispatched the writer Alton B. Meyers to write a biographical novel based on her life. It is easy to see what piqued Fox's interest. On Wednesday, February 6, 1889, the *New York Times* reported:

> Word has been received from Eufala, Indian Territory, that Belle Starr was killed there Sunday night. Belle was the wife of Cole Younger.... Jim Starr, her second husband, was shot down by the side of Belle less than two years ago.

> Belle Starr was the most desperate woman that ever figured on the borders. She married Cole Younger directly after the war, but left him and joined a band of outlaws that operated in the Indian Territory. She had been arrested for murder and robbery a score of times, but always managed to escape.

The only fact in the entire obituary was the report of Starr's death. Yet excited by Starr's legend, Meyers began to research her life for his biographical novel. Unable to get the cooperation of Starr's family, he created his story from secondhand accounts of neighbors and acquaintances. The resulting novel, *Belle Starr, The Bandit Queen, or The Female Jesse James,* sold thousands of copies, but it told little truth. Meyers had made up diary entries and letters from Starr to make the story appear authentic. Other biographies of Starr soon followed. Though many books and stories recount what they call the "real" story of Starr's life, few leave out the thrilling fabrications of the earliest biographical account.

The real Belle Starr did associate with criminals and flirt with lawlessness. Wearing fashionable velvet dresses and riding her horse sidesaddle, Starr rarely rode without her gun belt securely fastened around her waist. She hosted rough criminals in her home but presented herself in a ladylike manner. Yet her gracious manners did not prevent her from showing her temper, whipping her son, or aiming her gun at someone's face to make her point. Starr's early years explain her unusual combination of fashionable worldliness and criminal behavior.

A childhood in pre–Civil War Missouri

Starr was born Myra Maybelle Shirley near Carthage, Missouri, on February 5, 1848. At the age of eight, young "May," as her family called her, enrolled in the Carthage Female Academy, where she attended classes through the eighth grade. However, her education was disrupted as the area surrounding Carthage erupted in skirmishes between those living in the slave-holding state of Missouri and those in the free state of Kansas. Violence escalated throughout the region. When Kansas joined the Union as a free state in 1861, the battles grew ever more heated. Starr's brother joined the notorious William C. Quantrill raiding group and lost his life. After the death of Starr's brother, her father moved the family to Texas.

Descent into crime

The family prospered on a farm outside of Dallas. A smart young woman, Starr was bored in the local one-room schoolhouse and preferred spending time on the farm with her parents. In 1866 James C. Reed, a friend of Starr's in Missouri, moved with his family to Texas and became reacquainted with the young Belle. On November 1, 1866, they married. Within two years Starr had a baby girl she named Rosie Lee, whom she called "my pearl." Though she may have known the outlaw Cole Younger—he was a member of her late brother's raiding group in Missouri—she did not marry him and her first child was not his, contrary to what some stories say.

Jim Reed was a gambler and criminal who introduced Starr to criminal life. Although some stories suggest that Starr spent the late 1860s playing pianos in dance halls and frequenting gambling houses, she actually looked after her daughter and around 1870 or 1871 gave birth to a son, Edward, in Missouri. After Reed killed two men to avenge his brother's murder, he moved his family frequently to stay one step ahead of the law, ending up in California. Getting into

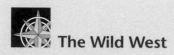

The Wild West

Belle Starr's life and the subsequent embellishment of it are products of the Wild West. Starr lived during a time when the West was a wild, unruly place. Gunfighters disrupted the life of growing towns with their seemingly random violence, and armed bandits sometimes made travel difficult and costly. Lawmen—like Sam Starr's nemesis, John West—attempted to keep the peace, but sometimes did so with violence of their own. Violence was a regular part of life, for westerners had few laws or authorities to enforce the law. However, this savage period in American history did not last very long. Prior to the Civil War (1861–65; a war fought between the Northern and Southern United States over the issue of slavery), violence had never been perceived as an epidemic. After the Civil War, however, the cowboy era brought hundreds of young, aggressive men into the frontier, where they clashed with thousands of settlers who had begun moving out into the western territories. Conscientious, solid citizens found the lawlessness of cowboys and other western characters a real threat to the civilization that they were trying to build. For example, the Cheyenne, Wyoming, *Daily Leader* declared that "Morally, as a class, cowboys are foulmouthed, blasphemous, drunken, lecherous, utterly corrupt. Usually harmless on the plains when sober, they are dreaded in towns, for then liquor has an ascendancy over them." The Wild West existed from approximately 1866 to 1890; it seemed so wild because the rudeness and violence of the frontier began to clash with the sensibilities of an encroaching civilization. Indeed, Starr's life parallels these changes on the frontier. Running with bandits in the 1860s and 1870s, she later attempted to conform to a more civilized life.

By 1890 the forces of civilization had generally triumphed in the West. Towns across Kansas barred the cattle trade and rid themselves of the wild cowboys at the same time. No longer able to live the free life of the cowboy, many men returned to farms and to the civilizing influence of families. Railroads stretched across the continent, bringing settlers to areas once remote. With the settlers came churches, civic organizations, family life, and, perhaps most importantly, law and order. In 1893 historian Frederick Jackson Turner noticed something that had probably become obvious to many: the frontier was closed, and the West was no longer wild. Yet the legendary characters of the Old West lived on in books and movies.

trouble by trying to pass counterfeit money, Reed and family soon fled California as well. In the early 1870s they sought refuge at the home of Reed's friend Tom Starr in Indian Territory, where Reed continued his criminal ways. In one robbery, Reed reportedly came away with about thirty thousand dollars. However, when Reed was killed in a gunfight in 1874, Starr was left in a "destitute condition," according to her sworn testimony for the U.S. commissioner in Dallas, which is quoted in Glenn Shirley's book *Belle Starr and Her Times*. She shipped her children to Missouri to live with relatives.

May Reed becomes Belle Starr

Although stories suggest that Starr had several lovers, little is known about the next few years of her life. In 1880 she married again, this time to Sam Starr, the half-Cherokee son of her first husband's friend, Tom Starr. About this time, she took the first name Belle; she kept the Starr surname for the rest of her life. Settled in her new marriage, Belle sent for her daughter, renaming her Pearl Starr. Living in Indian Territory along the Canadian River, the family operated a ranch, which doubled as an outlaw hideout. They reportedly hosted Jesse James and other fugitives from the law.

In 1882 both Belle and her husband faced Judge Isaac Parker—called the "hanging judge"—on charges of horse theft. Belle was the first woman ever sentenced by the judge and received less than one year in prison. During her incarceration, Belle wrote to her daughter, referring to her as Pearl Younger. Biographer Glenn Shirley explains the name change as Belle's attempt to save her daughter from legal problems. Her first letter, quoted in Shirley's *Belle Starr,* illustrates her concern for her daughter: "I shall be away from you a few months baby, and have only this consolation to offer you, that never again will I be placed in such humiliating circumstances and that in the future your little tender heart shall never more ache, or a blush called to your cheek on your mother's account."

When Belle and her husband were set free, they returned to their ranch and were reunited with Pearl; a year later, Edward rejoined the family. In 1885 burglary charges were brought against Sam Starr, and he left the ranch to hide

Belle Starr associated with criminals and flirted with lawlessness. Wearing fashionable velvet dresses and riding her horse sidesaddle, Starr rarely rode without her gun belt securely fastened around her waist.
(The Corbis Corporation. Reproduced by permission.)

in the wilderness. While her husband was in hiding, Starr faced two charges of horse theft, for which she was acquitted. After reuniting for a short time, Belle and Sam were separated forever when Sam was killed in a gunfight with John West, a Cherokee police officer, in 1886.

After Sam's death, Starr stopped housing fugitives. Neighbors stopped complaining to the police about their horses and cattle disappearing. By 1889, the widow Starr made a common-law marriage with the twenty-four-year-old Jim July, the adopted son of Tom Starr, Sam's father. Marrying another Cherokee allowed Starr to keep her property in Indian Territory. When July was arrested for attempting to steal a horse, Starr reportedly chastised him publicly and refused to pay his bail. She seemed to want to protect her newfound respectability.

Respectability … and death

Her peaceful life would not last long. Shortly after her third marriage, Starr died from a load of buckshot that blasted into her back; another load shattered her left shoulder and the side of her face. No one is sure who killed her—although there are several theories concerning her killer's motives and identity. Some commentators believe that an angry former lover was responsible for the killing. A few historians suspect Starr's eighteen-year-old son, Edward, who had a difficult relationship with his mother. Others speculate that the culprit was a neighbor named Edgar Watson, who had quarreled with her about land. Watson's criminal record, proximity to the killing, and his angry fight with Starr over a land lease prompt many historians to deem him the real killer. Although a neighbor found Starr before she died, Starr never named her killer.

Starr was buried at Younger's Bend, in a Cherokee ceremony: jewelry was laid in her coffin and a revolver was placed at her hand. Her daughter, Pearl, had a monument placed at the grave. It was inscribed with these words: "Shed not for her the bitter tear, / Nor give the heart to vain regret, / 'Tis but the casket that lies here, / The gem that fills it sparkles yet." Shortly after Starr was buried, her grave was robbed. To protect her mother's remains, Pearl had a two-foot rock vault built over Starr's grave.

For More Information

Green, Carl R., and William R. Sanford. *Belle Starr: Outlaws and Lawmen of the Wild West*. Hillsdale, NJ: Enslow Publishers, 1992.

Horan, James. *The Lawmen of the Authentic Wild West*. New York: Crown, 1980.

Prassel, Frank Richard. *The Great American Outlaw: A Legacy of Fact and Fiction*. Norman: University of Oklahoma Press, 1993.

Ross, Stewart. *Fact or Fiction: Cowboys*. Surrey, British Columbia: Copper Beech, 1995.

Shirley, Glenn. *Belle Starr and Her Times: The Literature, the Facts, and the Legends*. Norman: University of Oklahoma Press, 1982.

John Augustus Sutter

Born February 15, 1803
Kandern, Germany
Died June 18, 1880
Washington, D.C.

Pioneer

John Augustus Sutter has been heralded as one of the heroes of America's westward expansion. According to popular history, Sutter left Europe for the American frontier, where he realized his dream of creating an empire in the Sacramento Valley of the Mexican territory of California. At his California colony—named New Helvetia— Sutter welcomed the immigrants who streamed into the territory, especially after gold was discovered at his mill on the American River. However, Sutter claimed that miners ignored his claim to the land and deprived him of the wealth that should have come his way. Today he is remembered as one of the founding fathers of the state of California.

However, recent historians have established that Sutter was no saint: He built his reputation in America on a foundation of lies and borrowed money. He enslaved and mistreated the Native Americans who helped build New Helvetia. His mismanagement of his California empire was so complete that it led to financial failure. Despite all his faults, Sutter did play a pivotal role in opening California for American settlement. Sutter's story, then, is like many Western

"I have been robbed and ruined by lawyers and politicians.... my cattle were driven off by hungry gold-seekers; my fort and mills were deserted and left to decay; my lands were squatted on by overland immigrants; and, finally, I was cheated out of all my property. All Sacramento was once mine."

From Fool's Gold *by Richard Dillon*
John Augustus Sutter.
(Reproduced from the Collections of the Library of Congress.)

stories—it combines myth with reality, and it helps us understand that the settlement of the West was often based on luck, corruption, and lies.

Life as a European shopkeeper

Sutter was born Johann August Suter on February 15, 1803, in Kandern, Germany, a small village just north of Basel, Switzerland. His father, Johann Jakob Suter, served as a foreman in a paper mill. His mother, Christina Wilhelmina Stober, was the daughter of a pastor. Sutter left home at age fifteen to attend a military academy in Neuchâtel, Switzerland. He loved the romance and pageantry of the military, although he was never made an officer in the Swiss army (as he later claimed in America). He also began an apprenticeship (a period of learning under an experienced tradesman) as a publisher, printer, and bookseller.

After leaving school, Sutter became a clerk in a draper's shop in the Swiss town of Aarburg. He soon met Anna Dübeld and moved to her hometown of Burgdorf. He worked at several jobs, including grocery clerk. On October 24, 1826, he and Anna were married; the next day, Anna gave birth to their first child. Backed by Anna's family, Sutter opened a dry goods firm in Burgdorf. Like almost every venture Sutter ever engaged in, the business was a failure. Indeed, he piled up such an enormous debt by 1834 that it was clear he would be imprisoned for bankruptcy. In mid-May of that year he liquidated his assets, abandoned his family (he now had five children), and set out for the United States. According to historian Iris H. W. Engstrand, writing in *John Sutter and a Wider West*, "For more than a decade [Anna] Dübeld Sutter, the deserted wife and young mother, remained virtually a charity case, waiting vainly for her errant husband to rescue her from poverty and disgrace."

Starting over in America

When Sutter arrived in July 1834, the United States included twenty-six states, the Midwest beyond the Missouri River was free territory, and Texas had just become an independent republic. Mexico controlled most of the Southwest—

including the territory of California—and Britain, Russia, and the United States were vying for control of the Oregon Territory. To an immigrant fresh from Europe, the country seemed full of opportunity. Sutter quickly learned English, Americanized his name to John Sutter—adding the title "Captain" for good measure—and set out to build a new life.

Sutter soon headed west, spending the winter of 1834 in St. Louis. He tried farming but soon was drawn by the promise of riches to be had from trading goods on the Santa Fe Trail, which connected Missouri with the then Mexican city of Santa Fe. Sutter profited from his Santa Fe trade, though there were charges that he made money in part by cheating his trading partners. In 1837 Sutter moved to Westport, Missouri (now part of Kansas City), where he hired local Shawnee Indians to help him build a hotel. An observer of Sutter's actions in Westport claimed that Sutter exploited his Native American workers' weakness for hard liquor and showed a distinct fondness for young Shawnee women. With his business dealings once again falling apart, Sutter escaped his debtors and set out for Oregon in April 1838. His dream, he told his fellow travelers, was to create a new community in California, a land fabled for its abundance.

The road to California

Sutter accompanied the American Fur Company into the Oregon Territory and then joined a Hudson's Bay Company trapping expedition to Fort Vancouver. There were few ships sailing in this part of the world at the time, and Sutter learned that his best chance for reaching the main California port town of Yerba Buena (present-day San Francisco) would mean first traveling to Honolulu, Oahu, in the Hawaiian Islands (which were then called the Sandwich Islands). Sutter sailed aboard the *Columbia* to Honolulu and, while awaiting a ship to California, met the king of the islands, Kamehameha III.

Sutter told Kamehameha and others of his plans for building a community and trading post in California. Always a good storyteller, Sutter won the confidence of the king, who then offered to send eight men (Kanakas, or native Hawaiians) to help in this venture. In addition, most of the merchants traveling with him eagerly vowed their support. When Sutter and his followers finally obtained passage on the ship *Clementine,* he felt that his dreams were within reach. Traveling via Sitka, Alaska, Sutter arrived in Yerba Buena in July 1839.

The settlement of New Helvetia

Land was not free for the taking in California; first Sutter had to present his idea to Governor Juan Bautista de Alvarado at the territorial capital of Monterey, south of Yerba Buena. Sutter told Alvarado that he wanted to build a vast fort and trading post at the foot of the Sierra Nevada Mountains, inland from present-day San Francisco. The Mexican governor, believing that Mexico would benefit from a thriving community in the midst of the undeveloped valley, was enthusiastic about Sutter's plans. He proposed that Sutter could become a Mexican citizen—and the legal owner of a vast tract of land—if he developed the land within a year. Sutter was thus granted fifty thousand acres near the Sacramento River.

Before claiming his land, Sutter traveled to various Mexican, Russian, and American outposts throughout northern California, establishing relationships that would be necessary for the trading post. Sutter, his eight Kanaka laborers, and a handful of white settlers reached the juncture of the American and Sacramento Rivers in August of 1839. What they found was not quite a wilderness—several American Indian tribes had lived off the land for hundreds, or perhaps thousands, of years—but by white standards it was an "uncivilized" land, heavily forested and home to grizzly bear, deer, and elk. To Sutter, it seemed the ideal place to farm, graze livestock, and build a community.

Sutter first had to make peace with the Native American groups in the area. At first, he told the Miwok, Nisenan, and other Indians that he came in peace, and he offered them employment; later, he showed the Indians the three cannons that King Kamehameha had given the pioneers, thus warning the Indians that he would not hesitate to use force if necessary. With the help of the Native Americans, Sutter constructed a massive military-style structure, known as Sutter's Fort. The fort's eighteen-foot-high and three-foot-thick walls enclosed a trading post that included shops, small "factories," and personal dwellings. Outside the fort, farmland was cultivated, vineyards planted, and livestock grazed. Sutter called his community New Helvetia, which means "New Switzerland."

Sutter's empire

Sutter presided over his empire of New Helvetia with a mix of hospitality and despotism (absolute power and authority). To settlers—Mexican or American—who moved into the valley Sutter offered a warm welcome, a variety of goods, and cheerful assistance in getting established. He recognized that his business would profit from every settler who ventured into the region, and he did all he could to welcome newcomers. To the American Indians who performed the majority of the labor in New Helvetia, however, Sutter was neither kind nor generous. He paid his Indian laborers in coins that could only be exchanged for goods in his stores, and he never paid them well. Worse, he was not above enslaving Indians when he needed extra labor during harvest season. Sutter even gave Indian girls to his white trading partners, a practice that most historians stop just short of calling a slave trade. In New Helvetia, however, Sutter was king and could do as he liked.

In the 1840s Sutter's empire expanded in size and power. He tripled the size of his land holdings in 1841 when he purchased Fort Ross and the accompanying lands from the Russians. He exercised control over his holdings with the help of an Indian army of about two hundred men. This army—dressed in gaudy blue-and-green Russian uniforms—helped Sutter protect his land from Indian raids; they also coerced unwilling Indians into laboring in the fields during harvest season. In 1845, when the growing number of American settlers in California began to revolt against Mexican rule, Sutter switched his allegiance away from the Mexicans and used his army in service of the American cause. For his services Sutter was made an American citizen when California became a U.S. territory in 1847.

Gold on the American River!

In 1847, at the height of his influence in the region, Sutter and his workers built several mills powered by the many streams that flowed out of the mountains surrounding the valley. Sutter appointed a carpenter named James Mar-

Sutter's Mill in California's Sacramento Valley, the site of the gold discovery that started the California gold rush of 1849.
(© Robert Holmes. The Corbis Corporation. Reproduced by permission.)

shall (1810–1885) to oversee the construction of a sawmill in the Coloma Valley, about forty-five miles from Sutter's Fort on the south fork of the American River. On the morning of January 24, 1848, Marshall was surveying work on the mill when he spotted something sparkling in the river. Mill construction had disturbed the earth around the riverbed, and the moving water had washed away the gravel and sand to reveal what appeared to be gold. Picking out a few small nuggets, he ran back to the mill workers and shouted, "Boys, I believe I have found a gold mine," according to Rodman W. Paul's *The California Gold Discovery*.

The men discovered more of the gleaming, soft metal, and Marshall decided that he must present his find to Sutter. Together the two men tested the mineral. Amazingly, it *was* gold. Sutter hoped that he could keep Marshall's discovery secret. But word soon spread: there was gold on the American River.

A group of Mormons working on a flour mill on the same river discovered a second gold mine, which became known as Mormon Island. With this discovery, gold fever spread through New Helvetia. According to J. S. Holliday, author of *The World Rushed In: The California Gold Rush Experience*, "Sutter could not hold his workers. The flour mill stood unfinished, hides rotted in the warehouse. All his plans depended on a staff of assistants, field workers, carpenters, and tanners. Suddenly they were gone, with plans of their own." Once people across California—and throughout America—heard of the gold, they quickly left their jobs and rushed to the gold mines to strike it rich.

Gold rush disaster

Within a year after the initial discovery of gold, Sutter's Fort lay at the center of the greatest gold rush in American history. However, Sutter saw no profit from the boom: to him it must have seemed that the black cloud that had hovered over his previous business dealings had found him again, for gold-diggers from all over the world flocked to Sutter's property and "squatted" on his land (claimed the land with no legal basis) for the next three years. Ignoring Sutter's property claims and destroying his farm and ranch land, the squatters even took Sutter to court to challenge his property claims. Since the land was granted to Sutter under Mexican authority, those rights were now under question. Forced into lengthy and expensive court battles, Sutter had to sell much of his property and mortgage (borrow against) the rest. By 1852 John Sutter, once one of the most powerful men in California, was bankrupt.

Along with his family (who had finally rejoined him in 1850) Sutter moved to a small piece of property known as

The Transforming Power of the Gold Rush

The California gold rush, which began in 1848 with the discovery of gold at John Sutter's mill, transformed the state of California and indeed the entire nation. Before the discovery of gold, California was a distant and sparsely populated territory that the United States had acquired in a war with Mexico. Yet the discovery of gold and the ensuing publicity turned the trickle of immigrants coming into the territory into a steady flow and then a flood. An estimated thirty-two thousand people took the overland routes to California in 1849, and another forty-four thousand came in 1850. Many others came by sea. The territory of California now had enough inhabitants to petition for statehood, which was granted in 1850.

Though not all of the gold diggers struck it rich, many stayed in California and brought their families with them. The city of San Francisco exploded with growth and soon became an important port city. With California's statehood and the growing population there, the United States now had an official outpost on the West Coast, and the Pony Express (an early postal service), telegraph lines, and eventually the transcontinental railroad all connected east to west. These enhanced communication and transportation systems in turn helped populate the vast unsettled territory between California and Missouri. By speeding settlement in California, the gold rush also increased the pace of general westward expansion.

Hock Farm, on the Feather River near Marysville, California. From there he lobbied the California legislature for compensation for his losses, and the legislature finally voted to pay him $250 a month for five years. Even that amount seemed to provide little solace to the aging Sutter. To make matters worse, on June 21, 1865, a disgruntled worker burned down Sutter's home at Hock Farm.

Sutter left his beloved California in 1871 and settled in the German community in the town of Lititz, Pennsylvania. For the remaining years of his life he tried to convince the federal government to reimburse him for his losses, with no success. He was staying in a Washington, D.C., hotel on one of his many trips to petition Congress when he died in his sleep on June 18, 1880.

Although Sutter received no further reimbursement from Congress, he was remembered well for many years after his death. As California grew and successive generations looked back on the pioneer days, Sutter was held up as an important founding father, a noble visionary who brought prosperity and peace to California. However, beginning in the 1960s, historians presented Sutter as a much more complicated figure. They discovered accounts written by Sutter's contemporaries that portray him as a scheming, vain, drunken, but optimistic man who never quite managed to make the best of his opportunities. Josiah Royce's description of Sutter, penned not long after Sutter's death and quoted in *The California Gold Discovery*, perhaps captures the contradictory nature of the man best:

> In character Sutter was an affable and hospitable visionary, of hazy ideas, with a great liking for popularity, and with a mania for undertaking too much. A heroic figure he was not, although his romantic position as a pioneer in the great valley made him seem so to many travelers and historians. When the gold-seekers later came, the ambitious Sutter utterly lost his head and threw away all his truly wonderful opportunities. He, however, also suffered many things from the injustice of the newcomers. He died a few years since in poverty, complaining bitterly of American ingratitude. He should undoubtedly have been better treated by most of our countrymen, but, if he was often wronged he was also often in the wrong, and his fate was the ordinary one of the persistent and unteachable dreamer.

For More Information

Dillon, Richard. *Fool's Gold: A Biography of John Sutter.* New York: Coward-McCann, 1967.

Engstrand, Iris H. W. "John Sutter: A Biographical Examination."In *John Sutter and a Wider West,* edited by Kenneth N. Owens. Lincoln: University of Nebraska Press, 1994, pp. 76–92.

Holliday, J. S. *The World Rushed In: The California Gold Rush Experience.* New York: Simon and Schuster, 1981.

Lewis, Oscar. *Sutter's Fort: Gateway to the Gold Fields.* Englewood Cliffs, NJ: Prentice-Hall, 1966.

Marks, Paula Mitchell. *Precious Dust: The American Gold Rush Era: 1848–1900.* New York: William Morrow, 1994.

Owens, Kenneth N., ed. *John Sutter and a Wider West.* Lincoln: University of Nebraska Press, 1994.

Paul, Rodman W., ed. *The California Gold Discovery: Sources, Documents, Accounts, and Memoirs Relating to the Discovery of Gold at Sutter's Mill.* Georgetown, CA: Talisman Press, 1966.

Tecumseh

Born 1768
Chalahgawtha
(an Indian village near Springfield, Ohio)
Died 1813
Near the Thames River, Ontario, Canada

Warrior and tribal leader

At the height of his power in the first decade of the nineteenth century, Shawnee war chief Tecumseh was the single biggest obstacle to continued American expansion into what was known as the Old Northwest (the present-day states of Ohio, Indiana, and Michigan). Leading first his own people and then a confederacy (organized group) of Native American tribes, Tecumseh harassed Americans settling in the area and then defeated American military forces in several key battles. Despite allying themselves with the British during the War of 1812 (1812–14; a conflict between the British and the Americans over the control of the western reaches of the United States and over shipping rights in the Atlantic Ocean), Tecumseh's forces finally fell to the superior numbers and technology of the American forces.

Early life in the Ohio Valley

Tecumseh (probably originally pronounced te-kam-tha) was born near Chalahgawtha, a Shawnee village near present-day Springfield, Ohio. His father was Puckeshinwa, a respected Shawnee war chief, and his mother, Methoataske, was of Creek or possibly Cherokee origin. Although the exact number of children in the family is uncertain, Tecumseh had several siblings—including a set of younger triplet brothers.

Tecumseh was raised during a time of crisis for the Shawnee people. For hundreds of years they had inhabited the Ohio Valley, living in villages along the river, the women farming and the men hunting and fishing, and from time to time, warring with neighboring tribes. They had long been accustomed to contact with the "long knives," as they called the white frontiersmen; they traded with them and generally maintained good relations. But by the 1760s and 1770s whites began arriving in increasing numbers. They set up permanent settlements and clashed with the Indians over land and game. By 1774 the Shawnee were at war against the settlers. During one battle Tecumseh's father, Puckeshinwa, was killed.

Tecumseh's older brother Chicksika took it upon himself to school Tecumseh in the ways of a hunter and warrior. At fourteen Tecumseh joined his brother in battle. It was Tecumseh's first battle, and he turned and ran when violence erupted. His brother and the other warriors told him that fear in battle was acceptable once, but never again. Thereafter, Tecumseh was renowned for his bravery. Tecumseh also developed into a powerful public speaker, or orator. From an early age he could lead and inspire his people with his convincing and colorful arguments. Once, disgusted at the way his tribesmen burned, tortured, and killed their white prisoners, Tecumseh convinced his fellow warriors to give more humane treatment to enemies captured in battle.

Resisting white invasions

During the years following the Revolutionary War (1776–83), the U.S. government set about acquiring more Indian land to satisfy settlers and make up for financial losses from the war.

Government chiefs—the Indians' name for tribe leaders who were willing to sell land to the Americans—sold off huge tracts of land that they did not really own. Tecumseh's people tried to avoid these arrangements and never saw them as legitimate. It was probably during this time that Tecumseh came to believe that the land belonged to all the Indians in common and that, therefore, no one tribe or group had the right to sell any land.

During the late 1780s and early 1790s, Tecumseh and his fellow warriors honed their skills in guerrilla warfare, a method of fighting in which the Native Americans quietly stole up on unsuspecting settlements, attacked quickly, and disappeared into the woods. In the summer of 1788, Chicksi-ka—now the warriors' leader—was killed in an unsuccessful attack in Tennessee. Though some of the Shawnee returned home, Tecumseh remained in the South for another two years, hunting and raiding white settlements with a small party. He did not return home until 1790.

Washington sends troops to the Ohio Valley

While Tecumseh was away, the U.S. government had created the Northwest Territory out of the vast tract of land that lay between the Appalachian Mountains and the Mississippi River. Between 1785 and 1790 alone, nearly twenty thousand white settlers entered the region. Alarmed at the growing number of Indian attacks on American settlers, President George Washington (1732–1799) sent a force of fourteen hundred soldiers under General Josiah Harmar into the Ohio Territory. Believing he had scared the combined Shawnee, Potawatomi, and Chippewa forces into retreat, Harmar gave chase and suddenly found his troops in a deadly ambush. Indian forces, of which Tecumseh was a part, achieved their first major victory against the Americans.

Washington next sent a larger force under General Arthur St. Clair (1736–1818), but they were badly defeated in a battle along the banks of the Wabash River. Finally, Washington sent a force of three thousand soldiers under General "Mad" Anthony Wayne (1745–1796) to drive the Indians from the territory. Wayne met the force of thirty-five hundred Indians, including Tecumseh and his men, in a stand of storm-damaged trees known as Fallen Timbers. In a fierce battle, Wayne's troops defeated the combined Indian forces and forced them to sign a treaty granting all of present-day Ohio and much of present-day Indiana to the United States. This

Tenskwatawa, the Prophet

Two years after Tecumseh's birth, his mother had triplets. One of the triplets, Lowawluwaysica, earned a bad reputation as a clumsy, unlikeable boy. By the time he was a teen, he had begun to abuse alcohol and was seen as a disgrace to his family. He tried to study with the village medicine man, but his cures failed. Then, after drinking heavily one night, Lowawluwaysica had a vision in which the Great Spirit gave him a message for his people. According to this vision, the Great Spirit wanted the Indians to renounce the influence of the white man and return to their traditional ways. The Great Spirit had also given his messenger a new name, Tenskwatawa, which means "The Open Door."

In the years that followed, Tenskwatawa, who became known as The Prophet, joined his brother Tecumseh in helping to unite the Shawnee and other Indian tribes throughout the Midwest against the advance of the American settlers. Some historians have charged that Tenskwatawa was a fake whose "prophecies" were merely an attempt to ride along on Tecumseh's coattails. But Native Americans took The Prophet's message seriously, and many followed Tenskwatawa—up until the day when he led many warriors to their death at the Battle of Tippecanoe in 1811. After this battle, Tenskwatawa lost all honor and wandered from one village to another, despised and lonely.

treaty, the Treaty of Greenville, signed in August 1795, enraged Tecumseh, who dreamed of the next time Indians would stand together to defeat the American forces.

A time of peace

In the years following the Treaty of Greenville, Tecumseh and his people lived in relative peace with the American settlers. Settlers quickly moved into most of present-day Ohio; Tecumseh settled with his people along the White River, near present-day Indianapolis, Indiana. Tecumseh actually helped to maintain the peace between the peoples, negotiating several agreements that might have ended in bloodshed without him. But the pressure of Americans pushing their settlements westward soon ended this fragile peace. By 1805, with the Americans regularly scheming to break the treaty or trick the Indians into giving away more land, Tecumseh and his followers established a new village near Greenville, Ohio, in U.S. territory. He was daring the Americans to a fight, and this time he was not alone. Tecumseh was joined by one of his younger brothers, Tenskwatawa, who the Shawnee called The Prophet (see box on p. 202).

The Indian movement

Together, Tecumseh and Tenskwatawa exhorted the Shawnee and other Indian tribes that the time had come to put a stop to the white advance. Tecumseh's message was political: he visited other tribes in the region and tried to convince them that they would be stronger if they acted together under his leadership. Tenskwatawa's message was religious: he claimed that the whites were evil spirits and that the Native Americans could reclaim their land if they would reject the white man's influence and return to their traditional ways. The two leaders helped unite Indians in their determination to resist the whites.

William Henry Harrison (1773–1841), governor of the Indiana Territory, watched the Shawnee community closely, often sending messages to the Indians, asking them what they meant to do. Tecumseh and Tenskwatawa responded with reassurances of their peaceful intentions. By 1808, as game and other resources around Greenville were depleted, the brothers moved their supporters to a location near the meeting point of the Tippecanoe and Wabash Rivers in north-central Indiana. They named their new village Prophetstown, and it soon became a meeting point for the leaders of the Indian confederacy. Governor Harrison kept a careful eye on the settlement.

Between 1805 and 1810 Tecumseh ranged widely across the Indian territory, trying to build support for his Indian confederacy. Older, more conservative Indian leaders tended to reject Tecumseh's ideas, but younger leaders and warriors pledged their support. Tecumseh even visited with the British in 1808 to find out whether he would have their support if the Indians took arms against the Americans; the British pledged their friendship. Then, in September 1809, Governor Harrison convinced several chiefs to sign the Treaty of Fort Wayne, which granted the government about two and a half million acres of Indian land. This turn of events helped Tecumseh's recruiting: As word of the treaty spread among the northwestern tribes, a flood of warriors—disgusted with the leaders who had thus betrayed them—joined Tecumseh's cause.

In July 1810 Harrison met with Tecumseh at Vincennes in Indiana to try to negotiate a peace agreement. The commander of nearby Fort Knox described the party of Indians:

> They were all painted in the most terrific manner.... They were headed by the brother of the Prophet (Tecumseh) who, perhaps, is one of the finest looking men I ever saw—about six feet high, straight, with large, fine features, and altogether a daring, bold looking fellow.

At their meeting Tecumseh recited the long list of injustices that had been committed against the Indians. He spoke of his opposition to the Treaty of Fort Wayne and admitted that he headed a confederacy dedicated to preventing further invasion of Indian lands. The meeting ended without any resolution, but Harrison realized that he had a potent enemy.

The Battle of Tippecanoe

In the summer of 1811 Tecumseh traveled to the South on a mission to recruit more tribes into his alliance. Seeing Tecumseh's absence as an opportunity, Harrison quickly prepared his troops and marched toward Prophetstown. Learning that the army was near, Tenskwatawa claimed to have had a vision: he told his people that half of the white soldiers were insane and that their bullets could do the Indians no harm. During the night, the Indians surrounded Harrison's camp and attacked before dawn. The Battle of Tippecanoe lasted just over two hours. Though the Indians inflicted heavy losses among Harrison's troops, they lacked good leadership and soon retreated.

Harrison's troops retaliated by burning Prophetstown, destroying Tecumseh's Indian confederacy. With Tenskwatawa discredited and the Shawnee defeated, few tribes believed that they could resist the white advance any longer. But Tecumseh would get one more chance to fight against the Americans.

Rebuilding the confederacy

Following the Battle of Tippecanoe, Tecumseh set about rebuilding his confederacy. He assured Harrison of his peaceful intentions, but as the War of 1812 between the British and the Americans approached, Tecumseh decided to side with the British. Using his powers of persuasion, Tecumseh convinced other tribes to side with the British, and he joined in a number of battles in Canada and the Detroit area, helping the British gain an advantage. At the Battle of Brownstown, he turned back an army of more than 150 American troops with only 24 warriors.

For a time, Tecumseh and British general Isaac Brock worked together to coordinate the efforts of Indian and British forces. In fact, Brock so trusted Tecumseh that he placed him in command of all the Indian forces. Tecumseh played a vital role in the British conquest of Detroit on August 15, 1812. But Brock was soon ordered east to assist

William Henry Harrison (right, holding sword) and Tecumseh (left, holding tomahawk) were longtime foes in the struggle over control of the Old Northwest. *(Archive Photos, Inc. Reproduced by permission.)*

The Battle of the Thames, Tecumseh's last battle against Americans. *(Archive Photos, Inc. Reproduced by permission.)*

British forces there. He was replaced by Colonel Henry Proctor, who had no interest in the military tactics of people he thought of as savages. Under Proctor's cautious command the combined British and Indian forces suffered several setbacks late in 1812. In the spring of 1813 they learned that they must face a newly appointed American military leader, Tecumseh's old foe William Henry Harrison.

Proctor's leadership was ill fated, for the British triumphs of 1812 turned to defeats in 1813. After an ill-planned siege of the American Fort Meigs failed, Proctor led his forces on a retreat into Canada. Tecumseh and his forces guarded their rear, and on October 5, 1813, the British and Indians stopped to fight the Americans along the Thames River in Ontario. The night before the battle, Tecumseh had told his warriors that he would die the next day. His vision came true, for he was killed by a bullet through the heart. His warriors spirited his body away and disappeared into the surrounding woods.

The Americans won the War of 1812, thus ending British support for armed Indian resistance to white settlements throughout the Old Northwest. Without Tecumseh the Indian resistance fell apart, and most tribes simply moved further west to avoid confrontation with the white settlers. Tecumseh was remembered, by both friend and foe, as a brave and principled man who stood nobly for the dream that Indians could hold on to the lands of their ancestors. He was, in the words of his enemy William Henry Harrison, "one of those uncommon geniuses, which spring up occasionally to produce revolutions and overturn the established order of things."

For More Information

Cwiklik, Robert. *Tecumseh, Shawnee Rebel*. New York: Chelsea House, 1993.

Drake, Benjamin. *Life of Tecumseh and His Brother the Prophet*. 1841. Reprint. Lewisburg, PA: Wennawoods, 1999.

Eckert, Allan W. *A Sorrow in Our Heart: The Life of Tecumseh*. New York: Bantam, 1992.

Edmunds, R. David. *Tecumseh and the Quest for Indian Leadership*. Boston: Little, Brown, 1984.

Gilbert, Bill. *God Gave Us This Country: Tekamthi and the First American Civil War*. New York: Anchor/Doubleday, 1989.

Kent, Zachary. *Tecumseh*. Chicago: Childrens Press, 1992.

Schraff, Anne. *Tecumseh: The Story of an American Indian*. Minneapolis, MN: Dillon, 1979.

Shorto, Russell. *Tecumseh and the Dream of an American Indian Nation*. Englewood Cliffs, NJ: Silver Burdett Press, 1989.

Sugden, John. *Tecumseh: A Life*. New York: Henry Holt, 1998.

Sugden, John. *Tecumseh's Last Stand*. Norman: University of Oklahoma Press, 1985.

Mariano Guadalupe Vallejo

Born July 4, 1808
Monterey, California, New Spain (Spanish territory)
Died January 18, 1890
Lachryma Montis, near Sonoma, California

Rancher, politician

In the middle of the nineteenth century, one of the biggest boosters of the U.S. annexation of California was not a miner, an army soldier, or a U.S. politician, but rather a long-time Mexican rancher and landowner named Mariano G. Vallejo. In the first half of the nineteenth century, Vallejo had become one of the biggest landowners and most powerful politicians in the Mexican territory of California. But Vallejo had grown impatient with the mismanagement of Mexican rule, and he longed to bring his beloved country under the more democratic and enlightened rule of the United States. His crafty political maneuvering and well-forged alliances helped him survive the transition to American rule and play an important role in the growth of California as a state. Though not an American himself, Vallejo contributed greatly to the Americanization of the West.

Youth in a distant colony

Mariano Vallejo was born on July 4, 1808, in the coastal town of Monterey, the capital of the territory of Califor-

"We are republicans—badly governed and badly situated as we are—still we are all, in sentiment, republicans.... Why then should we hesitate still to assert our independence?"

Vallejo in a speech to Californians, urging them to push for annexation by the United States, quoted in General Vallejo and the Advent of the Americans

nia, at that time a distant outpost of the Spanish colony of New Spain (Mexico). His father was a government administrator and an engineer who never rose to a high position in the town of three hundred people. His son would do better. Mariano was one of three local boys who attracted the attention of the territorial governor, Pablo Vicente de Sola. Governor de Sola helped Vallejo obtain formal schooling from an English tutor, but perhaps more importantly, he taught Vallejo how to handle the delicate balancing act that defined early California politics.

During Vallejo's youth, California was in a precarious position. Because it was distant from the Spanish colonial government in Mexico (which declared independence from Spain in 1821), California received little official attention. Territorial governors like de Sola and his successors managed affairs without much interference from the Spanish government, and the territory was soon visited regularly by ships from Russia, Britain, France, and the United States. Each of these countries had some hope of claiming California, if the opportunity arose. Following Mexican independence, Spanish soldiers (including Vallejo's father) were given large land grants, and they became rancheros (ranchers). Vallejo joined his father on their nearly nine-thousand-acre parcel north of Monterey in 1822.

An important landowner

By the time he was twenty-two, Vallejo was already an accomplished young man. He had received military training in his teens, and in 1829 led a force of Californians to victory over a local Indian tribe. Moreover, he had already served as a member of the territorial legislature. In 1833 he married Francisca Benicia Carrillo, a beautiful, strong-willed woman who would remain his partner for life. That same year he was sent to establish a military post at Sonoma, about forty miles north of San Francisco. For his services, Vallejo was given a vast land grant of nearly sixty-six thousand acres that included the Sonoma Valley, the Sonoma Mountains, and the Petaluma River. Along with the land, he received six thousand cattle, six thousand sheep, a vast orchard, and numerous buildings and shops. "This land," writes Vallejo's biographer Alan Rosenus in *General Vallejo and the Advent of the*

Americans, "was Vallejo's to dispose of as he wished—the beginning of his personal empire."

General Vallejo

Vallejo and other ranchers who owned a lot of land and had become fairly powerful in California society grew to resent the influence of Mexican governors. When the well-liked Governor Figueroa died in 1835 and was replaced by the corrupt governor Nicolás Gutiérrez, the ranchers decided to take action. Organizing their own armies and encouraging some American settlers to pose as rebel armies, the ranchers intimidated Gutiérrez into resigning and named Vallejo military governor of the "Free State of Alta California." Vallejo was chosen for the position not because he was a fiery leader, but because he was a careful thinker who would not lead his peers into trouble. Vallejo's cousin, Juan Bautista Alvarado, was named civil governor. The cautious Vallejo made peace with Mexico; Mexico later acknowledged the wisdom of the takeover by confirming Vallejo's position and thanking him for his patriotism.

One of the biggest problems facing ranchers like Vallejo was the difficulty of finding colonists to settle in the region. Most Mexicans didn't want to travel north to the distant colony, and the Mexican government placed strict limits on the number of non-Mexicans who could live there. To the ranchers, it felt like the government was limiting their right to grow. Over the years, as Vallejo tried to develop his empire and negotiate with the Mexican government for policies that would help his empire grow, he became convinced that the best way to develop northern California was to welcome the small but growing stream of American settlers who were beginning to discover the region. In 1841 he offered his hospitality to the Bidwell-Bartleson party that had crossed the Sierra Nevada mountain range, not least because several of the party members had skills that were needed in his area. In the years to come, Vallejo would often ignore official restrictions on American immigration if he felt that the immigrants would benefit his community.

Vallejo's goal was the long-term prosperity of northern California. While he was certainly looking out for the good of the region, as the largest landowner he also stood to profit from the growth of towns, commerce, and agriculture in the region. Vallejo's pursuit of prosperity for his region often took unexpected forms. For example, in 1844 when it appeared that the troops he commanded might be asked to fight for the Mexican governor against some of his allies who resisted the governor, Vallejo simply dismissed Vallejo's troops and resigned from his position as general. Without troops, Vallejo could not participate in a coming civil war or be asked to expel American settlers. It was a subtle move that avoided armed conflict and furthered his own goal.

By 1845 outside influences began to speed California toward change. The former Mexican colony of Texas was admitted into the Union, and many in America thought that California would be an even better addition to the growing country. Also, the popularity of manifest destiny—the idea that the United States was destined to extend from the Atlantic to the Pacific Ocean—encouraged many to dream that one day the United States would control California. In that same year, 1845, an adventurer and explorer named John Charles Frémont (1813–1890; see entry) marched into California with 150 men. Settling in at Sutter's Fort (see John Sutter entry) in the Sacramento Valley (inland from Vallejo's ranch), Frémont's men would prove to be both a disruptive force and the catalyst that made California part of the United States.

The Bear Flag Republic

Soon after he arrived in California, Frémont began to stir things up among the American settlers who were already eager to see a change in California's government. Evicted from California by the governor for his disruptive activities, Frémont plotted to return and capture California for the United States. Frémont mistakenly believed Vallejo to be his opponent, and on June 14, 1846, he encouraged local settlers to storm Vallejo's compound in Sonoma. (Historians have debated whether Frémont was authorized by the U.S. government or acting on his own; most believe he was acting on his own.) Taking the compound peacefully, the raiders raised a flag that had on it a bear and a star; they declared themselves the leaders of the Bear Flag Republic. They took Vallejo and several of his allies hostage and imprisoned them at Sutter's Fort. Once Frémont determined that the raid had been a success, he resigned from the U.S. Army and took charge of the independent California Republic.

The Bear Flag Republic lasted less than a month, for Frémont rejoined the American forces when he learned that the United States and Mexico were at war (the Mexican-

American War, which lasted from 1846 to 1848 and was fought over the position of the southern border of Texas). After nearly a year of small-scale clashes and political maneuvering, American forces under army general Stephen Kearny secured all of California by January of 1847, helped along by the cooperation of ranchers in the northern part of the territory. The Treaty of Guadalupe Hidalgo, signed on February 2, 1848, made the conquest of California official and guaranteed California landowners that their property rights would be respected. Californios, the name for California's Hispanic inhabitants, would have to negotiate a new place in this new American territory.

Finding a place in the new order

Vallejo was released from his imprisonment on August 2, 1846, and he spent the remainder of the Mexican-American conflict—and indeed his life—trying to protect his position in the rapidly changing political order of California. One of his most pressing problems was the lack of respect American settlers paid to his land and property. Squatters set up homesteads on his property, and rustlers frequently stole his cattle and horses. Though he tried to reclaim his property through legal means, the courts would never return all of Vallejo's lost property to him. (He later received $48,700 in damages from the U.S. government, less than half of what he had claimed but still the largest payment made in all of California.)

Nevertheless Vallejo was far from powerless in the new California. Many of the U.S. officers and officials looked to him for his experience and judgment in dealing with local matters. Also, Vallejo controlled most of the best land in the fertile and beautiful Sonoma Valley. (He would later become involved in a complicated and ultimately failed attempt to provide the land for the state capitol.) Vallejo was asked to serve on a legislative committee to oversee the American settling of California, and he accepted the post on February 15, 1848. According to Rosenus, Vallejo "hoped to promote legislation that would benefit the country, and this would vindicate his faith in the course he had taken" (by allying himself with the Americans).

Fools Rush In: The California Gold Rush

The California gold rush that began in 1848 with the discovery of gold at John Sutter's mill (see John Sutter entry) transformed the once quiet Mexican territory of California into the fastest growing state in the United States. For Californios (Hispanic California natives) like Mariano Vallejo, the changes that swept California were nothing less than breathtaking. A quick look at the numbers reveals just how dramatically the gold rush transformed California.

In 1841, the non-Indian population of California numbered between sixty-five hundred and seven thousand Hispanics and fewer than four hundred foreigners of all nationalities (including American settlers). Those numbers rose slightly over the course of the decade, until 1849 when thirty-two thousand people entered California by overland routes, followed by another forty-four thousand in 1850. Many others came by sea. California officially became a U.S. territory in 1848, and only two years later it had enough inhabitants to petition for statehood. By 1852, the state was home to 250,000 people.

The Californios who had once exerted unquestioned rule over California soon found themselves overruled and outvoted by thousands of white American settlers who paid no heed to traditions and laws. The new settlers voted their representatives into power, took lands that belonged to Californios, and discriminated against Hispanic natives in a variety of ways. Vallejo, whose dream it was to draw settlers into the region, could never have expected what happened in California.

Gold rush and beyond

Vallejo might have returned to a position of real prominence in California were it not for one important event: the California gold rush. After the discovery of gold on John Sutter's land in the Sacramento Valley in 1848, thousands upon thousands of miners poured into California in pursuit of instant wealth. Many settled in California even if they didn't strike gold, snatching up whatever land they could and soon establishing such a large American presence in the state (statehood was granted in 1850) that political power was stripped from the once dominant figures of old California, including Mariano Vallejo. In Vallejo's account of the gold rush, titled "What the Gold Rush Brought to California," he complained bitterly about the "swollen torrent of shysters who came from Missouri and other states of the

Union," who "took from us our lands and our houses, and without the least scruple, enthroned themselves in our homes like so many powerful kings. For them existed no law but their own will and their caprice."

Vallejo was bitter about the fate he had been dealt, and he did lose most of his land and his fortune, which had been vast. He ended his days on a ranch north of Sonoma, operating a small farm and selling produce from the farm in local markets. Despite these difficulties, Vallejo had accomplished his dream: he had helped California achieve statehood, and his beloved country was now one of the most prosperous and quickly growing states in the Union. He was honored throughout California. According to Rosenus, "During the 1870s and 1880s, hardly a public event took place to which Vallejo was not invited—either as an honored guest or speaker." Late in life Vallejo wrote to his son, in a letter quoted in *General Vallejo,* "Everything turned out for the best.... [W]e are in the United States, soon to be the foremost nation on earth. Love everybody. Be good. Obey just laws.... Harbor no rancor in your heart."

The eighty-one-year-old Vallejo died in his home on January 18, 1890. His death was commemorated in ceremonies throughout the state, and he is remembered today as one of the men who made statehood possible. That he did so without bloodshed and with so little anger and hostility shows that he was one of the kindest-hearted builders of the modern United States.

For More Information

Comstock, Esther J. *Vallejo and the Four Flags: A True Story of Early California.* Grass Valley, CA: Comstock Bonanza Press, 1979.

Harlow, Neal. *California Conquered: The Annexation of a Mexican Province, 1846–1850.* Berkeley: University of California Press, 1982.

Rosenus, Alan. *General Vallejo and the Advent of the Americans.* Berkeley, CA: Heyday Books, 1999.

Vallejo, Mariano G. "What the Gold Rush Brought to California." In *The Course of Empire: First Hand Accounts of California in the Days of the Gold Rush of '49,* edited by Valeska Bari. New York: Coward-McCann, 1931.

Narcissa Prentiss Whitman

Born March 14, 1808
Prattsburg, New York
Died November 29, 1847
Waiilatpu, Washington (near present-day
Walla Walla, Washington)

Missionary

Though many emigrants moved west in the nineteenth century to establish farms, trap beaver, or dig for gold, others came on a holy mission to convert western Native Americans to Christianity. Narcissa Prentiss Whitman, along with her husband, Marcus Whitman, established their mission in Oregon Country in 1836, making Whitman the first white woman to cross the Rocky Mountains. The missionaries helped prepare the way for the great migration west along the Oregon Trail in later years, but they never succeeded at converting many Indians to their religion. In 1847 Indians slaughtered the Whitmans in their home.

A pious family

Narcissa Prentiss Whitman was born March 14, 1808, in Prattsburg, New York. Her parents had settled in the area when it was still the frontier (the western edge of American settlement), though by 1808 a number of towns had sprung up in the region. Whitman's mother was an enthusiastic Presbyterian, and many of Whitman's childhood memories were

"The missionary work is hard, up-hill work, even the best of it. There are no flowery beds of ease here."

Narcissa Whitman in a letter to her parents, October 6, 1841, quoted in Where Wagons Could Go

Narcissa Prentiss Whitman.

Women in the West

Women often played an important role in the settling of the West. As more and more families braved the dangers of the Oregon Trail and settled in the West, women came to play key roles in the building of western communities. In 1849, for example, Sarah Bayliss Royce established the first school in California in the mining camp of Grass Valley, using the Bible, a volume of John Milton's poetry, and a children's storybook for texts. The female members of Roman Catholic religious orders were also very active in establishing schools throughout the West in the 1870s.

Many western women opened businesses to serve the various mining and cattle towns that sprang up throughout the region. Doing work that men wanted to avoid, such as cooking and laundry, these women could often make more money than a man could, especially those men who searched fruitlessly for gold. Clara Brown, a former slave from Kentucky, earned so much money washing the clothes of California gold rush miners that she was able to purchase the freedom of her enslaved relatives in the East. Of course, many women also earned money as prostitutes serving the predominately male towns of the West. Though law-abiding and religious people condemned prostitution, brothels (houses of prostitution) were thriving businesses, offering some women a chance to earn more money than they could make any other way.

of Presbyterian services. Growing up, Whitman took special pleasure in singing hymns. Her voice would later become an important part of her missionary work; Indians from miles around would bring their children to hear her sing.

By her own account, Whitman decided to become a missionary when she was fifteen. She joined the Female Mite Society, one of several religious women's groups in Prattsburg, and began teaching Sunday school. At the same time, she pursued her own studies, first at Auburn Academy in nearby Auburn and then at Franklin Academy in Prattsburg. Later, in her mid-twenties, she taught school for a few years. In 1834 when her family moved to Amity, New York, a small village deep in the woods, she threw herself into church and Sunday school affairs. But she dreamed of becoming a missionary.

Are females wanted?

In 1834 Whitman heard a visiting Congregational minister, Samuel Parker, speak about his desire to gather missionaries and money to establish a mission, or religious outpost, among the Native Americans in Oregon Country. Whitman longed to join the mission, but Parker told her it was unlikely that the missionary board would authorize a woman for the journey. In December Parker wrote to the missionary board on Narcissa's behalf, asking, "Are females wanted? A Miss Narcissa Prentiss of Amity is very anxious....," according to Clifford M. Drury in *Marcus and Narcissa Whitman and the Opening of Old Oregon.* As Whitman and Parker expected, the application was rejected.

Nearby, however, a young doctor named Marcus Whitman had heard the same call for missionaries and had eagerly signed on. Learning that Narcissa—whom he had once met at a prayer meeting in the Prentiss home—was also interested, Marcus wrote to her and then visited Amity. Caught up in their shared enthusiasm for missionary work, the pair decided to marry. Their engagement, quickly decided upon in January 1835, was based not on love, but on a dream of the future that looked better if they pursued it together. Now twenty-seven years old, the tall and pretty Whitman was about to achieve her dream of becoming a missionary.

Thanks to her engagement with Marcus Whitman, Narcissa was accepted as a missionary. But she was not able to leave right away. Marcus had traveled west with Parker to survey the prospects for a mission. Joining with a party of trappers from the American Fur Company, Marcus traveled through the wilderness beyond the Rocky Mountains to the Green River in present-day Wyoming. In August 1835 he met with Nez Percé and Cayuse Indians from Oregon, who said they were eager to welcome missionaries among them. Excited by this news, Marcus Whitman returned to the East to help organize the party of missionaries to leave a year earlier than he and Narcissa had first planned.

Where wagons could go, women could go

Marcus and Narcissa began to make plans for their departure, but first they had to find other missionaries to go along with them. After a fruitless search, Narcissa suggested a friend of hers named Henry Spalding, a minister who was already organizing a mission among the Osage Indians of Nebraska. Spalding had once asked Narcissa to marry him, but she turned him down. He and his new wife, Eliza, agreed to go to Oregon instead of Nebraska.

Marcus and Narcissa were married on February 18, 1836, before a large crowd of family and friends. Quickly gathering supplies for their journey, the newlyweds embarked on their trip west in early March. The party traveled first by riverboat and then in a wagon train. Whitman found the going easier than she had expected. It helped that they were protected and guided by a large group of American Fur Company trappers. On July 4, Narcissa Whitman and Eliza Spalding became the first white women to cross the Continental Divide, the dividing line between the eastern and western watersheds of the Rockies.

The party of missionaries abandoned their wagons at Fort Boise (present-day Boise, Idaho) and proceeded on horseback for the remainder of their journey. They arrived at Fort Vancouver, near where the Columbia River empties into the Pacific Ocean, on September 12, 1836. They had covered more than 3,000 miles in 207 days, taking wagons further west than any party had before and opening an important stretch of what would soon be the famous Oregon Trail.

Waiilatpu

While the women stayed at Fort Vancouver, Marcus Whitman and Henry Spalding searched out suitable places for building their missions. In order to ease the increasing tensions between the two couples, the men chose separate locations for their missions. Marcus Whitman located a fertile spot east of Fort Vancouver on the Walla Walla River, twenty-five miles upstream from the Columbia and below the wooded slopes of the Blue Mountains. The Indians called the area Waiilatpu (pronounced wy-eee-laht-poo), or Place of the Rye Grass. (Spalding chose a spot in Nez Percé territory, about one hundred miles farther inland, on Lapwai—or Butterfly Valley—Creek.) After four weeks at Fort Vancouver, the women traveled east to join their husbands.

For two years, the Whitmans' missionary work went slowly but without major problems. They built a small house out of adobe (mud bricks mixed with grass and baked in the sun), set up a mill for grinding wheat into flour, and brought in farm animals. They both took pride in their newborn daughter, Alice Clarissa. Caring for the new baby helped ease Narcissa's growing homesickness. The mission soon became a popular stopping point for the travelers—mostly mountain men, fur company officials, and a few early settlers—who ventured through the region. Workers at the missions began the hard work of farming, building irrigation systems, and teaching the Cayuse and Nez Percé Indians about agriculture.

Marcus Whitman leads a prayer at South Pass as the Whitmans' wagon train crosses the Rocky Mountains.

(Reproduced by permission of Corbis-Bettmann)

Troubles at the mission

By 1840, frequent disputes between the Whitmans and the Spaldings made life increasingly difficult. The rivalry between the two missions was made worse by the arrival of additional missionaries sent by the missionary board. Soon even small decisions, such as whether to pray aloud or silently, became the cause for endless debate and argument. Though all shared in such problems, Narcissa was especially affected. She escaped to her room in tears when others expected her to make household decisions. The missionaries had expected to reach agreement in a spirit of Christian harmony; instead, they bickered and squabbled.

Equally troubling was the growing divide between white culture and Indian culture. Both sides expected something of the other that they did not receive. The Cayuse hoped they could share in the whites' technology, which seemed mysterious and powerful, without giving up their own ways. They did not wish to settle down on farms, for they were used to roaming widely in search of their food. And they could not comprehend the white notion of owning the land. The Indians believed that the land belonged to everyone and to no one.

The missionaries thought that the Indians should abandon Indian culture and embrace white ways, especially the Christian religion. At first the Cayuse had no trouble accepting the white man's god. They worshiped many spirits—tree spirits, river spirits, and the like—so they found it easy to add a new god to the list. But they did not like it when the missionaries expected the new god to become their only god. Their discomfort soon turned into resistance, and that resistance grew in the face of the Whitmans' increasing impatience with Indian ways.

Tragedy and survival

In June 1839 the Whitmans' beloved daughter Alice Clarissa had drowned in the nearby Walla Walla River. Narcissa fell into a deep depression, which made it even harder for her to deal with the Indians. According to Carlos Schwantes in *The Pacific Northwest,* Narcissa began to view the Native Americans as "filthy savages," ungrateful for what the Whitmans were trying to do for them. They in turn saw her as conceited.

The Whitmans' difficulties were compounded by the fact that they had been unable to convert many Indians to Christianity. In the fall of 1842, the missionary board decided to close the missions and transfer the Whitmans elsewhere. Unwilling to give up, Marcus traveled east to persuade the board to keep the missions open. He was convinced that the mission must remain a bastion of Christianity in the wilderness; the board agreed, and the mission remained open.

Reports of fertile, unclaimed land began to draw numbers of settlers westward by the early 1840s. The Whitmans and Spaldings had proven that women could survive the trip, and now whole families could consider moving to the West. Each year brought more settlers; by 1847 nearly five thousand settlers flooded across the Blue Mountains on their way west. The Whitman mission was a welcome outpost for weary travelers, who used it as a resting point on their way further west. The Cayuse, however, feared that the white people were an invading party eager to take Cayuse land.

The Indians also feared white diseases, against which they were defenseless. In 1847, in two months alone, a measles epidemic killed half the Cayuse. Whitman's efforts to nurse the Indians back to health met with little success. Children were hit especially hard by the disease. The white children who fell ill seemed to recover, but the Indian children did not. The Indians feared that the Whitmans might actually be poisoning their children. Their fears soon grew into open hostility, and they began committing aggressive acts against the mission, including throwing stones through mission windows.

Bloody end

On a cold, foggy November morning in 1847, the Indians decided to take their revenge on the hated missionaries. After a group of pioneer wagons had left the mission, a number of Cayuse entered the mission compound. While one Indian engaged Marcus Whitman in an argument about land, another crept up behind Whitman and beat him across the skull with a tomahawk; Whitman died within minutes. At the same time other Cayuse raided other parts of the house; one attacker shot Narcissa Whitman in the chest, and she died immediately. Eleven other whites were killed, and more than forty (mostly immigrants who had stayed there to rest) were captured.

The Whitmans' legacy

In the end, the Whitmans were unsuccessful missionaries, converting only about twenty Native Americans to Christianity in their decade of work. However, the Whitmans did serve as an example and a guide to the thousands of white settlers who came west after them. Narcissa Prentiss Whitman proved in particular that white women could survive the trip and prosper in the West, a land that until her arrival had been visited and populated almost entirely by men (who often married Indian women).

For More Information

Books

Drury, Clifford M. *Marcus and Narcissa Whitman and the Opening of Old Oregon.* 2 vols. Glendale, CA: Arthur H. Clark Company, 1973.

Drury, Clifford M., ed. *Where Wagons Could Go: Narcissa Whitman and Eliza Spalding.* Lincoln: University of Nebraska Press, 1997.

Jeffrey, Julie Roy. *Converting the West: A Biography of Narcissa Whitman.* Norman: University of Oklahoma Press, 1991.

Sabin, Louis. *Narcissa Whitman: Brave Pioneer.* Mahwah, NJ: Troll, 1997.

Schwantes, Carlos A. *The Pacific Northwest: An Interpretive History.* Lincoln: University of Nebraska Press, 1989.

Web Sites

"Narcissa Prentiss, American Martyr." [Online] http://www.prenticenet.com/roots/prentice/bios/narcissa.htm (accessed June 15, 2000).

"Whitman Mission National Historic Site." [Online] http://www.nps.gov/whmi (accessed June 15, 2000).

Sarah Winnemucca

Born c. 1844
Near Humboldt Lake, in Nevada
Died October 16, 1891
Henry's Lake, Idaho

**Native American rights advocate,
author, interpreter, and lecturer**

A s tensions between Native Americans and whites increased on the frontier in the late 1800s, Paiute Indian Sarah Winnemucca won regard as a steadfast peacemaker. Winnemucca was a valued spokeswoman for her people to white society. Unwavering in her insistence on peace, she dedicated her life to improving the lives of Indians and eventually became a nationally known lecturer and lobbyist for Indian causes.

"We will look on her as our chieftain, for none of us are worthy of being chief but her."

Chief Winnemucca quoted in Sarah Winnemucca: Northern Paiute Writer and Diplomat.

Early years

Sarah Winnemucca was born about 1844 near Humboldt Lake, in the part of Utah Territory that later became Nevada; she was the fourth child of Chief Winnemucca, called Old Winnemucca, and Tuboitonie. They named her Thocmetony, meaning Shell Flower. Her grandfather and father were influential leaders of the Paiute Indians and both promoted friendly relations with whites. Sarah grew up listening to her grandfather, Captain Truckee, preach a story that explained how whites and Indians were related. He had traveled with John C. Frémont (1813–1890; see entry) to Califor-

Sarah Winnemucca.
(The Granger Collection, New York. Reproduced by permission.)

Captain Truckee's Story

Sarah Winnemucca's grandfather, Captain Truckee, was convinced that Indians and whites were related. Indeed, when he first heard of whites traveling eastward from California, he rejoiced, saying, "My white brothers my long-looked-for white brothers have come at last!" Despite the great suffering the Paiutes experienced at the hands of whites, Captain Truckee was steadfast in his belief that whites and Native Americans were related. He would tell the following story to explain why they had been separated so long:

In the beginning of the world there were only four, two girls and two boys. Our forefather and mother were only two, and we are their children.... One girl and one boy were dark and the others were white. For a time they got along together without quarreling, but soon they disagreed, and there was trouble. They were cross to one another and fought, and our parents were very much grieved. They prayed that their children might learn better, but it did not do any good; and afterwards the whole household was made so unhappy that the father and mother saw that they must separate their children; and then our father took the dark boy and girl, and the white boy and girl, and asked

nia in 1846 and later aided him in the Mexican-American War (1846–48; a conflict over the position of the southern border of Texas). Truckee enjoyed easy relations with whites thanks in part to his letter of recommendation from Frémont, which he carried until his death.

However, as a young girl Sarah Winnemucca was afraid of whites because she thought they ate people. She assumed this after hearing a garbled version of the Donner Party's cannibalism. (The Donner Party was a group of travelers who became stranded in the Sierra Nevada Mountains of California in the winter of 1846 and 1847 and resorted to cannibalism to survive.) Sarah's mother, who was also afraid of whites, tried to run when she heard that they were coming to the Indians' camp. Carrying her small daughter, Elma, and dragging young Sarah by the hand, she was unable to keep up with the rest of the women in her tribe. Sarah's mother dug a shallow hole in the ground and covered her girls with sagebrush. Frightened to move for fear of being discovered, the girls spent the day listening for the white "cannibals." Later in the evening, their mother returned and dug out the girls,

them, "Why are you so cruel to each other?" They hung down their heads, and would not speak. They were ashamed. He said to them, "Have I not been kind to you all, and given you everything your hearts wished for? … You see, my dear children, I have the power to call whatsoever kind of game we want to eat; and I also have the power to separate my dear children, if they are not good to each other." So he separated his children by a word. He said, "Depart from each other, you cruel children; —go across the mighty ocean and do not seek each other's lives."

So the light girl and boy disappeared by that one word, and their parents saw them no more, and they were grieved, although they knew their children were happy. And by-and-by the dark children grew into a large nation; and we believe it is the one we belong to, and that the nation that sprung from the white children will some time send someone to meet us and heal all the old trouble. Now, the white people we saw a few days ago must certainly be our white brothers, and I want to welcome them. I want to love them as I love all of you.

Source: Catherine S. Fowler, foreword to Life among the Piutes: Their Wrongs and Claims, by Sarah Winnemucca Hopkins (edited by Mrs. Horace Mann). Reno: University of Nevada Press, 1994, pp. 6–7.

who were unharmed. The horror of that day never left Sarah. She later wrote in her autobiography, *Life among the Piutes*, "Oh, can any one imagine my feelings, *buried alive*, thinking every minute that I was to be unburied and eaten up by the people that my grandfather loved so much?"

Coming to terms with whites

Apart from this frightening episode, Winnemucca's family tradition of peaceful relations with whites would dominate her life. Her grandfather wished so much that his family would learn the customs of white people that he sent Sarah with her siblings and mother to live with whites in California in 1851. The women could earn money as cooks and household help. Sarah performed housework for several white families as a girl. While living with a white family as a domestic worker in her early teens, she learned about Christianity and took the name Sarah, which she kept the rest of her life. With the whites Sarah did learn much about white customs; she learned to use tables and chairs, to sew, and to speak both

English and Spanish. And to fulfill her grandfather's dying wish, she attended a Catholic school in California in 1860, but she was forced to leave when white parents complained about their children associating with a Native American. Though never embracing her grandfather's love of whites, Winnemucca grew to accept their differences and tried to understand their culture.

Despite her limited formal education, Sarah learned languages quickly and devoured books whenever she could. As an adult, she could speak five languages and write English proficiently. As a member of her tribe's most prominent family, Sarah was well positioned to have a great impact on lives of her people in her adulthood.

Changing times for the Paiutes

As Sarah grew, the lives of her people were changing dramatically. Once able to roam their homelands, which included parts of present-day Idaho, Nevada, and Oregon, the Northern Paiutes soon found waves of settlers encroaching on their way of life. With the discovery of the Comstock Lode (a vast silver deposit at Virginia City, Nevada), miners poured into the Paiute lands, taking the Paiute grazing land and indiscriminately raping and killing Indians. To try to keep peace in their homeland, the Paiutes signed a treaty with the whites. But in early 1860, when whites kidnaped and abused two young Indian girls, the Paiutes and white settlers fought for three months. The brief war ended with a compromise that established Indian reservations on the Paiute homeland around Pyramid Lake and the Walker River. But a series of poor Indian agents (government officials in charge of protecting Indians and distributing government aid to them) failed to keep whites from using Indian land as pastures for livestock, from fishing in Pyramid Lake, from stealing Indian timber, from squatting on the most fertile tracts of land, or from tricking Indians out of their supplies. Sarah noted in 1866 the she and her brother "got along very poorly, for we had nothing to eat half of the time," according to Ellen Scordato in *Sarah Winnemucca: Northern Paiute Writer and Diplomat.*

Unable to survive on the land devoted for the reservation, many of the Paiutes, including Sarah and her brother

Natchez, moved to Fort McDermit in northeastern Nevada in the 1860s, where the soldiers fed them and gave them supplies. Sarah earned money at the fort by working as an interpreter and scout. In 1868, Natchez brought Old Winnemucca and 490 of his followers to Fort McDermit, but Old Winnemucca did not want to live according to white customs and left again to live his more traditional, roaming lifestyle.

After the end of the Civil War (1861–65; a war fought between the Northern and Southern United States over the issue of slavery), the army could no longer care for the Indians at Fort McDermit, and a new Indian agent, Major Henry Douglass, took on the difficult task of making the Indian reservations in Nevada livable for the Indians. Douglass restricted the reservation land to Paiutes alone and made plans to improve the reservations. But Douglass was appointed a U. S. marshal and had to leave his plans unfinished. By 1873, several corrupt Indian agents had left the reservations in shambles. Throughout these years, Winnemucca saw her people fall on very hard times, but she emerged as a skillful translator and a strong, outspoken advocate for Indian welfare and the maintenance of peace. She occasionally earned money by working for the army as an interpreter.

By 1875, Winnemucca and many of her tribe had moved to the Malheur reservation in Oregon. With a kindly Indian agent named Sam Parrish, the Paiutes lived relatively well. Upon their arrival, Parrish announced to the Indians that "The reservation is yours. The government has given it to you and your children." Sarah acted as interpreter and teacher on the reservation and found Parrish and his wife to be generous, kind people. But in 1876, Parrish was replaced by a new, corrupt agent at Malheur Reservation, who promptly fired Winnemucca and began cheating the Indians out of the rations sent by the government. The Paiutes did not have enough food or clothing, and Winnemucca could not persuade the federal government or the nearby army officers to help.

A daring rescue

Troubles between whites and Indians were not limited to the Paiutes and their Indian agent. A nearby tribe called the Bannocks began what Winnemucca called "the greatest

Indian war that ever was known," according to Scordato. The Bannocks attacked whites as well as Paiutes and wanted "nothing better than to kill Chief Winnemucca's daughter," for supposedly siding with the army against the Bannocks, notes Scordato. Hearing of the war, Sarah Winnemucca had offered her services as an interpreter and scout.

During one attack, the dreaded Bannocks captured Winnemucca's father and other members of the tribe. Winnemucca learned of their plight while out scouting for the army. Upon hearing the news, Winnemucca mounted a horse and rode more than one hundred miles to save them. Disguising herself as a man, she rode into the camp and helped them escape during the night. But they were pursued by the Bannocks. Winnemucca kept her father's band ahead of the Bannocks by not sleeping for two full days. When she delivered her people to army protection, Sarah had ridden 223 miles. "It was," she remembered in her autobiography, "the hardest work I ever did for the army." But Sarah's work was not done; she and her sister-in-law Mattie continued to act as scouts, interpreters, and guides for the army, helping to track hostile Indian bands and witnessing many battles between the Bannocks and the army. According to Scordato, Natchez declared his sister a "warrior," and Chief Winnemucca honored Sarah's bravery before the tribe by saying, "Oh! how thankful I feel that it is my child who has saved so many lives, not only mine, but a great many, both whites and her own people. Now hereafter we will look on her as our chieftain, for none of us are worthy of being chief but her."

With the end of the war, the Paiutes were to be returned to the Malheur Reservation, but to Winnemucca's distress, the Bureau of Indian Affairs in Washington, D.C., insisted that the Indians march 350 miles north to the Yakima reservation in Washington Territory, forcing them to live alongside tribes that had sided against them during the Bannock war. It was winter, and the Paiutes did not have adequate clothing for the long walk. Many died during the terrible trip, and others, including Mattie, died soon after.

The change in relations between the Paiutes and whites troubled Winnemucca. Her people were starving, and promises of land and supplies from whites had been almost universally broken. Her father had come to believe that whites were a weak race because of their short memories. As relations with whites worsened, Winnemucca was in a unique position to help her people. Able to speak and to write English, she brought her people's grievances to the attention of the Indian agents in charge of the reservations, and when she could, she spread news of the Indians' plight and tried to negotiate better accommodations for Indians. In 1879, in San Francisco, Winnemucca gave her first lecture on the plight of her tribe. Dressed in a spectacular feather headdress, a cape, a buckskin dress adorned with beads, and embroidered moccasins, she gave an impassioned speech on a stage decorated like a forest. She told of the dishonest Indian agents and how some of her tribe had been exiled along with their enemies to a reservation in Washington Territory.

Speaking out for her people

Her speeches were so moving that members of the audience would spontaneously shout agreement or affirm statements they knew to be true. A taste of her speeches can be found in her autobiography:

> Oh, dear friends.... We shall never be civilized in the way you wish us to be if you keep on sending us such agents as have been sent to us year after year, who do nothing but fill their pockets and the pockets of their wives and sisters, who are always put in as teachers and are paid from fifty to sixty dollars per month, and yet do not teach. The farmer is really his cousin, his pay is nine hundred dollars a year, and his brother is paid as clerk.... Year after year, the government officers have been told of their wrongdoings.... Yet it goes on, just the same as if they did not know it.... Our agent made my people give every third sack of grain to the agent, and the same of everything else. Every third load of hay is given. My people ask why, as he had not given them seed for planting, nor did the farmer pay to help them to plant. They did not see why they should pay, but the agent told them that was the order from Washington ... they must pay it or he would take their wagons away.

After her lecture in San Francisco, she was labeled "The Princess Sarah"—a title that would stick—in the *San Francisco Chronicle.* Her lecture was described as "unlike anything ever before heard in the civilized world—eloquent, pathetic, tragical at times; at others her quaint anecdotes, sarcasms and wonderful mimicry surprised the audience again and again into bursts of laughter and rounds of applause," according to Dorothy Nafus Morrison in *Chief Sarah: Sarah Winnemucca's Fight for Indian Rights*.

News of her lectures reached the nation's capital, and in 1880 she was invited to meet with the president. Together with Chief Winnemucca and her brother Natchez, she met with Secretary of the Interior Carl Shurz and, very briefly, with President Rutherford B. Hayes (1822–1893). However, Winnemucca was not allowed to lecture or talk to reporters in Washington, D.C., and her small group was given promises that were not kept. Despite the lack of action on the government's part, Winnemucca was able to continue to rally audiences with her stories of mistreatment on the reservations. In 1883, seventy-nine-year-old Elizabeth Palmer Peabody and her younger sister, Mary Peabody Mann, the widow of Horace Mann (an American educator who helped revolutionize public education), helped arrange speaking engagements for Winnemucca in Boston and many other cities in the East. The sisters would remain Winnemucca's enthusiastic financial supporters for many years. They encouraged her to write, as well as speak. Winnemucca wrote many letters, at least one magazine article, and the first English language autobiography of an Indian. Though she sent messages, complaints, and entreaties to anyone she thought might help, her people received little from the government or the Indian agents.

Peabody and Mann also encouraged Winnemucca in her dream to start an all-Indian school, arranging to pay one hundred dollars per month to support it. Winnemucca had been an assistant teacher to the kindly Mrs. Parrish on the Malheur Reservation and greatly enjoyed children. In 1884, she founded the Peabody School for Indian children near Lovelock, Nevada. It was to be a model school where Indian children would be taught their own language and culture as well as learning English. Peabody and Mann could not support the school alone, however. Unable to get government funding or approval, Winnemucca was forced to close the school after four years.

Winnemucca's life was cut short a few years later by disease. After her brief marriage to First Lieutenant Edward Bartlett (whom she married in 1871 and left a few months later after discovering him to be an alcoholic) and then to Joseph Satwaller (whom she married in 1876 and left in

1878), she had married Lewis H. Hopkins in 1881. He traveled east with her when she went to lecture there. A habitual gambler, Hopkins proved as poor a husband as Winnemucca's first two. He died at their ranch at Lovelock on October 18, 1887, of tuberculosis. On October 16, 1891, Sarah Winnemucca died—probably of tuberculosis—at the home of her sister Elma at Henry's Lake, Idaho. In his book called *Famous Indian Chiefs I Have Known*, General Oliver Otis Howard said of Sarah's army career, "She did our government great service, and if I could tell you but a tenth part of all she willingly did to help the white settlers and her own people to live peaceably together, I am sure you would think, as I do, that the name of Thocmetony should have a place beside the name of Pocahontas in the history of our country."

Though she never wavered in her commitment to aiding her people, Sarah died believing that she had failed to make the changes she had worked so hard for. Nevertheless, she has not been forgotten. Her name is in most reference books about North American Indians. Many books have been written about her life and accomplishments, several especially for young people. The book she wrote in 1883, *Life among the Piutes: Their Wrongs and Claims,* was republished in 1994 and remains an important source on the history and culture of the Paiutes. In Nevada, on the McDermit Indian Reservation, there is a historical marker, erected in 1971, honoring Sarah Winnemucca with the words "she was a believer in the brotherhood of mankind." The name of Sarah Winnemucca stands high among Native Americans who have fought for the rights of their people.

For More Information
Canfield, Gae Whitney. *Sarah Winnemucca of the Northern Paiutes.* Norman: University of Oklahoma Press, 1983.

Hopkins, Sarah Winnemucca. *Life among the Piutes: Their Wrongs and Claims.* Edited by Mrs. Horace Mann. Foreword by Catherine S. Fowler. Reno: University of Nevada Press, 1994.

Howard, O. O. *Famous Indians Chiefs I Have Known.* 1908. Reprint. Lincoln: University of Nebraska Press, 1989.

Morrison, Dorothy Nafus. *Chief Sarah: Sarah Winnemucca's Fight for Indian Rights.* Portland: Oregon Historical Society Press, 1990.

People of the Western Range. Alexandria, VA:, Time-Life Books, 1995.

Scordato, Ellen. *Sarah Winnemucca: Northern Paiute Writer and Diplomat.* New York: Chelsea House, 1992.

Woodward, Grace, Harold Howard, and Gae Canfield. *Three American Indian Women: Pocahontas, Sacajawea, Sarah Winnemucca.* New York: Fine Communications, 1995.

Zanjani, Sally. *Sarah Winnemucca.* Lincoln: University of Nebraska Press, 2001.

Brigham Young

Born June 1, 1801
Whitingham, Vermont
Died August 29, 1877
Salt Lake City, Utah

Religious leader

Through most of the nineteenth century, the American West was considered the land of opportunity. Settlers and entrepreneurs moved westward for the diverse economic opportunities: to dig for gold, to herd cattle, or to farm. Yet for the Mormons, the West offered religious freedom and an escape from the persecution the religious group faced elsewhere. The leader of the Church of Jesus Christ of Latter-Day Saints (the Mormons), Brigham Young led his followers on a trek across the American plains to the Great Salt Lake Valley in present-day Utah. There he oversaw the establishment of a Mormon city and agricultural society. Known as Salt Lake City, it quickly became an important stopping point for travelers headed to points further west; it was one of the first major cities in the Rocky Mountain region.

A spiritual journey

Born in Whitingham, Vermont, on June 1, 1801, Brigham Young was the ninth child of John and Abigail Young. Struggling to succeed as farmers, his family moved to

Mormon leader Brigham Young led his followers on a trek across the American plains to the Great Salt Lake Valley in present-day Utah.

Brigham Young.
(The Corbis Corporation. Reproduced by permission.)

western New York when Brigham was three years old. He spent his youth in terrible poverty; in fact, he often had to miss school in order to work long hours on the family farm. In his lifetime he received just eleven days of formal education, but his strict Methodist parents made sure that he read the Bible regularly. Brigham absorbed the strict religious values of his parents and claimed never to have stolen, lied, gambled, drunk alcohol, or disobeyed his parents. Yet as Brigham reached his mid-twenties, he became dissatisfied with the Methodist Church and began to learn about other religions.

At age sixteen Brigham had left home to apprentice as a woodworker in Auburn, New York. He soon became a skilled carpenter and builder. By 1824 he had married Miriam Angelina Works and started a family. During the mid-1820s, western New York was swept by a series of religious awakenings, great outbursts of religious interest spurred by traveling preachers and tent revivals. Historians have called this period the Great Awakening, for these revivals inflated church membership and even inspired the creation of new religious movements. One such movement was started by Joseph Smith (1805–1844) of Macedon, New York, a self-proclaimed prophet and the founder of the Church of Jesus Christ of Latter-Day Saints. Smith claimed to have translated the sacred Book of Mormon from a set of golden plates. His religion offered clear answers to questions about life and the afterlife and promised that it could bring about the salvation of the world through the work of church members, also called Saints. The Mormon Church offered Brigham Young the answers he was searching for, and after the death of his wife in 1832, he dedicated his life to the church.

Becomes Mormon leader

After his wife's death, Young moved to Kirtland, Ohio, where he helped establish a community of some thirteen hundred Saints. Young quickly moved up in the church leadership, eventually becoming one of the senior leaders, or Apostles, of the Mormon Church. However, life as a Mormon was not easy. Outsiders often resented the close-knit, self-supporting Mormon communities, charging that they discriminated against non-Mormons. Also, outsiders were uncomfortable

Mormon Prophet Joseph Smith

While many religions trace their beginnings to ancient times, the Mormon Church was started less than two hundred years ago by an American named Joseph Smith (1805–1844). At the age of twenty-two, Smith claimed that angels had led him to some golden plates near Indian burial mounds outside his home in western New York. He contended that he then translated the plates, which turned out to be a history by Mormon, an American prophet and historian of the fourth century. This history recounted the story of two Jewish groups who had migrated to North America and whom Jesus visited after his ascension.

Using the Book of Mormon as a guide, Smith founded a restored Christian church and proclaimed himself a "seer, a Translator, a Prophet, an Apostle of Jesus Christ and Elder of the Church." He soon attracted a band of followers whose devo-tion to Smith's teachings drew the hostility of outsiders. Settling in Kirtland, Ohio, the Mormon community evolved into a communal experiment in which the church held all property and each family received sustenance from a common storehouse.

To his followers, Smith was a prophet whose teachings came directly from God. When he directed them to abstain from tobacco and alcohol, exclude blacks from the Mormon priesthood, or take multiple wives, his words were taken as holy law. To outsiders, Smith was a charlatan, a religious fraud who deceived people in order to increase his own power. This may have been the belief of an angry mob that brutally murdered Smith on June 27, 1844. Brigham Young assumed the leadership of the church that Smith had founded, leading his people to their promised land in present-day Utah and helping to build a religion that thrives to this day.

with Mormon religious doctrine and doubted the authenticity of Smith's claim to be a prophet. Persecution from outsiders, which sometimes included attacks on Mormon communities by angry mobs, soon drove the Mormons westward. They settled first in the town of Far West, Missouri, but were driven from there by a militia organized by Missouri governor Lilburn Boggs. Then they formed the community of Nauvoo in Illinois, which soon attracted large numbers of Mormons.

By 1841, Young had been named president of the Quorum of Twelve Apostles, a position second only to Joseph Smith. In the early 1840s Smith revealed to his church members a controversial doctrine, the doctrine of plural marriage. Plural marriage called for Mormon men to take many wives, and although Young did not like the doctrine at first—he was quite happy with his second wife, Mary Ann Angell—he deferred to his church superior and began to take on more wives. The policy of plural marriage, or polygamy (having more than one spouse), only increased the anger that outsiders directed at the Mormons. Angry mobs began attacking Mormons living in Nauvoo, and government officials were inclined to look the other way. In 1844 Joseph Smith was imprisoned after a clash with members of a nearby community; a mob broke into the prison and killed Smith. Now the sole leader of the Mormon Church, Young began to look for a safe place to lead his people. He heard of a great valley in the West that contained a large salt lake. There, he thought, the Mormons might live free of persecution.

The journey westward

In 1846 thousands of Mormons, led by Brigham Young, began leaving Nauvoo to journey westward. They didn't travel far that first year, settling on the Missouri River at a place they called Winter Quarters (near present-day Omaha, Nebraska). Young supervised the construction of homes in which to spend the winter and the building of wagons they would need to cross the prairie the next year. In April 1847 Young commanded an advance party of some 150 people who left Winter Quarters to blaze the trail—known as the Mormon Trail—to the Great Basin in Utah.

The trek to Utah was an arduous one. The day began at five o'clock in the morning with breakfast and prayer, followed by hours of crossing bumpy prairie and rapid rivers; it ended with lights out at nine o'clock at night. On June 1 the party arrived at Fort Laramie, the largest outpost on the Oregon Trail. It was there that the group received the valuable advice of mountain man Jim Bridger (1804–1881; see entry), who helped Young determine the best path to the Great Salt Lake Valley. The Mormons followed the Oregon Trail to Fort Bridger, in southwestern Wyoming, and then made their way down through the mountains and into the Great Salt Lake Valley on July 24, 1847. Here, in this wide valley ringed with

mountains, Young hoped his people could find peace to build their religious community.

Building a thriving community

Young's party was the first in a great exodus of Mormons who traveled west to the Great Salt Lake Valley in the coming years. Guided by Young, who assumed the title of prophet in 1847, the Mormons planted crops and built homes after their arrival in the area, creating a thriving Mormon community. Young shuttled back and forth for several years, encouraging the further migration of Mormons from the eastern United States. Moreover, Mormon missionaries to Europe recruited many hundreds of people, paying their way to come to America and join the great "Zion," or religious community. By 1848 more than five thousand settlers lived in the valley.

In the isolated Great Salt Lake Valley, the Mormons found the freedom from persecution that they long desired. However, their isolation would not last. The American victory in the Mexican-American War (1846–48; a war fought between Mexico and the United States primarily over the southern border of Texas, but in which the United States gained large amounts of territory in the Southwest) made Utah a United States territory, and President Millard Fillmore (1800–1874) named Young governor of the territory in 1850. This secular (nonreligious) authority combined with Young's religious authority made him the powerful ruler of the Utah Territory. Newspaper editor Horace Greeley (1811–1872) visited the territory in 1859. In his subsequent book, *An Overland Journey from New York to San Francisco in the Summer of 1859,* Greeley remarks that Young "carries the territory in his breeches pocket without a shadow of opposition." The Mormons also came into contact with great numbers of travelers heading west to California—especially after the gold rush of 1849—and were able to profit by selling supplies to the travelers. Yet as the Mormons had learned earlier, such contact with the outside world did not bode well for the Mormons' future.

Soon the Mormons living in Salt Lake City were under attack from outsiders. Government officials appointed to positions in Utah complained that Young's influence was too strong and that he was leading a theocracy, a government in which church and state are one. Moreover, the official adoption of plural marriages in the 1840s created a public outcry against Mormon immorality and rekindled charges that Mormons believed that they could live outside the law. In 1857, convinced that the Mormons were considering rebellion, President James Buchanan (1791–1868) sent two thousand troops to Utah to install a new governor, Alfred Cumming. Fearful of renewed persecution and bloodshed, Young ordered the Mormons to evacuate Salt Lake City and hide in Mormon communities to the south. In June 1857, after the U.S. troops marched without attack into Salt Lake City, a peace commission negotiated a deal that made Cumming governor but left the real power in Young's hands. The "Mormon War" was over, and life returned to normal.

Under Young's leadership, the Mormons continued to develop a society in Salt Lake City that favored church members. They settled the best land in the territory, and voted church members into significant positions of power. In 1868 Young established the Zion's Cooperative Mercantile Institution, a group that ensured that Mormons retained the best access to goods and services. For church members, Salt Lake City and the other Mormon communities that dotted the territory were ideal places to live. Towns were safe, there were no rowdy drinking and gambling houses, and a strict code of morality prevailed. At long last, the Mormons had succeeded at creating their dream.

Brigham Young died after a brief illness on August 29, 1877. At the end he called out "Joseph! Joseph! Joseph!" which his family believed to be a greeting to church founder Joseph Smith. Young left behind twenty-six wives and fifty-seven children. Thousands of mourners filed past his casket, which was placed in the Mormon Tabernacle (a great church building). They called Young the American Moses, for he had led his people to the promised land. The Mormon Church officially abandoned the practice of polygamy in 1890; six years later Utah was admitted to the Union as the forty-fifth state. The Church of Jesus Christ of Latter-Day Saints is today one of the fastest growing religions in the world.

For More Information

Books

Arrington, Leonard J. *Brigham Young: American Moses*. New York: Knopf, 1985.

Bernotas, Bob. *Brigham Young*. New York: Chelsea House, 1992.

Bringhurst, Newell G. *Brigham Young and the Expanding American Frontier*. Boston: Little, Brown, 1986.

Greeley, Horace. *An Overland Journey from New York to San Francisco in the Summer of 1859*. New York: Knopf, 1964.

Sanford, William R., and Carl R. Green. *Brigham Young: Pioneer and Mormon Leader*. Springfield, NJ: Enslow, 1996.

Web Sites

"Brigham Young." [Online] http://www.pbs.org/weta/thewest/wpages/wpgs400/w4young.htm (accessed on May 16, 2000).

"Brigham Young." [Online] http://www.mala.bc.ca/~mcneil/youngb.htm (accessed on May 16, 2000).

Index

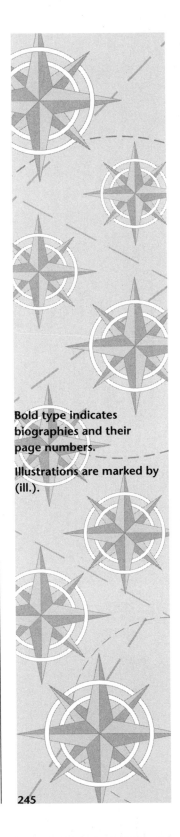